Methods in Behavioral Research

Methods in

 Mayfield Publishing Company

Behavioral Research

Paul C. Cozby
California State University, Fullerton

CREDITS

The author thanks the following publishers for permission to reprint quotations, figures and statistical tables from their publications:

American Psychological Association
Biometrika Trust (Table C.4)
Hafner Press (Table C.6)
Institute of Mathematical Statistics (Tables C.3 and C.5)
Longman Group Ltd. (Table C.2)
Psychology Today
Psychonomic Society, Inc.
W. H. Freeman and Company

ACKNOWLEDGMENTS

The author thanks Paul Rosenblatt and Ellen Berscheid of the University of Minnesota, Norman Miller of the University of Southern California, and many students at California State University, Fullerton, for the help they have given, both directly and indirectly, in producing this book.

Library of Congress Catalog Card Number: 76-56505
International Standard Book Number: 0-87484-383-9

Manufactured in the United States of America

Mayfield Publishing Company
285 Hamilton Avenue, Palo Alto, California 94301

This book was set in Souvenir and Avant Garde Book by Chapman's Phototypesetting and was printed and bound by the George Banta Company. Sponsoring editor was Alden C. Paine, Carole Norton supervised editing, and Zipporah Collins was manuscript editor. Michelle Hogan supervised production, the book was designed by Nancy Sears, and Martha Weston prepared the chapter opening and cover art.

CONTENTS

v

PREFACE

This book is a general introduction to the methods of behavioral research. The ordering of chapters reflects a progression from fundamental considerations prior to conducting research and the actual conducting of research to complex experimental designs, and finally to some issues in research, such as generalization and ethics. I have tried throughout to discuss methodological concepts in a variety of contexts, to maintain continuity and to facilitate learning and retention of the concepts. In addition, the book discusses both experimental and correlational approaches to research. The potential advantages of each approach are stressed.

Instructors vary considerably in the emphasis given to statistics in a course on research methods. Statistical concepts are discussed at three points in the book. In Chapter 2, a very general overview of statistical significance is given, to enable the student to intelligently read published research reports. Chapter 8 is devoted to a more detailed discussion of the logic of statistical significance tests. Finally, Appendix B contains calculational formulas and examples for several statistical tests. It is hoped that this format will allow the instructor sufficient flexibility to introduce statistics in the way which is appropriate for a particular class.

As a general text on research methods in the behavioral sciences, the book is intended to be appropriate for courses in a variety of disciplines. The concepts of research methodology that are presented are relevant to research in psychology, sociology, education, human services, communications, speech, and other disciplines that focus on the nature of behavior. My background is in psychology, and the examples used in the book reflect this background. Nevertheless, I have tried to choose examples that will be of interest to students in many disciplines, and I hope that the book will appeal to a variety of students, irrespective of their primary areas of interest.

I would like to invite instructors and students to send to me or to the publisher your comments (good, bad, or indifferent) concerning this book. I am always interested in ways that the concepts of research methodology can be best presented to the students who are eager to learn about behavior.

Methods in Behavioral Research

1

WHY STUDY BEHAVIOR SCIENTIFICALLY?

This is a book about research methods in the behavioral sciences. Scientific research is one of the most important tools that we can use to study behavior and possibly solve our many social problems. Indeed, learning about human behavior and gaining insights into potential solutions to problems such as aggression, violence, crowding, overpopulation, mental health, interpersonal communication, racism, and sexism are probably the major reasons you and many other students decided to take courses in the behavioral sciences in the first place.

This introductory chapter contains a discussion of ways that knowledge of research methods can be useful to you, as a professional in various occupations and as a concerned and informed citizen. That is followed by an examination of the characteristics of a scientific approach to the study of behavior.

USING RESEARCH METHODS

A knowledge of research methods facilitates assessment of the value of research reported in the popular press. Your daily newspaper, *Time, News-*   **3** *week, Psychology Today,* and other media are continually reporting research results—"Link between coffee drinking and heart attacks found," or "Smoking linked to poor grades." Many articles and books, for example, make claims about the beneficial effects of particular diets or vitamins on your sex life, your personality, or your health. How does the average person evaluate such reports? Do you just accept the findings because they are supposed to be scientific? You shouldn't. A background in research methods helps you to read these reports critically. *If* you can appraise the methodology employed, you can decide if the findings are valid.

It is likely that your occupational role will require you to use research findings. Psychologists who work in clinical settings, for example, need to know about recent research on therapy techniques, testing procedures, and so on. Business executives are interested in research in consumer psychology. Educators must keep up with research on such subjects as the role of personality factors in pupil performance. Knowledge of research methods and the ability to read and evaluate research reports are useful in many fields.

A knowledge of research methodology may motivate you to conduct research. This does not necessarily mean that you will decide to become a research scientist at a university or research center—although undoubtedly many students will pursue such a profession. Rather, you may come to realize that many aspects of your life are researchable. A teacher must determine the best seating arrangements for class discussion, for group problem-solving, and for individual learning. Architects and city planners are interested in learning which aspects of the environment are related to neighborhood satisfaction. A counselor must decide on the optimal group size for group therapy with alcoholics. A business person considers the value of a program that purports to ensure that employees feel they are doing important work. Answers to such problems can be found through research.

New programs are proposed and tried in both business and government organizations. The Head Start program for disadvantaged youngsters is an example of a national program. You can probably think of many local programs. Here in California, several of my students are working in a program designed to help adults pass a high school equivalency test so that they can pursue career programs in the community colleges. Shouldn't there be some means of evaluating these projects to determine whether they are effectively accomplishing their goals? If they are not effective, different approaches should be tried. Donald Campbell (1969) has advocated such an approach to reform programs and social experiments that are tried out in limited areas.

It is possible that after you have achieved an understanding of research methods you will want to conduct research to help answer questions in your own life.

THE SCIENTIFIC APPROACH

What makes the scientific approach different from other ways of learning about behavior? It is certainly true that people have always observed the world around them. People observe the world and seek explanations for what they see. Philosophers, novelists, and lay persons have always sought the same goals as scientists—explanations of how and why things happen as they do.

But most people do not use scientific means of attaining these goals. Let's take an example from philosophy. In his *Rhetoric,* Aristotle (1954) was concerned with the factors that determine persuasion or attitude change. One principle set forth by Aristotle deals with the credibility of the speaker: "Persuasion is achieved by the speaker's personal character when the speech is so spoken as to make us think him credible. We believe good men more fully and readily than others." Thus, Aristotle would argue that we are more persuaded by a speaker who seems prestigious, trustworthy, and respectable than by one who seems ordinary, dishonest, and disreputable.

Skepticism and science

Does the scientist accept Aristotle's arguments? Aristotle is considered an authority, and the fact that his works have been valued for more than two thousand years gives him a great deal of prestige. Despite this, the answer is no. The scientist does not accept on faith the pronouncements of anyone, regardless of the person's prestige or authority. Nor does a scientist unquestioningly accept his or her own intuitions—the scientist recognizes that his or her ideas are just as likely to be wrong as are anyone else's. *Scientists are skeptical.*

The essence of the scientific method is the insistence that all propositions be subjected to an empirical test. Only after this has been done does the scientist decide to accept or reject a proposition.

As it turns out, Aristotle's proposition has been tested and generally found to be true. For example, one study tried to change subjects' attitudes toward the sale of antihistamines (Hovland & Weiss, 1951). All subjects[1] read the same persuasive article. Half of the subjects were told that the article had been written by someone with high credibility, and the other half of the subjects were told that the article was written by a person with low credibility. The results of the experiment showed that the attitudes of the subjects who believed the article was written by a person with high credibility changed more than the attitudes of those who believed it was written by a person with low credibility.

Description and explanation

The experiment on speaker credibility was successful in *describing* the effects of speaker credibility. Now you may be wondering *why* the highly credible person is more effective in changing attitudes. Describing the world is one goal of the scientist. However, another goal of the scientist is to explain what occurs in the world. In other words, the goals of the behavioral scientist are to describe behavior and then to explain it.

In the experiment on credibility and attitude change, the researchers attempted to explain the effects of speaker credibility by stating that subjects are more willing to believe what is said by a person with high credibility than by one with low credibility. This explanation may be correct, but there could be other explanations. It is usually much more difficult to provide an explanation for behavior than it is to describe it.

The behavior that has been labeled schizophrenia provides a good illustration of the difficulty of explaining behavior. Although researchers have discovered a great deal about schizophrenic behavior, we still don't have an adequate explanation of schizophrenia. Researchers continue to examine the validity of various explanations. Genetics, family interaction, and biochemical and physiological factors are all being studied, and each new piece of research brings us closer to an adequate explanation.

---

1 Psychologists and other behavioral scientists generally refer to the objects of their investigations as *subjects*. A subject may be a rat, monkey, child, college student, or non-college adult, for example.

In recent years, students and the general public have been demanding that research be relevant. I won't deny that research that has immediate practical applications has its attractions, but basic, theory-oriented research is important, too. Often it is not possible to predict the eventual usefulness of research. Insistence that all research have obvious and immediate applications could result in the neglect of potentially important areas of research. Psychologist B. F. Skinner's basic research on operant conditioning was conducted in the 1930s. Yet only in recent years have the results of this research been applied in behavior modification therapy techniques. Research with no apparent practical value may ultimately be very useful.

Although you may not realize it, scientific thinking is a familiar aspect of everyday experience. You are probably always trying to figure out the causes of your own behavior and that of others. Harold Kelley (1967) and others have suggested that when you do this, you use methods which are not very different from the methods used by research scientists.

Try to remember what you thought about Patty Hearst and her behavior after she became associated with the Symbionese Liberation Army. You probably entertained a number of hypotheses that could explain her behavior. One hypothesis might have been that she was brainwashed to believe in SLA ideology. Another might have been that she was forced into saying and doing some things but that her basic beliefs didn't really change. Yet another hypothesis might have been that she was a believer in the SLA even before she was abducted. As the news media reported the events in which Patty Hearst was involved, you probably evaluated your hypotheses and decided which one was correct.

Scientists form hypotheses to explain the world, and they try to assess the accuracy of their hypotheses. Scientific methodology uses formal procedures to test hypotheses and a technical and precise language. But the basic process is the same.

In the remainder of this book, we will explore the methodologies available to you and to any researcher who wants to investigate a particular problem. When you understand these methodologies, you will have a basis for evaluating the research of others and for conducting your own research. I hope you will find this exploration interesting and exciting.

STUDY QUESTIONS

1 *Why do you think scientific skepticism is useful in furthering our knowledge of behavior?*

2 *What is the difference between a description of behavior and an explanation of behavior?*

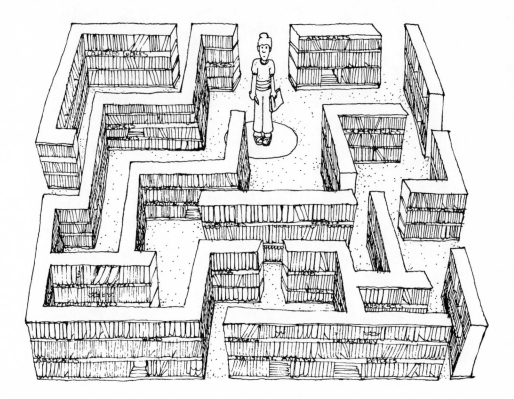

2

WHERE TO START

Where would you begin if you wanted to conduct a research project? Where would you get ideas about problems to study? And how would you find out about other people's ideas and research on a problem? In this chapter, we'll explore some sources of scientific ideas. We'll also consider the nature of research reports published in professional journals.

SOURCES OF IDEAS

It isn't easy to say where good ideas come from. You and I and many others are capable of coming up with worthwhile ideas, but verbalizing the process by which ideas are generated is difficult. Cartoonists know this—they show a brilliant idea as a lightbulb flashing on over the head of the person having it. But where does the electricity come from? Let's consider five sources of ideas: common sense, observation of the world around us, theories, past research, and practical problems.

Common sense

One source of testable ideas is the body of knowledge called common sense—the things we all believe to be true. Researchers usually prefer to work with ideas that run counter to what you would expect on the basis of common sense. But testing a common sense idea can be valuable, because common sense notions don't always turn out to be correct.

An example of an experimental hypothesis based on common sense comes from a study by Jonathan Freedman, Simon Klevansky, and Paul Ehrlich (1971) on the effects of crowding. If you were to ask a number of people to tell you about the effects of crowding, you would probably hear about all sorts of undesirable behaviors, including crime, delinquency, and mental illness. Common sense tells us that crowding is bad. Freedman and his colleagues tested the hypothesis that if people are crowded together, a deterioration in performance on mental tasks will result. High school students were exposed to densities ranging from a relatively high density of 4 sq. ft. per person to a relatively low density of 32 sq. ft. per person. While exposed to these densities, subjects worked on various mental tasks, such as crossing out numbers and thinking of unusual uses for common objects. The researchers then compared the level of performance of the subjects who worked under crowded conditions with that of subjects who worked under uncrowded conditions. And they found that the common sense view was not correct. The performance level of the crowded subjects was just as good as the performance level of the uncrowded subjects. Obviously, a more complex view of crowding is needed—one that transcends our common sense notions. Failure of the research to support the common sense view of crowding forces us to go beyond a common sense theory of behavior.

Observation of the world around us

Your observations of things that happen to you and to others can provide you with hypotheses to test. When something you notice intrigues you, you may ask yourself why it happened.

Elliot Aronson found himself in just such a situation. Back in 1961, President John Kennedy engineered an attempt to invade Cuba at the Bay of Pigs. The attempt failed and quickly became known as "the Bay of Pigs fiasco." What intrigued Aronson was that, according to a Gallup poll, President Kennedy's personal popularity increased shortly after the fiasco. Ordinarily we like people who are competent. And so it seemed strange to Aronson that **13** such a blunder would cause an *increase* in popularity. Why would this happen? Aronson describes his idea:

> One possibility is that John Kennedy may have been "too perfect." He was young, handsome, bright, witty, charming, and athletic; he was a voracious reader, a master political strategist, a war hero, and an uncomplaining endurer of physical pain; he had a beautiful wife . . . and a talented, close-knit family. Some evidence of fallibility (like being responsible for a major blunder) could have served to make him more human in the public eye and, hence, more likable (1972).

This certainly is an interesting idea, but it has not yet been proven. The Gallup poll data showing that Kennedy's popularity increased shortly after the Bay of Pigs fiasco does not demonstrate a connection between these two phenomena. In the real world, many events occur simultaneously. Thus, some factor other than Kennedy's blunder may have caused the increase in popularity. In order to rule out the influence of these other events, Aronson, Willerman, and Floyd (1966) conducted a laboratory experiment to test the hypothesis that a blunder committed by a perfect person will result in increased liking for that person. In the experiment, male college students listened to a tape recording of another student who was a candidate for the "College Quiz Bowl." The tape contained an interview in which the candidate was asked a series of difficult questions by an interviewer. The subjects' task was to form impressions of the candidate. Two versions of the tape were made. In one the candidate was presented as a nearly-perfect person; in the other the candidate was presented as an average person. The nearly-perfect person was pretty fantastic. He answered 92 percent of the questions correctly, and in the interview he disclosed that in high school he had been an honor student, yearbook editor, and member of the track team. The average person answered only 30 percent of the questions correctly, had been just an average student in high school, a proofreader on the yearbook staff, and had failed to make the track team. Half the subjects heard the tape with the nearly-perfect person; the rest of the subjects heard the tape with the average person.

The experimenters created a blunder condition by adding a variation to each of the tapes, near the end of the recording. Half the subjects who heard the superior person being superior also heard him make a clumsy blunder—they heard him spill coffee all over his new suit. Half the subjects who heard the average person being average also heard him make the same clumsy blunder. Thus, there were four experimental conditions: (1) one-fourth of the subjects heard a nearly-perfect person who committed a blunder; (2) one-fourth of the subjects heard a nearly-perfect person who didn't commit a blunder; (3) one-fourth of the subjects heard an average person who committed a blunder; (4) the remaining subjects heard an average person who didn't commit a blunder.

After listening to the candidate's performance on the tape recording, each subject was asked to rate how much they liked the candidate. Aronson's hypothesis was supported—the most liked person was the nearly-perfect person who had blundered. Interestingly, the average person who had committed the very same blunder was the one the subjects liked the least.

It is important to note that Aronson's experiment does not prove that the increase in Kennedy's popularity was caused by the blunder. Some other factor may have caused the increase. But the results of Aronson's experiment are consistent with his hypothesis. The world is full of phenomena that are as testable as the one observed by Aronson. You just have to be on the lookout for them.[1]

Theories

Much research in the behavioral sciences tests theories of behavior. Theories serve two important functions in increasing our understanding of behavior. First, theories *organize and explain* a variety of specific facts. Specific facts about behavior are not very meaningful by themselves, and so theories are needed to impose a framework on them. This framework makes the world more comprehensible by providing a few abstract concepts around which we can organize and explain a variety of behaviors. As an example, consider how Darwin's theory of evolution organized and explained a variety of facts concerning the characteristics of animal species.

Second, theories generate *new* knowledge by focusing our thinking so

1 Another example of research stimulated by events in the real world is the study of helping behavior done by Bibb Latané and John Darley. Several years ago a woman named Kitty Genovese was stabbed to death in New York City while thirty-eight of her neighbors looked on without helping. Latané and Darley's research indicates that a major factor in helping is the number of people who witness an emergency: the greater the number of bystanders, the less likely it is that the victim will receive aid. See B. Latané and J. Darley, *The unresponsive bystander: Why doesn't he help?* New York: Appleton-Century-Crofts, 1970.

that we notice new aspects of behavior—theories guide our observations of **15** the world. New knowledge is generated by theory-testing research. The theory makes predictions about behavior, and the researcher conducts research to see if those predictions are correct. If the predictions are confirmed, the theory is supported. A theory is never proven. Research can provide support for the correctness of a theory, but research also reveals weaknesses in a theory and forces the researcher to modify the theory or develop a better one.

We needn't delve too deeply into the nature of theories. A brief description of one very small and limited theory should suffice. Reactance theory was developed by Brehm (1966) to explain what happens when a person's freedom to choose between alternatives is threatened. Earlier research and theory dealt with what happens when a person freely chooses between alternatives; Brehm focused on situations in which an attempt is made to force the individual to make a particular choice. Brehm's reactance theory assumes that people react to the loss of freedom of choice by trying to reestablish the freedom of choice that has been lost. One way an individual can reestablish freedom of choice is by rejecting the alternative he has been forced to choose and simultaneously increasing his desire for the unavailable alternative.

Let's look at a study (Driscoll, Davis & Lipetz, 1972) that tested reactance theory. This research deals with a situation in which parents try to interfere with and break up the relationship between two young people. Reactance theory makes a clear prediction in this situation. The parents are attempting to restrict the couple's freedom of choice by telling the couple that they are not to love each other. Reactance theory predicts that the couple will reassert their freedom of choice by increasing their love for each other.

The research described earlier—Freedman's investigation of crowding and Aronson's study of blunders—used the *experimental method*. The basic feature of the true experiment is that the researcher directly controls the situation experienced by the subjects. For example, in the Freedman study, the experimenters created both crowded and uncrowded conditions. The parental interference study makes use of a second approach to behavioral research, the *correlational method*. The researcher who uses the correlational method doesn't directly control the situation experienced by subjects; instead he or she looks for existing situations that provide the conditions his study requires. If Freedman and his co-workers had found one group of people who lived in a high density neighborhood and another group of people who lived in a low density neighborhood and then had taken measures to see how each of these groups did on the various performance tasks, they would have been using the correlational method. The difference between the experimental and correlational methods may not seem significant. However, the difference has important implications for how the research findings can be interpreted.

In a study that used the correlational method, the group of researchers tested the hypothesis that parental interference strengthens romantic bonds. The researchers gave questionnaires to forty-nine couples who had been dating seriously for an average of eight months. The questionnaire included questions designed to measure the amount of parental interference each couple had experienced during their relationship. Other questions were designed to measure how much love each person felt for his or her partner. This investigation is an example of the correlational method because the amount of parental interference experienced by the subjects was *not* controlled by the researchers. (Indeed, it would be highly unethical to even try to manipulate parental interference.)

As you might expect, the amount of parental interference reported by some subjects was quite low, and the amount reported by other subjects was quite high. The amount of love reported by the couples also varied. When the researchers looked at the couples' parental interference scores and their love scores, they found a relationship between the two variables. The greater the parental interference score, the greater the love score. Thus, the prediction from reactance theory was confirmed.

Past research

A fourth source of ideas is past research. When a study yields interesting results, the researcher may write a report of the research for publication in a professional journal. Such journal articles often stimulate further research. You might disagree with the researcher's methodology and wish to use a different approach to test his hypothesis; you might think of a logical extension of the results of the research; you might want to try to generalize the results to males if the original study used females; you might be able to apply the results to a practical problem; or you might think of some alternative explanation for the results of the original research. Research studies usually provide some answers to the original question, but they also raise many new questions that can only be answered by further research.

Practical problems

Research is also stimulated by practical problems that require immediate solutions. For example, an automobile manufacturer might want to conduct research on different kinds of car seats to determine which one will minimize driver fatigue. Groups of city planners and citizens might survey bicycle riders to determine the most desirable route for a city bike path. On a larger scale, researchers have been asked to guide national policy by conducting research on the effects of marijuana, the effects of exposure to pornographic materials, and so on. Much research in the behavioral sciences is aimed at solving practical problems such as these.

LIBRARY RESEARCH
Before any research project is conducted, the investigator must have a thorough knowledge of earlier research findings. Even if the basic idea has been formulated, a review of past studies will aid the researcher to clarify his or her idea and to design the study. Thus, it is important that you know how to search the literature on a topic and that you know how to read research reports in professional journals.

The nature of journals
If you've walked through the periodicals section of your library, you've probably noticed the enormous number of professional journals. It is in these journals that researchers publish the results of their investigations. After a research project has been completed, the study is written up. Many of these reports are then submitted to the editor of an appropriate journal. The editor solicits a review of the paper from a scientist in the same field, who decides if the report is to be accepted for publication. Because each journal has a limited amount of space and receives many more papers than it has room to publish, most papers are rejected. Those that are accepted are published about a year later.

Most psychology journals specialize in one or two areas of human or animal behavior. Even so, the number of journals in many areas is so large that it is almost impossible for anyone to read them all. For instance, research in the area of social psychology can be found in the *Journal of Personality and Social*

Psychology, Journal of Experimental Social Psychology, Sociometry, Journal of Applied Social Psychology, Representative Research in Social Psychology, Journal of Social Issues, and *Journal of Social Psychology.* This list doesn't include any journals published outside the United States, nor does it include the titles of any journals that specialize in related fields, such as personality or developmental psychology. If you were seeking research on a single specific topic—such as the effect of crowding on human behavior, or the effect of television violence on aggression—it would be impractical to look at every issue of every journal in which relevant research articles might be published. Fortunately, you don't have to.

Psychological Abstracts
Psych Abstracts publishes "nonevaluative summaries of the world's literature in psychology and related disciplines." It is published monthly by the American Psychological Association, and each volume contains approximately twelve thousand abstracts of published articles. To find articles on the topic in which you are interested, you use the index at the end of each volume.

The summaries of the articles give you brief descriptions of the research findings. On the basis of this information, you can decide whether a particular article is relevant to your interests. If it is, you can go to the journal and read the article. The reference section of your library has abstracts of literature in many disciplines. For example, sociology journal articles are abstracted in *Sociological Abstracts.*

Literature reviews
Articles that summarize the research in a particular area are also useful. The *Psychological Bulletin* publishes reviews of the literature in various topic areas of psychology. The *Annual Review of Psychology* each year publishes articles that summarize recent developments in various areas of psychology. A number of other disciplines have similar annual reviews.

ANATOMY OF A RESEARCH ARTICLE
Once you have selected a research article, what can you expect to find in it? Journal articles usually have five sections: (1) an *abstract* similar to the ones found in *Psychological Abstracts;* (2) an *introduction* that explains the problem

under investigation and the specific hypothesis being tested; (3) a *method* **19** section that describes in detail the exact procedures used to test the hypothesis; (4) a *results* section in which the findings are presented; and (5) a *discussion* section in which the researcher may speculate on the broader implications of the results, propose alternative explanations for the results, discuss reasons why a specific hypothesis was not supported, or suggest directions for future research on the problem. Let's look at each of these sections in detail.

Abstract

The abstract is a summary of the research report and is usually no more than 150 words in length. If you write a research report for a laboratory class, you may find that the abstract is the most difficult part to write. It's hard to squeeze a great deal of information into 150 words. The abstract usually includes the hypothesis and information about the origin of the hypothesis, a brief description of the procedure (sometimes including the sex and number of subjects), and the general pattern of results. The discussion section is the least important part of the abstract; often it is a single sentence, such as "Implications of the results for future research are discussed."

Introduction

In this section, the researcher describes the problem that has been investigated. Past research and theories relevant to the problem are described in detail. The specific expectations of the researcher are given, often as formal hypotheses. In other words, the investigator introduces you to the research in a logical format that shows how past research and theory are connected to the research problem and to the expected results.

Method

The method section is divided into subsections; the number of subsections is determined by the author and depends on the complexity of the research design. Sometimes the first subsection presents an overview of the design to prepare the reader for the material that follows. The next section describes the characteristics of the subjects. Were they male, or female, or were both sexes used? What was the average age? How many subjects participated? How were the subjects recruited? Were they volunteers or was participation a course requirement? Was there any monetary compensation for participation in the study? Did these subjects have any unusual characteristics? The next subsection details the procedure used in the study. The author describes exactly what the subjects experienced when they participated—the instructions they were given, the situation they were exposed to, the questionnaires they filled out, and so on. It is important here that no potentially important detail be omitted. Readers of the article may find fault with specific aspects of the procedure, or they may want to attempt a replication of the study. And so they will need a detailed description of the procedure. The remaining subsections detail other aspects of the study, such as the apparatus or testing materials used. These are important as well.

Results

In the results section the author presents his findings, usually in three ways. First, there is a description in narrative form—for example, "It was found that subjects who listened to the more credible speaker changed their attitudes more than did subjects who heard the less credible speaker." Second, the results are usually presented in statistical language. And third, the material is often depicted in tables and graphs, which summarize the data in visual form.

The statistical terminology of the results section will probably seem quite incomprehensible to you. However, lack of knowledge about the calculations isn't really a deterrent to understanding the article or the logic behind the use of statistics. They are a tool the researcher uses in evaluating the outcomes of the study. We'll discuss statistics in somewhat more detail after looking at the last section of the research article, the discussion.

Discussion

In this section the author discusses the research from various perspectives. Do the results support the hypothesis? If they do, the author should give all of the possible explanations for the results and should discuss why one explanation is superior to another. If the hypothesis has not been supported, the author should offer suggestions to explain this. What might have been wrong with the methodology, the hypothesis, or both? The author may also discuss how the results fit in with past research on the topic. And this section may also include suggestions for possible practical applications of the research and about future research on the topic.

You now have some idea of what a research article contains. At this point, you will find it useful to read a research article. Start by reading the abstract and then skimming the body of the article. Then read the article in detail.

Finally, you will want to *critically* read the article in order to evaluate it. Re- member that scientists are not perfect, and the things they write can be criticized. Right now, you may feel that you don't know enough about research methodology to be able to do this. Hopefully, by the time you finish this book you will feel qualified to generate such criticism.

A LITTLE BIT ABOUT STATISTICS

When you read journal articles in the behavioral sciences, you will encounter many statistical terms. What do these terms mean? Why did the researcher use statistics? Basically, statistics are a tool the researcher uses to evaluate the results of the research. The remainder of this chapter is devoted to a brief overview of the use of statistics in research. Chapter 8 and Appendix B contain more detailed discussions of statistics. Let's start by studying a description of a research experiment. This one happens to be about self-disclosure.

Self-disclosure—revealing information about yourself to another person— has received increasing attention in recent years. Part of this attention has resulted from the intrinsic interest of the subject. In addition, many clinicians have stressed the importance of self-disclosure in mental health and effective interpersonal relationships. A well-established finding is that we reciprocate the disclosure level of others. If another person discloses a particular amount of information to you, you will disclose a similar amount of information in return. An experiment on disclosure reciprocity might go as follows.

There would be two groups of subjects—a low disclosure group and a high disclosure group. Subjects in the low disclosure group would talk with someone who would reveal only a small amount of information about himself or herself. Subjects in the high disclosure group would talk with someone who would reveal highly intimate information. The amount of disclosure by each subject would then be measured—let's say that subject disclosure could range from a score of 1 (no disclosure) to a score of 7 (very high disclosure). If reciprocity is taking place, we would expect that the amount of subject disclosure would be greater in the high disclosure group than in the low disclosure group.

The subjects for the experiment are sampled from a *population of interest* and then randomly assigned to either the low disclosure group or high disclosure group. *Random assignment* is necessary to make sure that the groups are equivalent before the experiment. The process of random assignment assures that each subject has an equal chance of being assigned to either of the two groups. It is unlikely, then, that high revealers would be assigned to one group, and low revealers would be assigned to the other group. If the groups are equivalent before the experiment, any differences in the groups after the experiment can be attributed to the *experimental manipulation*. In other words, if subjects in the high disclosure group reveal more about themselves than subjects in the low disclosure group, this difference can be interpreted as a result of the differences in the disclosures made to the two groups.

Now let's examine a hypothetical set of data from such an experiment. Table 2-1 shows the disclosure scores of twenty subjects—ten subjects in each of the two groups. The first task of the researcher is to describe this set of data. The data can be described on two dimensions. The first is *central tendency*. Measures of central tendency provide a single index of each group *as a whole*. The most common measure of central tendency is called the *mean* (symbolized as $\overline{X}$). The mean is the sum of all subjects' scores divided by the number of subjects. In the data in Table 2-1, the mean score of the low group is 2.6 and the high group mean is 4.6. On the average, then, subjects in the high group disclosed more than subjects in the low group.

The second dimension on which the data can be described is *variability*

Table 2-1 **Results from a hypothetical experiment on disclosure reciprocity**

Scores of subjects in low disclosure condition	Scores of subjects in high disclosure condition
1	4
1	5
2	5
2	5
4	4
3	2
6	6
2	7
3	2
2	6
$\Sigma = 26$	$\Sigma = 46$
$\overline{X} = 2.6$	$\overline{X} = 4.6$

about the group mean. Notice that the different subjects in each group have different scores. Thus, the scores in each group vary on either side of the group mean. A measure of variability called the *variance* (symbolized as s^2) gives a single number that indicates how much the scores are spread about the group mean. The researcher uses information based on central tendency and variability to evaluate the significance of the results.

The means of the two groups differ, and the researcher must determine whether this difference is significant. Our discussion of random assignment emphasized that the groups must be equivalent prior to the experiment. If the experimental manipulation has no effect, you would expect the groups to be equivalent after the experiment as well. However, whenever you compare a sample of two groups, there will almost always be *some* difference in the means. Random assignment is not a perfect technique, especially with small sample sizes, and so the groups are not *exactly* equivalent.

To illustrate, the people in your class have a specific mean grade point average (GPA). You could compute this by having each student turn in a piece of paper on which his or her GPA is written. Now, if you divided the class into two groups by random assignment, and computed the GPA of each group, the means of the two groups should be identical, right? Right, except that error in the assignment procedures would probably produce slightly different mean GPAs. A significance test is needed to determine whether the difference is meaningful or merely reflects error.

The problem is similar for the results of the self-disclosure experiment. The means of the two groups would almost certainly be different even if the manipulation of the researcher's disclosures did not influence the subjects' disclosures in any way. If the difference between the means was probably caused by the manipulated variable, the results are said to be *significant*. If the difference between means was probably caused by error factors, the results are said to be *nonsignificant*.

To evaluate the mean difference, the researcher uses statistical significance tests. The statistical tests tell the researcher the probability that the difference between means was due to error. There are a variety of statistical tests available for this purpose. The appropriate test is determined by the research problem and the data gathered. A common test for evaluating the difference between means is the *F test*.[2] The basic consideration in the F test is whether

---

2   The calculational formulas for the F test do not concern us here. See Appendix A for exact calculations.

influence of the experimental manipulation is greater than the effect of *random error*. The influence of the manipulated variable is called *systematic variance;* the random error factor is called *error variance.*

To determine whether the results are significant, the researcher compares the amount of systematic variance to the amount of error variance. To make this comparison, we need an index of these two sources of variance. Systematic variance is indexed by the difference between the means. The greater the difference between means, the greater the systematic variance. As the difference between means becomes larger, so does the likelihood that the results are significant. As the difference increases, the likelihood that error could have caused the difference decreases.

Error variance is indexed by the amount of variability about the group means. The smaller the spread of scores about the group means, the smaller the error variance. The *F* test involves a ratio of systematic variance to error variance. A researcher hopes for a relatively large amount of systematic variance and a small amount of error variance.

The statistic, *F,* is equal to the amount of systematic variance divided by the amount of error variance. The larger this ratio—the greater the value of *F*—the more likely it is that the results are significant. A large *F* ratio indicates that the results were probably due to the operation of the manipulated variable.

Statistical significance is expressed in terms of *probabilities.* A result is said to be significant when there is a *low* probability that the results were due to error factors (indicating a high probability that the results were due to the experimental manipulation).

The concept of probability is a familiar one in everyday life. Weather forecasters use this concept when, for example, they predict rain. Probabilities range from a low of 0.0 (absolutely no chance of rain tomorrow) through 0.50 (a fifty-fifty chance that rain will fall) to a high of 1.0 (absolute certainty that rain will fall).

In psychology it has become common practice to use the .05 probability level as the standard for determining whether results are significant. Thus, a probability of .05 or less (for example, .01 or .001) is considered enough to rule out error as a factor in the results. When the probability of error is higher (for example, .15 or .50), we conclude that error might have produced the difference in means—the results are considered nonsignificant, and the researcher doesn't interpret the results as supportive of the hypothesis.

Researchers who use a probability of .05 or less for determining significance are being quite cautious. Most scientists feel that they should be cautious and not take a result seriously unless there is a very small probability that error caused the results. Still, the decision to use a particular probability in making judgments of significance is an individual matter; sometimes a larger probability (such as .10) or a smaller probability (such as .001) is justified.

Let's return to the data from the disclosure experiment. I computed a significance test and found an F value of 8.04. By consulting an appropriate statistical table, such as the ones found in Appendix C, I find that the probability of finding an F this large, if error factors caused the difference between means, is less than .05. That is, there is only a 5 percent chance, or less, that the difference in the means of the high and low disclosure groups is a fluke.

This discussion of statistics should give you a basic background for interpreting statistical terms when you encounter them in journal articles and other texts. I hope that when you see these statistics being used, you'll recognize what they mean. The phrase "$p < .05$" means that "the probability of this result occurring through error factors is less than .05." Similarly, the phrase "the results were significant at the .01 level" means "there is less than one chance out of one hundred that the results are a fluke."

Now let's examine some of the research methods that are available to anyone who wants to study behavior.

STUDY QUESTIONS

1 *Describe the five sources of ideas for research. Do you think any one source is better than the others, or that one source is used more frequently than the others? Why?*

2 *What are the two functions of a theory?*

3 *What information does the researcher communicate in each of the sections of a research article?*

4 *What does a researcher mean when he or she states that "the results were significant (p < .05)"?*

3
EXPERIMENTAL AND CORRELATIONAL METHODS

In the preceding chapter, I made a distinction between the experimental method and the correlational method. The experimental method involves control or *manipulation* of the situation being studied. The correlational method lacks this element of control; it is nonmanipulative. An investigator using the correlational method merely observes the situation. Thus, you can see that Aronson's study on blunders used the experimental method, since the situation involving the blunder was under Aronson's direct control. In contrast, the study that investigated parental interference and romantic love used the correlational method. The investigators didn't control or manipulate the amount of parental interference; they observed it by questioning a number of couples. In the rest of this chapter, we will explore the implications of this difference between the two methods.

RELATIONSHIPS BETWEEN VARIABLES

When a researcher conducts research, he or she is attempting to find out whether there is a relationship between two variables. In the study on speaker **27** credibility, the researchers were attempting to discover whether there is a relationship between speaker credibility (the first variable) and attitude change (the second variable). In this case a relationship was found: The greater the credibility of the speaker, the greater the attitude change. Similarly, Freedman's experiment on crowding was an attempt to discover whether there is a relationship between crowding and task performance. In this study, no relationship between the two variables was found; crowded subjects did just as well on the tasks as uncrowded subjects.

A *variable* is a general class or category of objects, events, or situations. Within this general class, specific instances are found to vary. *Speaker credibility* is one such general category. Within this category there are a number of levels or values of speaker credibility. One speaker may have extremely low credibility, a second may have extremely high credibility, and a third speaker may have a moderate level of credibility. *Crowding,* or *density,* is another variable. When talking about density, you can identify numerous levels or values of this variable. One level of the density variable is 1 sq. ft. per person. Another level of density is 30 sq. ft. per person. The number of levels or values of density are virtually infinite. The important thing is that you recognize that levels of the variable are spread along a continuum. Some variables, such as density, have many possible levels; others, such as sex, have only a small number of levels. There are only two levels of the sex variable — male and female.

When a researcher tries to discover whether there is a relationship between two variables, he wants to know whether the levels of the two variables vary systematically together. If you ask whether there is a relationship between speaker credibility and attitude change, you are asking whether changes in levels (values, amounts) of speaker credibility are accompanied by changes in levels (values, amounts) of attitude change. Is an increase from low credibility to high credibility accompanied by an increase from small amounts of attitude change to large amounts of attitude change?

TYPES OF RELATIONSHIPS

The type of relationship between two variables is the general way in which changes in the values of one variable are associated with changes in the values of the other variable. Behavioral scientists generally encounter only a few types of relationships. These include the linear positive, the linear negative (or *monotonic* relationships), the curvilinear (or *nonmonotonic*) relationship, **29** and, of course, the situation in which there is no relationship between the variables. These relationships are best illustrated by line graphs that show the way changes in one variable are accompanied by changes in another variable. The four graphs in Figure 3-1 represent these four types of relationships.

Figure 3-1   Four types of relationships between variables

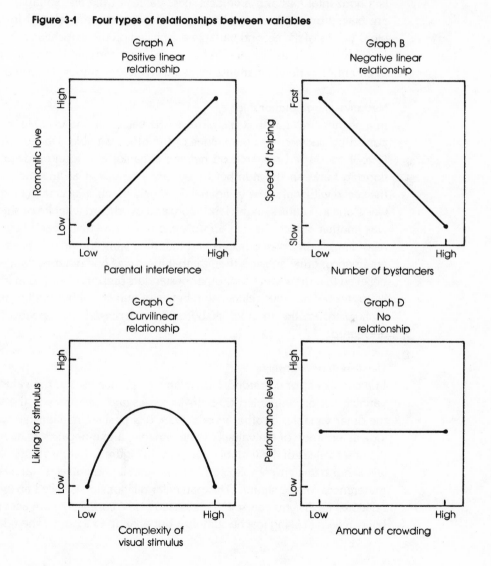

Positive linear relationships

In a positive linear relationship, increases in the values of one variable are accompanied by increases in the values of the second variable. Graph A in Figure 3-1 illustrates the relationship between parental interference and romantic love. This is a positive linear relationship. In a graph such as this, there is a horizontal axis and a vertical axis. Values of the first variable of interest are placed on the horizontal axis and these values are labeled from low to high. Values of the second variable are placed on the vertical axis and labeled from low to high. In Graph A in Figure 3-1, you can see that greater amounts of parental interference are associated with greater amounts of romantic love.

Negative linear relationships

In a negative relationship, increases in the values of one variable are accompanied by *decreases* in the values of the other variable. Darley and Latané (1968) conducted research on helping behavior and found a negative relationship between the number of bystanders present at an emergency and the speed with which the victim received help. Each subject in the experiment was alone in a cubicle in the laboratory and overheard what he or she thought was another subject having an epileptic seizure (actually each heard a tape recording). Some subjects believed that they were the only ones to hear the emergency; other subjects thought that there was one other bystander; others believed that there were four other bystanders present. Graph B in Figure 3-1 illustrates the negative relationship between number of bystanders and speed of helping. As the number of bystanders *increased,* the speed of helping *decreased.*

Curvilinear relationships

In a curvilinear or *nonmonotonic* relationship, increases in the values of one variable are accompanied by *both* increases *and* decreases in the values of the other variable. In other words, there is a positive relationship when you look at a portion of the values of one variable, and a negative relationship for the other values of the variable. Graph C in Figure 3-1 shows a curvilinear relationship between complexity of visual stimuli and subjects' ratings of their preferences for the stimuli. This particular relationship is called an *inverted-U* relationship. As you can see, increases in visual complexity are accompanied by increases in liking for the stimulus, but only up to a point. The relationship then becomes negative; further increases in visual complexity are accompanied by *decreases* in liking for the stimulus (Vitz, 1966).

No relationship

When there is no relationship between the two variables, the graph is simply a flat line. Graph D in Figure 3-1 illustrates the relationship between crowding and task performance found in the Freedman study discussed earlier. In this experiment, the level of task performance was the same regardless of the amount of crowding. Such a finding produces a flat line. Increases in the amount of crowding are accompanied by no changes in the amount of task performance.

These graphs illustrate several kinds of "shapes" that describe the relationship between two variables. Almost any shape can describe the relationship between two variables. From time to time you may encounter other relationships that are described by more complicated shapes than those in the graphs in Figure 3-1.

Remember that these are *general patterns* of relationships. Even if, in general, there is a positive linear relationship, that does not necessarily mean that everyone who scores high on one variable will also score high on the second variable. There may be individual deviations away from the general pattern. In addition to knowing the general type of relationship between two variables in an experiment, you also need to know the strength of the relationship. Sometimes two variables are strongly related to one another, and there is very little deviation from the general pattern. In other situations the two variables are not highly correlated.

CORRELATIONAL METHOD VERSUS EXPERIMENTAL METHOD

The correlational method is nonmanipulative. The researcher goes out and observes persons on the first variable of interest and also observes the same persons on the second variable of interest. The correlational method is entirely observational; both variables are *observed* as they occur naturally.

The experimental method involves both manipulation and observation. The researcher manipulates the first variable he wishes to study and then observes the responses of subjects on the second variable.

The study of crowding and task performance discussed earlier can be used to illustrate the differences between the two methods. If you were going to study the relationship between crowding and task performance using the correlational method, you would find two situations in which the levels of crowding were different but the people were performing the same tasks. If a relationship existed, the people who were less crowded would have different task performance scores than the people who were more crowded. For example, you could give a set of mental tasks to people who live in a high density neighborhood and also to people in a low density neighborhood. You could then observe whether task performance is different in the two groups. You would be using the correlational method because you would not manipulate either of the variables.

Let's say you found that the people who live in the crowded neighborhood scored lower on task performance than the people who live in the uncrowded neighborhood. You could then state that there is a negative relationship between the two variables, because *increases* in the amount of crowding are accompanied by *decreases* in the amount of task performance.

There are two major problems in interpreting results obtained using the correlational method. These problems make the correlational method less desirable than the experimental method.

Direction of cause and effect

The first problem is one of direction of cause and effect. When you use the correlational method, you cannot tell which variable causes the other. In other words, you can't say that crowding *causes* a deterioration in task performance. Although there are plausible reasons for this particular causation pattern, there are also factors that could explain the opposite pattern, in which poor task performance causes crowding. This isn't as implausible as it sounds; perhaps people who don't do well on mental tasks seek out crowded situations in an effort either to have others available for help, to seek solace among the masses, or to reduce their visibility. Clearly, it is impossible to tell which variable caused the differences observed by the researchers.

This problem of direction of cause and effect is not the worst problem of the correlational method. Scientists are fond of pointing out that astronomers have been able to make very accurate predictions even though they cannot manipulate any variables. In addition, the direction of cause-and-effect is often not crucial because, for some pairs of variables, the causal pattern may operate in both directions. For instance, there seem to be two causal patterns in the relationship between the variables of similarity and liking: Similarity causes people to like each other, and liking causes people to become more similar.

The "third variable" problem

When the correlational method is used, we don't know whether there is *any* direct causative relationship between the two variables. It may be that crowding doesn't cause lower task performance *and* that low task performance doesn't cause crowding. Perhaps there is a relationship between the two variables because some other variable causes both crowding and task performance. This is known as the *third variable problem* —any number of other, third, variables may be responsible for an observed relationship between two variables. In the crowding study, one such third variable could be social class. People of lower social class might live in more crowded neighborhoods *and* do poorly on the various mental tasks devised by psychologists; similarly, people of a higher social class might live in less crowded neighborhoods *and* do well on the mental tasks. If social class is the determining variable, then there is no direct cause-and-effect relationship between crowding and task performance. The relationship observed was caused by a third variable, social class.

You may have wondered whether the study that showed a relationship between parental interference and romantic love also showed that parental interference *causes* an intensification of love. The correlational method can only demonstrate whether there is an association between two variables; it does not provide information about cause and effect. Thus, that study found that parental interference tends to be accompanied by romantic love. However, that finding could mean that interference causes love, that love causes parents to interfere, or that some third variable operates that causes a relationship between the two variables.

These two problems are serious limitations of the correlational method. Often they are not considered in media reports of research results. For instance, you may have seen newspaper accounts of the results of a correlational study that found a positive relationship between amount of coffee consumed and likelihood of a heart attack. It is easy to see that there is not necessarily a cause-and-effect relationship between the two variables. Numerous third variables (such as type of occupation, personality, or genetic predisposition) could cause both a person's coffee drinking behavior and his likelihood of heart attacks. Similar criticisms can be made of any study that employs the correlational method to study the relationship between two variables. Inevitably the results of such studies are ambiguous.

The experimental method reduces such ambiguity of interpretation. Remember that in the experimental method, one variable is manipulated while the second variable is observed. In Freedman's crowding experiment, the researchers determined the degrees of crowding to which the subjects were exposed and then observed their performances on various mental tasks. When the experimental method is used, the researcher can say something about the direction of causality. Note, in the crowding experiment, that the degree of crowding came first in the sequence of events. Thus, task performance could not have determined amount of crowding.

The experimental method uses two techniques—direct *experimental control* and *randomization*—to eliminate the influence of any extraneous third variables. Thus, any relationship between the two variables is real, because the two variables are directly related.

Experimental control

Experimental control means that all extraneous variables are kept *constant*. If a variable is held constant, it cannot influence the results. For example, one extraneous variable to be controlled in a crowding experiment is room temperature. Great care must be taken to ensure that the temperature is the same in both the crowded room and the uncrowded room. If the temperature variable were not controlled, the crowded room would be warmer than the uncrowded room. Any observed differences in task performance might then be due to the temperature variable, rather than the crowding variable. Other variables to be kept constant would include the attractiveness of the rooms, the method of recruiting subjects, and the person who reads instructions to subjects. It is not difficult to imagine how such variables could affect the results. For example, what would happen if the person reading instructions to the crowded subjects had an unintelligible foreign accent?

Randomization

Sometimes it is difficult to keep a variable constant. The most obvious such variable is any characteristic of the subjects. If, in a study using the experimental method, you have one group of subjects in the crowded condition and a different group of subjects in the uncrowded condition, the subjects in the two conditions might be different on some variable, such as social class. This difference could cause an apparent relationship between crowding and task performance.

The experimental method eliminates the influence of such variables by *randomization.* Randomization assures that the extraneous variable is just as likely to affect one experimental group as it is to affect the other group. To eliminate the influence of subject characteristics, the researcher assigns subjects to the two groups in a random fashion. Randomization assures that the subject characteristic composition of the two groups will be almost identical. This ability to randomly assign subjects to groups is an important difference between the experimental and correlational methods. Recall that in a correlational study a third variable such as social class could be responsible for the results. In a correlational study of crowding and performance, subjects in the low and high crowding groups could be different in social class. In a study using the experimental method this could not happen because the subjects would be randomly assigned to the two groups.

Any other variable that cannot be held constant is also controlled by randomization. For instance, often an experiment is conducted over a period of several days or weeks. Because all subjects in both conditions can't be run simultaneously, the researchers use a random order of running subjects. (*Running subjects* is the process of collecting data from the individuals who participate in the study. It is a perhaps unfortunate bit of jargon that may have its origins in the process of running rats through mazes.) This procedure prevents a situation in which only the uncrowded condition is studied during the first few days and only the crowded condition is studied during the last few days. Similarly, the uncrowded condition will not be studied only during the morning while the crowded condition is studied only in the afternoon.

Direct control and randomization eliminate the influence of any extraneous variable. Thus, the experimental method allows a relatively unambiguous interpretation of the results. Any difference between groups on the observed variable can be attributed only to the influence of the manipulated variable.

The experimental and correlational methods both are attempts to discover a relationship between variables. In the correlational method, both variables are observed by the researcher. In the experimental method, one variable is manipulated while the other variable is observed. The manipulated variable is called the *independent variable,* and the observed variable in the experi mental method is called the *dependent variable.*

INDEPENDENT AND DEPENDENT VARIABLES

The distinction between independent and dependent variables seems to be one of the most difficult things that the psychology student is asked to commit to memory. One way to remember the difference is to relate the terms to what happens to a subject in an experiment. The researcher devises a situation with which he or she confronts the subject. This situation is the manipulated variable; it is called the *independent variable* because the subject has nothing to do with its occurrence. In the next step of the experiment, the researcher observes the subject's response to the manipulated variable. The subject is responding to what happens to him; the researcher assumes that what the subject does or says is caused by the independent (manipulated) variable. In other words, the subject's behavior is *dependent* on the effect of the inde- pendent variable. The independent variable, then, is the variable *manipulated by the experimenter,* and the dependent variable is the *behavior of the sub- ject* that is assumed to be caused by the independent variable.

When the relationship between an independent and a dependent variable is presented on a graph (as in Figure 3-1), the independent variable is *always* placed on the horizontal axis and the dependent variable is *always* placed on the vertical axis. If you look back to Figure 3-1, you will see that this graphing method was used to present the four relationships.

PREDICTION VERSUS CONTROL

Two goals of science are prediction and control of behavior. In many ways, the distinction between prediction and control parallels the distinction be- tween the correlational and experimental methods. The correlational method allows prediction of behavior, and the experimental method allows control of behavior.

Let's say that, in a correlational study of crowding and task performance, you found that crowding is associated with poor performance. Can you now predict anyone's performance level on the basis of the amount of crowding in his neighborhood? The answer is yes; the correlational method does allow prediction of behavior. You can make such a prediction if you know that there is a relationship between the two variables.

Can you go one step further and control a person's level of task performance by changing the degree of crowding in his neighborhood? The findings of this correlational study do not indicate that this could be done. If the relationship between crowding and performance was caused by the operation of a third variable such as social class, then a change in amount of crowding would have no effect on task performance. Only a change in the *causal* variable would result in a performance change.

There are other interesting implications of the prediction–control distinction. When college administrators use such things as the Scholastic Aptitude Test (SAT) scores or high school grades to determine whether to admit an applicant, they are making a prediction of future behavior (success in college) on the basis of the results of research that uses the correlational method. Research has shown that a person's *observed* behavior on one variable (performance on the SAT) is associated with that person's *observed* behavior on another variable (grades in college). College administrators don't know why scores on the SAT predict college grades, and they probably don't care. They would be just as happy if size of earlobe predicted success in college; if this were true, an earlobe questionnaire would be mailed to all applicants. Could someone control a person's college grades by having him memorize the answer sheet for the SAT (or stretching his earlobe)? These tactics would probably not influence the person's college grades, because grades are caused by various factors (third variables) that also cause the person's score on the SAT. To have any kind of control over a person's college grades, you would have to change the variables that actually *cause* college grades.

USES OF THE CORRELATIONAL METHOD

Now that you know that the experimental method has distinct advantages, you may wonder whether researchers ever use the correlational method and, if so, why. The correlational method remains a popular research technique, because there are many situations in which the correlational method is the most practical—or perhaps the only—method available.

Exploratory research

When a researcher is just beginning to explore the relationship between variables, the first step may be a correlational study. In this early stage, the researcher is primarily interested in knowing whether *any* relationship exists between the two variables. If a relationship does exist, the researcher can then turn to the experimental method to learn more about the precise nature of the relationship.

Ethical and practical considerations

Some variables may not be studied experimentally because manipulation of these variables would be unethical or impractical. For instance, child-rearing practices would be very difficult to manipulate. Even if it were possible—for example, to randomly assign one group of parents to a withdrawal of love condition and another group to the physical punishment condition—such manipulation would be unethical. Instead, such variables are usually studied as they occur in natural situations. Many important research areas present similar problems. Among these are studies of the factors that lead to suicide, mental illness, alcoholism, divorce, or drug abuse, and studies of the effects of father or mother absence on sex-role identification. But we do not have to ignore such problems because we cannot use the experimental method. Instead, we can use the correlational method. Finally, some variables cannot be manipulated. The study of sex differences, for instance, requires use of the correlational method.

Making successful predictions

In many real-life situations, accurate predictions of future behavior are required, but no information is needed about the causes of that behavior. For example, a company president might need to predict whether an applicant will succeed in a specific job. In this situation, a test related to job performance could be used. On such a test, applicants who would be successful employees would score high and applicants who would be unsuccessful employees would score low. Thus, the company president could use the test results to screen applicants. These predictions of future behavior would eliminate the cost of training employees who would not become successful employees, as well as some of the pain and embarrassment that results from having to fire an employee.

The company president needs only accurate predictions of future behavior. He or she probably doesn't care *why* high scores on the test are related to job success. In theory, the actual content of the test is unimportant as long as test scores are related to job performance. A test that asks about movie preferences could, theoretically, be used to predict success as an accountant, if in fact a relationship exists. Use of such a strange predictor may strike you as unfair, however. And the United States Supreme Court has agreed with you. Because of recent Court decisions, any test used to make hiring decisions must have a surface relationship to the behavior being predicted. Thus, in practice, the test that is used usually examines the behavior of interest.

I have made a strong case for the superiority of the experimental method as a research tool, although there are situations in which the correlational method is preferable. Moreover, in attaining the ultimate goal of a thorough understanding of behavior, both methods are necessary and desirable. The experimental method permits relatively unambiguous inferences concerning cause and effect. Remember, though, that the high degree of control over extraneous variables along with the ability to strongly manipulate the variable of interest may also present problems of interpretation. An experimental finding that seems important under controlled conditions may be unimportant in the real world. Ideally, scientific progress involves dependence on information acquired under natural circumstances, further clarification obtained by the use of experimental methods, and then additional testing under natural conditions. This process constitutes a scientific discipline that is both precise and truly descriptive of events that occur in the everyday environment. A variety of techniques are used in this approach to the study of behavior. No single approach is sufficient. Each is appropriate under particular circumstances, and all are necessary in the development of a complete science of behavior.

STUDY QUESTIONS

1 *What is a* variable*? Try to think of at least five different variables, and then specify the* levels *of each variable.*
2 *Describe the four general types of relationships between variables. Draw graphs depicting these relationships.*

3 *What is the difference between the correlational method and experimental method? What is meant by the* direction of cause and effect problem *and the* third variable problem? *How does the correlational and experimental method distinction correspond to the distinction between prediction of behavior and control of behavior?*

4 *How do direct experimental control and randomization control for the influence of extraneous variables?*

5 *What is the difference between an independent variable and a dependent variable?*

6 *What are the primary reasons for using the correlational rather than the experimental method?*

4

MEASUREMENT OF BEHAVIOR

Whether a researcher uses the correlational method or the experimental method, observation or measurement of behavior is involved. In the correlational method, both variables are measured; in the experimental method, the independent variable is directly manipulated and the dependent variable is then measured. Thus, the observation or measurement of behavior is of central importance to the researcher. In this chapter, we will explore some of the fundamental concepts of measurement as well as some of the types of measurement techniques available to the researcher.

OPERATIONAL DEFINITIONS

The first point to consider is that a "variable" is an abstract concept that must be translated into concrete forms of observation or manipulation. Thus, a variable such as "aggression," "liking," "amount of reward," or "psychological health" must be defined in terms of the specific method used to measure or manipulate it. Scientists refer to the *cperational definition* of a variable. **43**

This is a definition of the variable in terms of the operations or techniques the researcher uses in measuring or manipulating the variable.

It is necessary to operationally define variables in order to empirically study them. Thus, a variable such as "speaker credibility" might be operationally defined as a "speaker described to listeners as a Nobel Prize recipient" or as a "part-time instructor at Central High School." Similarly, "liking" might be operationally defined as "a check mark on a 7-point scale ranging from dislike extremely to like extremely." Researchers must always translate the variables into specific operations for manipulating or measuring them.

The task of operationally defining a variable forces the scientist to discuss abstract concepts in concrete terms. Often this process results in the realization that the variable is too vague to study. This does not necessarily indicate that the concept is meaningless, but rather that systematic research is not possible until the concept can be operationally defined. Sometimes scientific study of a concept is dependent on development of a technology that makes operational definition possible. For instance, the scientific study of dreaming was facilitated by development of electrophysiological techniques for studying brain wave patterns during sleep.

Operational definitions also facilitate communication of our ideas to others. If someone wishes to tell me about *aggression,* I need to know exactly what he or she means by this term because there are many ways of operationally defining aggression. For example, aggression could be defined as: (1) the number and duration of shocks delivered to another person, (2) the number of times a child punches an inflated toy clown, (3) the number of times a child punches other children during recess, (4) homicide, or (5) warfare. My communication with the other person will be easier if we agree on exactly what we mean when we use the term *aggression* in the context of our research.

There is rarely a single, infallible method for operationally defining a variable. A variety of methods may be available, each of which has advantages and disadvantages. Researchers must decide which method is best for studying the problem at hand. Since no one method is perfect, it is clear that complete understanding of any variable involves studying the variable using a variety of operational definitions. We can now turn to some of the methods used to measure behavior.

We will examine five approaches to measuring behavior: (1) archival data sources, (2) self-report measures, (3) behavioral measures, (4) physiological measures, and (5) field observation. These methods represent general ap-

proaches that can be used when operationally defining a variable that is
to be measured.

METHODS FOR MEASURING BEHAVIOR
Archival data

The term *archival data* refers to existing information. The researcher doesn't actually collect the original data. Instead he or she analyzes existing data, such as statistics that are part of the public record, reports of anthropologists, or the content of letters to the editor. Archival data are used in investigations of historical variables and in cross-cultural research.

Historical research studies the changes in variables over time. One such study examined achievement motivation in American history. The investigators, de Charms and Moeller (1962), rated the amount of achievement imagery expressed in the themes of children's readers published between 1800 and 1950. The researchers had predicted that the achievement values expressed in the readers would be related to technological development. Indeed, they found that increases in achievement imagery were followed by increases in the number of patents issued several years later by the U.S. Patent Office. Declines in achievement imagery were associated with declines in patents. Analysis of these two types of archival data—children's readers and patent information—allowed the researchers to investigate how achievement motivation and technological development are related in a nation's history.

Archival data can also be used to establish a link between scientific research and the humanities. For many years historians have argued about the authorship of several of *The Federalist* papers—were they written by James Madison or Alexander Hamilton? To investigate this question, researchers counted the number of times specific words and value statements were used in works known to be authored by Madison and in works by Hamilton. Comparison of these data with similar information from the disputed papers led the researchers to conclude that the disputed papers were written by James Madison (Mosteller & Wallace, 1964; Rokeach, Homant, & Penner, 1970).

Archival data is also used in cross-cultural research. Cross-cultural research examines aspects of social structure that differ from society to society. A variable such as the presence or absence of monogamous marital relationships cannot be studied in a single society. In the United States, for example, monogamy is the rule, because bigamy is illegal. By looking at a number of cultures, some monogamous and some not, we can increase our understanding of the reasons that one system or the other comes to be preferred.

Cross-cultural research is also useful in determining the generalizability of results obtained in one culture. For example, research conducted in the United States has shown that removing a person's sense of individuality results in increased aggressiveness. In laboratory research conducted in the United States, subjects who were dressed in large lab coats and had hoods placed over their heads (loss of individuality) behaved more aggressively than subjects dressed in ordinary clothes and identified by name (Zimbardo, 1970). A valid question for research is whether the relationship between individuality and aggression is limited to modern-day United States society.

To study this question, Robert Watson (1973) used anthropologists' reports of warfare practices in a number of societies. He rated each society on the basis of whether warriors changed their appearance before battle, using body and face paint, wearing special clothes, and so on. He also rated the amount of aggression in warfare displayed by each society. Highly aggressive societies engaged in such practices as torturing prisoners, killing enemies on the spot, and headhunting. Less aggressive societies did not show such behaviors. Watson's results showed that loss of individuality is related to aggression in other cultures. Societies in which warriors change their appearance engage in more aggressive warfare than societies in which warriors do not make such changes.

The use of archival data allows researchers to study interesting questions that could not be studied in any other way. Archival data provide a valuable supplement to more traditional data collection methods. There are at least two major problems with the use of archival data, however. First, the desired historical records may be difficult to obtain, because often records have been lost or destroyed. Second, we can never be completely sure of the accuracy of information collected by someone else.

Self-report
Self-reports are the replies given by subjects in response to interviews and questionnaires—the two methods used most frequently by behavioral scientists to study behavior. Most people at some time have been asked to fill out a questionnaire or have been interviewed in a survey. Often respondents

are asked to rate their reactions to the independent variable. A questionnaire
item designed to measure liking might look like this:

How much do you like this person?

Dislike   Like
very much   very much

The subject places a check at the point on this 7-point scale that best represents his or her feelings toward the person being rated.

There are two basic ways of asking people about themselves. The first is to use a paper-and-pencil measure that asks the respondent to describe herself or himself on a written form. The second is the interview, which involves face-to-face contact between an interviewer and the respondent. Each approach has some advantages and some disadvantages. Paper-and-pencil measures are easy to administer and allow subject anonymity. Interviews are costly because a paid interviewer must interact individually with each person. However, interviews involve a real, interpersonal interaction and may provide a great wealth of unique information about the individual.

Surveys Self-report measures are used in surveys and opinion polls. Survey data can provide an accurate description of what is happening in an entire population. Polling organizations, such as Gallup and Harris, survey a relatively small number of people from a very large population to determine what people are thinking about issues such as gun control, capital punishment, and nuclear power, or to obtain data on preferences in political candidates and television programming. When scientific sampling techniques are used, the survey results can be interpreted as an accurate representation of the opinion of the entire population. Such accuracy can be achieved by sampling an extremely small percentage of a very large population, such as that of the United States.

Surveys on a much smaller scale are going on all the time. You may be asked by your school to be part of a student survey. Most large corporations survey employees to find out what they think of current operations. Or you may be contacted by a manufacturer who wants to know what you think of a product. The results of such surveys are generally used as a basis for instituting changes.

A questionnaire mailed out to individuals is the least expensive method of obtaining survey information. However, it is easier to throw away a questionnaire received in the mail than it is to refuse to respond to an interviewer. Persistent interviewers are usually successful in making sure that the entire sample takes part in the survey. When accuracy is very important—as it is in predicting the winner of a political contest—face-to-face interviews are usually preferable.

Aptitude and interest measures   Self-report measures are used in studies of aptitude and interest. Typically, such measures are designed for applied purposes. The Strong Vocational Interest Blank, for example, is given to many high school and college students to help them decide which vocations they might find most satisfactory. Aptitude tests are frequently used to predict an individual's future performance in a job. For example, people who apply for flight training in the armed forces may be given a test that will identify those individuals who are most likely to complete the training. Those who are not selected for the flight training may be given other tests to identify their aptitudes.

Personality measures   Self-report is frequently used in personality assessment. In clinical work, paper-and-pencil measures, diagnostic interviews, or a combination of both may be used in personality assessment. A well-known paper-and-pencil measure used in clinical diagnosis is the MMPI—the Minnesota Multiphasic Personality Inventory. The MMPI consists of 550 self-description items, such as "I have trouble making new friends." By saying whether each item is descriptive of himself or herself, the respondent provides a thorough self-description. The MMPI is generally used for diagnostic purposes. The items are divided into ten clinical scales, such as hypochondriasis, depression, and schizophrenia.

The MMPI, which is used primarily in clinical work, was developed by testing persons with known psychiatric disorders. Other personality assessment instruments, developed with normal subjects, are designed to measure dimensions of normal personality. One such test that is used frequently is the Personality Research Form (PRF) developed by Douglas Jackson. The PRF consists of self-descriptive items that measure "normal" personality traits such as achievement, dominance, and nurturance. Such tests are generally used in basic research on the structure of personality and the nature of personality traits.

Problems with self-report measures   Use of self-report measures, although widespread, presents several problems that should be recognized.

Interviewer bias   Several biases can affect the outcome of an interview. For example, because the interview is a face-to-face interaction, the interviewer can subtly influence the respondent's answers by inadvertently showing approval or disapproval of answers. Another bias, sometimes described as "seeing what you are looking for," can interfere when the interviewer must interpret the person's answers, as happens in a diagnostic interview.

This problem was nicely illustrated in an experiment conducted by Langer and Abelson (1974). Clinical psychologists were shown a video tape of an interview in which the person being interviewed was described to the psychologists as either an applicant for a job or a patient. Half of the psychologists were told that the person was a job applicant; the other half were told that the person on the tape was a patient. In fact, all of the psychologists saw the same tape. The psychologists later rated the person as more "disturbed" when the person was a patient than when he was a job applicant. This bias was much more pronounced among traditional therapists than among behavior-oriented therapists. Presumably, the behavior-oriented therapists focused more on the actual behavior of the person, and so were less influenced by the expectations stemming from the label of "patient."

Response sets   A response set—which is a tendency to respond to all questions from a particular perspective rather than to provide answers that are directly related to the questions—can affect the usefulness of data obtained from self-reports.

The most common response set is called *social desirability,* or "faking good." The social desirability response set leads the individual to answer in the most socially acceptable way—the way he thinks most people respond or the way that reflects most favorably on him. If a survey asked people to admit to behavior they may consider undesirable, the results may be considered suspect. I have even found it difficult to get college students to admit to the mildly undesirable activity of watching television.

The opposite of the social desirability bias is a tendency to respond in a socially undesirable way, or "faking bad." Faking bad is most often found in hospital and mental health settings among individuals who feel they have something to gain by being diagnosed as ill. The behavior of Corporal Klinger in the television series "M*A*S*H" is a humorous example of faking bad. Klinger wears women's clothing in an unsuccessful attempt to get a discharge from the army. The MMPI, which was constructed for use in clinical settings, includes a scale that is effective in identifying individuals who are faking bad.

Another problem is presented by the tendency of some respondents to consistently agree or disagree with survey questions. The solution to this problem is relatively straightforward—questions are posed in both positive and negative directions. For instance, a scale designed to measure attitudes toward marijuana might include two items such as: "There should be no criminal penalties for the use of marijuana" and "Persons who use marijuana are dangerous criminals." If someone agrees—or disagrees—with both items, his or her answers are definitely suspect.

Psychologists who use self-report measures realize that respondents do not always tell the truth—they may fake good or fake bad and thus provide inaccurate information. As a result, a researcher may attempt to conceal the purpose of his or her study from the respondents, in the hope that they will act naturally. In the next section we will explore techniques that can be used in situations in which self-report data may be inadequate.

However, we may have overestimated the tendency of people to misrepresent themselves. Sidney Jourard (1969) has argued that people are most likely to lie when they don't trust the researcher. Jourard asserts that if the researcher openly and honestly communicates the purposes and uses of the research, and gives assurances that there will be feedback concerning the results, then respondents will also be honest.

Behavioral measures

Behavioral measures use direct observation of behavior instead of self-reports. The difference between self-report and behavioral measures is the difference between asking a person how much and what kind of television programs she or he watches and electronically monitoring viewing behavior by attaching an instrument to the TV set.

Behavioral measures are used for a variety of reasons. For example, they must be used when the subject is unable to give verbal or written responses. Such situations occur in research that involves small children and species other than humans (although recent efforts to teach language to chimpanzees may lead to self-report data from other species).

Behavioral measures are also used to avoid the problems caused by faking. And they are used when the research demands observations of behavior in real-life situations. For example, researchers studying helping usually employ behavioral measures. They have found that social desirability bias can be a problem, because most people overestimate the extent to which they would help someone. Also, the typical helping experiment involves setting up an "emergency" situation in which, for example, a confederate has an epileptic seizure. The logical measure is to observe whether the subject who witnesses the emergency actually helps in the situation.

Data obtained from behavioral measures are valuable as supplements to data from self-report measures. When both approaches can be used, researchers can use the results from one approach as a check on the validity of the results obtained using the other approach. Liking, for example, can be measured by asking a person to indicate in a questionnaire whether he or she likes or dislikes another individual. And liking can be observed by measuring the physical distance that one person places between himself or herself and another individual. It is useful to know whether the self-report measure of liking and the behavioral measure of liking yield similar results.

Physiological measures

Physiological measures are recordings of the physiological responses of the body. Such measures provide one obvious solution to the problems of self-report. An individual has complete control over his or her responses in a self-report measure; physiological responses, however, are not easily controlled. The use of lie detectors is based on the assumption that physiological responses recorded by mechanical instruments will reveal the truth. The lie detector uses several physiological recording instruments that are believed to reveal emotional responses when a lie is told.

There are several commonly used physiological measures. The galvanic skin response (GSR) test is used as a measure of general emotional arousal and anxiety. The GSR is a measure of the electrical conductance of the skin, which changes when sweating occurs. Another physiological measure is the electromyograph, or EMG, which measures muscle tension. The EMG is frequently used as a measure of tension or stress.

Physiological measures are also used when the researcher wants information about the relationship between brain and behavior. The electroencephalograph (EEG) measures electrical aspects of brain activity. The EEG is generally used as a measure of cortical arousal. It can be used to record activity in different parts of the brain as learning occurs. The EEG has also shown that different brain wave patterns occur during the alert waking state, during relaxation, and during different stages of sleep. Research on brain activity during sleep has produced information on dreaming. And recent research on *bio-*

feedback shows that people can control the nature of their brain activity when given feedback from an EEG machine. With such feedback, people can learn, for example, to control their brain wave patterns so that they relax.

Other physiological measures are available to researchers. These three are the ones most frequently used and most illustrative of the usefulness of physiological recording.

Field observation

Field observation techniques of studying behavior involve a much more general methodological approach than the techniques we have been examining. It does not focus on specific measurement of a specific behavior. In the typical field observation study, the researcher makes observations in a natural setting (the field) over an extended period of time. Field observation is commonly used in anthropology. An anthropologist lives with a group in another culture and then writes a report that includes the observations and interpretation of these observations. An example is Margaret Mead's (1938) classic study of adolescence in Samoa. Mead concluded that Samoan adolescents do not experience the psychological problems seen in United States adolescents because the Samoan culture has less restrictive attitudes toward sex than does ours. Jane Goodall's observations of primate behavior over a long period of time under natural conditions in Africa provide another example of the field observation method.

A rather dramatic example of the use of field observation in psychology is provided by David Rosenhan's (1973) study, "On Being Sane in Insane Places." Rosenhan was concerned with a number of questions involving psychiatric diagnoses and hospitalization. Can sane individuals be distinguished from the insane? Do the characteristics of the mental hospital setting cause people to show abnormal behaviors? To answer these and other questions, Rosenhan devised an innovative scheme. The first step was to see whether sane individuals could be hospitalized as insane. Eight normal people (including Rosenhan) became pseudopatients—they went to a number of mental hospitals claiming that they had been hearing voices. They did not report or exhibit any other abnormal behaviors. All eight of the pseudopatients were admitted for hospitalization, and all but one were diagnosed as schizophrenic. After they were hospitalized, the pseudopatients behaved normally and indicated that their original symptoms had disappeared. Even so, their sanity was never detected. These individuals were hospitalized for an average of nineteen days, then discharged with a diagnosis of "schizophrenia in remission." Although a number of their fellow patients suspected that the pseudopatients were faking, none of the staff members at any of the various hospitals harbored any such suspicions. Instead, the staff members labeled the patients as "sick" and then perceived the patients' behaviors as evidence of the illness. (This finding fits the description of "seeing what you are looking for" discussed earlier). Rosenhan cites evidence gathered from psychiatrists, case summaries, and reports by the pseudopatients of incidents they experienced.

All of the pseudopatients kept extensive notes on their experiences which provided data for this study. These notes provide insights into the experience of hospitalization. Rosenhan describes in detail the extent to which patients and staff are isolated from one another and the small amount of time spent by staff members with patients. Many dramatic incidents occurred that indicate the extent to which institutionalized patients are depersonalized and powerless. Patients received excessive punishment from attendants. And staff members often treated the patients as if they were not actually present. For example, a nurse unbuttoned her uniform and adjusted her brassiere in front of a number of male patients. According to Rosenhan, she did this as if the patients were not there. Such treatment may indeed contribute to the bizarre behavior exhibited by institutionalized individuals.

Rosenhan's study is valuable. The data he presents were collected in a real setting and provide a rich description and interpretation of life in a mental institution. You should note that the methodology of field observation is very general and relies heavily on anecdotal evidence based on the specific experiences of the observers.

At least two general issues must be considered when evaluating field observation data. The first is whether the observer is concealed or nonconcealed. Are the subjects aware of the fact that someone is observing them? The anthropologist living among people in another culture is nonconcealed. The pseudopatients in Rosenhan's study attempted to conceal their note-taking, but quickly discovered that the staff paid no attention to this behavior. In general, concealed observation is preferable because the presence of the observer may influence and alter the behavior of those being observed. However, concealed observation sometimes involves excessive invasion of privacy—consider the example of researchers (Henle & Hubbell, 1938) who hid under beds in dormitory rooms to discover what college students talk about!

Another issue is whether the observer is a participant or nonparticipant in the setting in which the observations are made. A nonparticipant observer is an outsider who does not become an active part of the situation. A participant observer, however, is an active participant who observes from the inside. The pseudopatients in Rosenhan's study were participant observers. As participants they were able to observe many aspects of the hospital that they would not have seen as outsiders, and they were able to *experience* the effects of hospitalization. A potential problem in participant observation is that the observer may lose the objectivity that is necessary in scientific investigation. The observer may come to like the members of the group being studied and may even become converted if, for example, he is studying a religious or political group. Loss of objectivity results in biased observations that are of little value.

EVALUATING MEASURES OF BEHAVIOR

Now that you are familiar with some of the specific techniques for measuring or observing behavior, we can turn to some general considerations that are important in evaluating any measurement technique.

The problem of reactivity

A measure is reactive if awareness of being measured changes the subjects' behavior. Reactivity can be a problem when subjects are aware that their behavior is being observed. In other words, a reactive measure tells us what the person is like when being observed, but it doesn't tell us how the subject would behave under natural circumstances.

Reactivity is most likely to be a problem in self-report measures. We have already examined the problems of social desirability and other misrepresentations that may occur when using self-report. Reactivity can also be a problem in behavioral observation if the subjects know they are being observed. A participant observation technique with concealed observation would seem to be the ideal solution to reactivity, but even here the personality and behavior of the observer may change the subjects' behavior.

Fortunately, there are a number of ways to minimize or eliminate reactivity. The reactivity of self-report measures can be reduced by honesty between researcher and subject. Also, when people know that they are being observed—as in physiological recording or nonconcealed observation—the researcher should allow enough time for the subjects to adapt to the presence of the observer. After a period of time, subjects become used to the recording equipment or the observer, and it is expected that their behavior will be natural.

Reactivity can also be countered by the use of measures in which the subjects are totally unaware that their behavior is being studied. Such techniques are called *unobtrusive measures*. Observation of the distance that two people place between themselves is an unobtrusive measure, if the subjects do not know that that distance is being recorded. Archival records are unobtrusive measures, since such records usually have been collected as part of normal record keeping.

A number of examples of unobtrusive measurement techniques are described in a book by Webb, Campbell, Schwartz and Sechrest (1966). Some of these are quite humorous. For instance, in 1872 Sir Francis Galton used archival data to examine the efficacy of prayer in producing long life. Galton wondered whether British royalty, who are frequently the recipients of prayers by the populace, live longer than other people. He checked death records and found that members of royal families actually led *shorter* lives than other people, such as men of literature and science. The book by Webb and his colleagues is a rich source of such unobtrusive measures and has influenced researchers to seek alternatives to traditional self-report measures.

Reliability

A reliable measure is one that is consistent. And because it gives a stable measure of a variable, a reliable measure is precise.

A reliable measure of length, for example, would yield the same measurement of a table each time the table is measured. A measuring device that says today that a table is two meters long will yield an identical measure tomorrow. If it doesn't, then the device lacks perfect reliability and contains measurement error. Similarly, a measure of intelligence would be unreliable if it measured the same person as average one week, dull the next week, and then bright the following week.

Any measure can be thought of as made up of two components: (1) a *true score,* which is the real score on the variable, and (2) *measurement error.* An unreliable measure of intelligence contains measurement error and so does not provide an accurate indication of an individual's intelligence. In contrast, a reliable measure of intelligence—one that contains little measurement error—would yield an identical (or nearly identical) intelligence score each time the same individual is measured.

We can visualize the concepts of true score and measurement error as follows. Suppose that you have two intelligence tests. One test has high reliability; the other is not reliable. An obtained score of 102 on the two tests might be

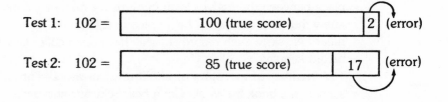

Test 1:   102 = | 100 (true score) | 2 | (error)

Test 2:   102 = | 85 (true score) | 17 | (error)

Test 2 is a less reliable measure of intelligence than Test 1. It would not yield a consistent or precise measure of intelligence.

The importance of reliability is obvious. An unreliable measure of length would be useless in building a table; an unreliable measure of a variable such as intelligence is useless in studying that variable. Researchers cannot use unreliable measures to discover relationships between variables. When the measure of the variable lacks reliability, the variable will usually not be related to other variables.

The reliability of a measure can be assessed in several ways. All are based on a statistic called a *correlation coefficient* (symbolized as r). The correlation coefficient is a number ranging from +1.00 to −1.00 and is used to indicate the strength of relationship between two variables. When the correlation coefficient approaches plus or minus 1.00, there is a strong relationship. A positive number (for example, +1.00) indicates that there is a positive relationship, and a negative number (for example, −1.00) shows that there is a negative relationship. A correlation of 0.00 indicates no relationship.

One commonly used method for assessing reliability is called *test-retest* reliability. The same individuals are measured at two different points in time. A correlation coefficient is computed to see whether scores on the first measure are related to scores on the second measure. (Recall that reliability is described as the consistency of a measure.) High test-retest reliability is indicated by a correlation coefficient which approaches +1.00. A high correlation coefficient tells us that each individual's score on the first measure is very similar to that individual's score on the second measure. Thus, the measure shows consistency over time.

After we know that a measure is reliable, we can ask about its *validity*. A valid measurement device actually measures what it is supposed to measure. A measure of scholastic aptitude (such as the Scholastic Aptitude Test, or SAT) is designed to measure the ability to succeed in school. To assess the validity of such a test, you would investigate whether the test does, in fact, measure this ability.

Face validity   There are several types of validity. The simplest is *face validity,* which tells us whether the measure appears (on the face of it) to measure what it is supposed to measure. A measure of ability to succeed as an accountant *could* ask questions concerning movie preferences, but such a measure would lack face validity. A measure that asks respondents to solve accounting problems would have face validity as a measure of ability to succeed as an accountant. Face validity is not very sophisticated, because it is based only on the appearance of the measure. However, it is useful as a first approximation of validity, and most researchers prefer to use measures that have face validity.

Criterion validity   A second type of validity is called *criterion validity*. The criterion validity of a measure is a matter of whether the measure allows the researcher to predict individuals' behavior on some criterion. Criterion validity is important in applied settings when researchers are interested in using a test to predict future behavior—the criterion. Tests that are given to applicants for a job, training program, or school are used to predict future performance and are called *predictor measures.* The criterion of a test of "pilot ability" is whether the test actually measures ability to complete flight training. I have already noted the usefulness of such tests as guides to the selection of job applicants. The researcher who is conducting criterion validity research must show that there is a relationship between scores on the predictor measure and scores on the criterion measure.

Construct validity   *Construct validity* is an important concept in basic, theoretical research. A measurement device that actually measures the theoretical variable or construct that it is supposed to measure is said to have construct validity. An example should help clarify the meaning of this term.

Psychologist Sandra Bem (1974, 1975) was interested in the concepts of masculinity and femininity. While recognizing that an individual might be highly masculine or highly feminine, Bem proposed that individuals might also be characterized as *androgynous*—as having both masculine and feminine characteristics. Bem's theory of the androgyny construct states that the androgynous person is free from traditional sex-role stereotypes and behaves in either a masculine or feminine way, depending on which is more appropriate in a particular situation. The exclusively masculine or feminine individual is limited to traditional sex-stereotyped behaviors.

Bem first had to construct a measurement device that would provide an operational definition of the androgyny variable. She developed a paper-and-pencil measure that asks respondents to describe themselves on twenty masculine characteristics, such as "ambitious" or "dominant," and on twenty feminine characteristics, such as "affectionate" or "gentle." Androgynous individuals describe themselves as having both masculine and feminine characteristics; others describe themselves as exclusively masculine or feminine. Bem called her measure the Bem Sex Role Inventory (BSRI). Is the BSRI reliable? Bem found the test-retest reliability of the BSRI to be .93, indicating high consistency over time.

Next she had to determine the construct validity of the BSRI. Does this test of androgyny measure what it is supposed to measure? That is, does the BSRI allow her to successfully test the proposed theory of the androgyny variable? The measure has construct validity if it is useful in testing Bem's theory of androgyny. Bem conducted research that supports the construct validity of the BSRI. She found that individuals who described themselves (on the paper-and-pencil test) as either masculine or androgynous exhibited masculine independence when placed in a conformity situation. And individuals who described themselves as feminine or androgynous exhibited feminine behavior when playing with a kitten. The results support the theory: Androgynous individuals engage in both masculine and feminine behaviors, while others are limited to either masculine or feminine behavior. The fact that the test devised to measure the androgyny construct is successful in testing the theory of androgyny is evidence for the construct validity of the measure.

Now that you have a basic understanding of the measurement techniques that are fundamental to all types of research, we are ready to turn to a detailed discussion of the design of experiments.

STUDY QUESTIONS

1 *What is an* operational definition *of a variable? Why may there be more than one operational definition of any variable?*

2 *Describe the five methods for measuring behavior. What advantages and disadvantages are associated with each of these methods?*

3 *How does the field observation method differ from the other methods discussed?*

4 *What is a reactive measure? What methods are available to reduce the problems of reactivity?*

5 *What is meant by* reliability *of a measure? Distinguish between* true score *and* measurement error.

6 *What is meant by* validity *of a measure? Distinguish between face validity, criterion validity, and construct validity.*

5

EXPERIMENTAL DESIGN: PURPOSES AND PITFALLS

The experimental method involves control of all extraneous variables. Suppose you think that crowding leads to poor task performance. To test your hypothesis, you put one group of people in a crowded room and another group in an uncrowded room. The people in each of the groups are then given identical tasks. Now suppose that the people in the crowded group do not do as well on the tasks as those in the uncrowded room. Can you attribute this difference between the groups to the difference in crowding? You can, *if* there is no other difference between groups. What if there *is* some other difference between the groups? Suppose that the room in which the crowded group was placed had no windows, but the room used for the uncrowded group did have windows. In this situation it would be impossible to know whether the poor performance of the crowded group was due to the crowding or the lack of windows.

This chapter contains a discussion of the fundamental principles of experimental design. Recall that the experimental method has the advantage of allowing an unambiguous interpretation of results. The researcher manipulates the independent variable to create groups that differ in the *levels* of the variable, and then compares the groups in terms of their scores on the dependent variable. All other variables are kept constant, either through direct *experimental control* or through *randomization*. If the scores of the groups are different, the researcher can conclude that the independent variable caused the results, because the only difference between the groups is the manipulated variable.

Although the task of designing an experiment seems simple, researchers sometimes make mistakes and use designs that look perfectly acceptable but actually contain serious flaws. We will take a detailed look at the flaws in such designs so that you will understand the advantages of good experimental designs.

CONFOUNDING AND INTERNAL VALIDITY

In this hypothetical crowding experiment, the variables of crowding and window presence are *confounded*. Confounding occurs when the researcher fails to control some extraneous variable. A variable other than the manipulated variable has been allowed to exert a *differential effect* in the two conditions. If the window variable had been held constant, the presence or absence of windows might have affected subject performance. Windows might improve performance, but the effect of the windows would be identical in both conditions. Thus, the presence of windows would not be a factor to be considered when interpreting the difference between the crowded and uncrowded groups. When the variables of crowding and windows are confounded, the effect of the window variable is *different* in the crowded and the uncrowded conditions.

In the crowding experiment, both rooms should have had windows or both rooms should have been windowless. Because one room had windows and one room did not, any differences in the dependent variable (performance) cannot be attributed solely to the independent variable (crowding). An alternative explanation can be offered—the difference in performance may have been caused, at least in part, by the window variable.

Good experimental design involves eliminating possible confounds that result in alternative explanations. You want to be able to say that your independent variable caused the results. You can only do this when there are no competing explanations.

When you can confidently attribute the results to the effect of the independent variable, the experiment is said to have *internal validity*. To achieve
internal validity, the researcher must design and conduct the experiment so
that only the independent variable can cause any effect that results. Internal
validity can be contrasted with the *external validity* of an experiment. When
an experiment has internal validity, the results are valid within the confines of
the experimental procedure used. When an experiment has external validity,
the results can be generalized to other subject populations, other situations,
and so on. Any good experiment must have internal validity; otherwise the
results are meaningless. If the results are internally valid, you can then ask
questions about generalizability—about external validity.

When you design an experiment or read about someone else's research,
it is important to consider internal validity. Several different experimental
designs that have been described by Campbell and Stanley (1966) nicely
illustrate the internal validity problem. We will look at three poorly designed
experiments that lack internal validity and two well designed experiments
that are internally valid.

POORLY DESIGNED EXPERIMENTS

The missing control group

In our first design, there is only one group. Suppose you want to test the hypothesis that sitting close to a stranger will cause the stranger to move away.
You might then try sitting next to a number of strangers and measuring the
number of seconds which elapse before the stranger leaves. Your design would
look like this:

subjects → Group 1: IV (Sit next to subject) → DV (Measure time until leaves)

Suppose you find that the average amount of time before the subjects leave
is 9.6 seconds. Such a finding is meaningless and uninterpretable. You do
not know whether subjects would have stayed longer if you had not sat down
or whether they would have stayed for 9.6 seconds anyway. It is even possible
that they would have left sooner—perhaps they liked you!

The design (called a "one-shot case study") lacks a crucial element of an experiment—a control or comparison group. A control condition, in which you do *not* sit next to the stranger or sit at a greater distance, is necessary.

One way to provide comparison would be to measure the subjects before manipulation (pretest) and then again afterward (posttest). An index of change from the pretest to the posttest could be computed. While this sounds fine, there are some major problems.

The pitfalls of a one-group pretest-posttest design

Consider a program designed to reduce prejudice. Using the design I just described, you would select a group of subjects, administer a test of prejudice, present the program to reduce prejudice, and then readminister the prejudice test. Hopefully, you would find that the average score on the prejudice measure was lower the second time. Your design would look like this:

(Subjects) → Group 1: DV pretest (Prejudice measure) → IV (Program)
→ DV posttest (Prejudice measure)

If you did find a reduction in prejudice, would it be safe to assume that the result was due to your prejudice reduction program? The problem with this design is that it has failed to take into account a number of competing alternative explanations arising either from the design itself or from external factors.

History   History refers to any event that occurs between the first and second measurements but is not part of the manipulation. For example, subjects in the prejudice study might hear a speech or see a program on television urging them to be unprejudiced. Any such event is a potential confounding variable that would invalidate the results.

Maturation of subject   People change over time. In a relatively brief period they become bored, fatigued, perhaps wiser, and certainly hungrier; children over a longer period become more coordinated and analytical. Any changes that occur systematically over time are called *maturation*. Maturation is a problem in our design because it could result in a change from the pretest to the posttest. Note that these differences might have occurred anyway, even if you hadn't introduced your manipulation.

Testing   Testing is a problem to the extent that simply taking the pretest changes a subject's behavior. Suppose that taking a test makes you aware of the attitude being tested. Such awareness might then cause a reduction in prejudice that would be reflected in a lower score on the posttest. If this occurred, note that your prejudice reduction program didn't cause the change;

simply taking the pretest was enough. Similarly, the experience of taking the pretest might make the subject more sophisticated about the matter being tested, or more adept at the skill being tested—again, the experiment would not have internal validity.

Instrument decay   Sometimes the basic characteristics of the measuring instrument change over time. This is particularly true when human observers are used to measure behavior. Interviewers may become more skilled, so that the manner in which they ask questions—and perhaps also the ways in which they record observations—also change. An observer may gain skill, lose energy, or change the standards on which observations are based.

Statistical regression   Statistical regression is sometimes called *regression toward the mean*. It is likely to occur whenever subjects are selected because they score extremely high or low on some characteristic. When such subjects are retested, their scores tend to change in the direction of the mean. Extremely high scores are likely to become lower, and extremely low scores are likely to become higher.

Statistical regression would be a problem in our prejudice reduction program if participants were selected because they scored high on the prejudice test. If the average score in the population were, say, 50 (on a scale from 0 to 100), and the selected subjects scored between 90 and 100, the chances are that the posttest scores would show an apparent reduction in prejudice. Such a change could be due to statistical regression, not to the program.

Statistical regression can be seen when we try to explain events in the "real world" as well. A columnist in the sports section of the *Los Angeles Times* frequently writes about the hex that awaits an athlete who appears on the cover of *Sports Illustrated*. It seems that the performances of a number of athletes have nosedived after they were subjects of *Sports Illustrated* cover stories. While it is possible that cover stories cause the lower performance (for example, the notoriety could result in nervousness and low concentration), statistical regression is also a likely explanation. An athlete is selected for the cover of *Sports Illustrated* because he or she is performing at an exceptionally high level. The principle of statistical regression says that high performance is likely to deteriorate. We would know this for sure if *Sports Illustrated* also did cover stories about athletes who were in a slump and became a good omen for them.

All of these problems can be eliminated by the use of an appropriate control group. A group that does not receive the experimental treatment gives you an adequate control for the effects of history, statistical regression, and so on. For example, outside historical events would have the same effect on both the experimental and control group. If the experimental group changes *more* than the control group, you can attribute this greater change—the difference between the changes in the two groups—to the effect of the experimental manipulation.

In forming a control group, you must make sure that subjects in the experimental condition and the control condition are equivalent. If subjects in the two groups are different *before* the manipulation, it is likely that they will be different *after* the manipulation as well. The next design illustrates this problem.

The nonequivalent control group design

This design employs a separate control group, but the subjects in the two groups—the experimental group and the control group—are not equivalent. Subject differences becomes a confounding variable that provides an alternative explanation for the results. This problem, which is called *selection differences,* usually occurs when subjects who form the two groups in the experiment are chosen from existing natural groups. Their participation in those earlier groups was a form of self-selection that will be reflected in their participation in the experimental and control groups. Suppose that your prejudice-reduction program consists of participation in an encounter or sensitivity training group. The design might look like this:

(Subjects)→ Group 1:IV (Sensitivity training) → DV (Prejudice measure)

(Subjects)→Group 2:IV (No sensitivity training) → DV (Prejudice measure)

The subjects in Group 1 were given the prejudice measure after they had completed a sensitivity training course. The subjects in Group 2 were people who had not participated in any sensitivity training courses. The researcher does not have any control over which subjects are in Group 1 and which are in Group 2. Rather, subjects in Group 1 chose to participate in the sensitivity training, while subjects in Group 2 chose not to participate. The problem of selection differences arises because people who participate in sensitivity training groups may be different from people who do not choose to participate. Perhaps people who seek out the sensitivity training are already less prejudiced. If this is true, any difference between the groups on the prejudice measure could reflect preexisting differences rather than the effect of sensitivity training.

Would a pretest solve the problem of selection differences? The results of a pretest would tell you whether the groups were equivalent before the manipulation. Thus, use of a pretest would improve this design. But it wouldn't completely solve the selection differences problem, because the two groups could still differ on other (unmeasured) variables.

Sometimes a research problem requires an approach that doesn't allow all the niceties of a true experiment. In such situations, the best we can do is to try to approximate a true experiment by making efforts to eliminate alternative explanations. Campbell has recently advocated using such quasi-experimental designs when real-world problems make true experiments impossible. Some of these designs will be discussed in Chapter 13.

WELL DESIGNED EXPERIMENTS

Now that you have a clear picture of how an experiment is designed and an understanding of some of the problems to be avoided, let's look at a well-designed experiment.

The simplest possible experimental design has two variables—the independent variable and the dependent variable—and two groups—an experimental group and a control group. Researchers must make every effort to assure that the only difference between the two groups is the manipulated variable. Remember, the experimental method involves control over extraneous variables. That control keeps extraneous variables constant (experimental control) or uses randomization to make sure that any extraneous variables will affect both groups equally. The simple experimental design can take one of two forms. The first is a posttest-only design. The second is a pretest-posttest design.

Posttest-only design

A researcher who uses the posttest-only design must (a) obtain two equivalent groups of subjects, (b) introduce the independent variable, and (c) measure the effect of the independent variable on the dependent variable. Such a design would look like this:

Subjects → Group 1: IV (experimental group) → DV (measurement)
Subjects → Group 2: IV (control group) → DV (measurement)

Thus, the first step is to choose the subjects and assign them to the two groups. The subject assignment procedures used must achieve equivalent groups in order to eliminate the problem of selection differences. Groups can be made equivalent by randomly assigning subjects to the two conditions or by having the same subjects participate in both conditions.

Next the researcher must choose two levels of the independent variable. This might involve an experimental group that receives a treatment and a control group which does not. For example, manipulating amount of reward could mean rewarding correct answers in one condition while not rewarding correct answers in the other. In a study of the effectiveness of a type of therapy, people who are given the therapy could be compared with an equivalent group of people who are not given therapy. Another approach would be to use two different amounts of the independent variable—to use a higher reward for the experimental group than for the control group, or more therapy for the experimental group than for the control group. Either of these approaches would provide a basis for comparison.

The final part of this design involves measuring the effect of the independent variable. The same measurement procedure is used for both groups, so that comparison of the behaviors of the two groups is possible. Since the groups were equivalent to begin with, and various factors—such as history and maturation—affect both groups equally, any difference between the groups must be attributed to the effect of the independent variable. The result is an experimental design that has internal validity. In actuality, statistical significance tests would be used to assess the difference between the groups. However, we don't need to be concerned with statistics at this point. An experiment must be well designed, and confounding variables must be eliminated. If not, the results are useless and statistics will be of no help at all.

Pretest-posttest design

The only difference between the posttest-only design and the pretest-posttest design is that in the latter a pretest is given before the experimental manipulation is introduced. This design makes it possible to ascertain that the groups were, in fact, equivalent at the beginning of the experiment. However, this precaution is usually not necessary if subjects have been randomly assigned to the two groups. With a sufficiently large sample, random assignment will produce groups that are almost identical in all respects. Although there are no clear-cut rules for specifying a "sufficiently large" sample, ten subjects per group probably is the absolute minimum. The larger the sample, the less like- lihood there is that the groups will differ in any systematic way.

Advantages and disadvantages of the two designs

Each design has some advantages and some disadvantages that become factors in the decision to include or to omit a pretest. Although randomization is likely to produce equivalent groups, it is possible that even with randomization the groups will not be equal. This would be particularly true with small samples. The knowledge that the groups are equivalent is reassuring. If the groups turn out to be nonequivalent, a third variable may have been operating and you would not have achieved a basis for interpreting the effect of the manipulated variable.

Sometimes a pretest is necessary to select a particular type of subject. In a prejudice reduction program, the researcher would probably want to use subjects who are highly prejudiced. These people, after all, are the target of your program. In addition, the researcher who uses a pretest can measure the extent of change in each subject. In a prejudice reduction program, the researcher could see whether the program was more effective for some people than for others. If it was, the researcher could try to find out why.

A pretest is necessary whenever there is the possibility that subjects may drop out of the experiment. For example, if your prejudice reduction program lasts over a long period of time, some people may drop out of the program. The dropout factor in experiments is called *mortality*. People often drop out for reasons unrelated to the experiment, such as illness. However, mortality sometimes is related to the experimental manipulation. Even if the groups are equivalent to begin with, different mortality rates could make them non-equivalent. In a program designed to reduce prejudice, who is most likely to drop out? The most prejudiced subjects in the experimental group might drop out, but the most prejudiced subjects in the control group probably would remain. If this did actually happen, the most prejudiced people in the original experimental group would not take the posttest. Use of a pretest makes it possible to assess the effects of mortality—you can look at the pretest scores of the dropouts and know whether mortality affected the final results. Mortality is most likely to be a problem when the experimental manipulation extends over a long period of time. In such a situation, a pretest is a very good idea.

One disadvantage of a pretest is that it may sensitize subjects to what you are studying, enabling them to figure out your hypothesis. If this happens, the subjects may then react differently to the manipulation than they would have without the pretest. For example, subjects in the prejudice reduction study might figure out from the pretest that researchers were studying prejudice. Then, when they experienced the experimental manipulation, they would think, "This is supposed to reduce my prejudice." And that might lead them to reduce their prejudice on the posttest. When a pretest affects the way subjects react to the manipulation, it is very difficult to generalize the results of the experiment to people who have not received a pretest. In other words, the independent variable may not have an effect in the real world where pretests are rarely given—a prejudice reduction program might have less influence on a group that does not realize the intent of the program than it has on a group of pretested subjects.

The pretest can provide a cue that tells subjects what the researcher is trying to find in his experiment. Such cues are called *demand characteristics* of an experiment. A demand characteristic is any aspect of the experiment that *demands* that the subject behave in a particular way. When such demand characteristics are present, the researcher's ability to generalize his findings to real world situations, where the demands aren't present, is diminished.

When use of a pretest is desirable, the researcher should try to disguise the pretest. Perhaps unobtrusive measures can be used so that subjects are not aware of the testing. Or perhaps the pretesting can be done in a completely different situation by a different experimenter. When reading about an experiment in which a pretest-posttest design was used, you should try to determine whether such precautions were taken.

The problem of confounds

Even though an experimenter has used one of the two good designs, you cannot assume that there are no design problems. A researcher might inadvertently fail to control all extraneous variables. This happened in a now famous experiment on achievement motivation (Horner, 1970). Female subjects were asked to respond to a story about a person named Anne, who finished at the top of her medical school class. Male subjects were asked to respond to a story about John, who finished at the top of his medical school class. The females wrote about all the social and emotional problems faced by Anne after her success. The males did not anticipate such problems for John when he achieved success. Note, however, that these responses do not tell us whether only female subjects see the problems of success, or whether both males and females react negatively when a female succeeds. The variables of sex of subject and sex of successful person were confounded. Another experiment (Monahan, Kuhn, & Shaver, 1974) was necessary to study the reactions of both male and female subjects to both Anne and John.

Remember, everything in the two conditions must be kept constant. Nothing but the independent variable can be allowed to vary. Subjects must be treated in the same way in both conditions. It would not be proper, for example, for the researcher to smile more at subjects in the experimental group than at subjects in the control group. Careful experimental procedures usually eliminate such problems.

Now that you have a basic understanding of the characteristics of good experimental designs, it is time to discuss how an experiment is actually conducted. The process of actually testing a hypothesis is challenging and fun.

STUDY QUESTIONS

1 *What is meant by confounding?*

2 *What is meant by the internal validity of an experiment?*

3 *Describe the various threats to internal validity discussed in the text: history, maturation, testing, instrument decay, statistical regression, selection differences, and mortality.*

4 *Why does having a control group eliminate the problems associated with the second "bad design"—the one-group pretest-posttest design?*

5 *Why do the two good experimental designs eliminate the problem of selection differences?*

6 *Distinguish between the posttest-only design and the pretest-posttest design. What are the advantages and disadvantages of each?*

6

CONDUCTING AN EXPERIMENT

After you have decided on a hypothesis to test, you must do a great deal of planning before you actually conduct the experiment. Before an abstract idea can be turned into a research project and tested, a number of choices have to be made.

A hypothesis proposes a relationship between two conceptual variables. To test your hypothesis, you will have to decide how you are going to manipulate the independent variable and how you are going to measure the dependent variable. Remember, usually a variable can have many operational definitions—you will have to decide on one. This will require consideration of how to maximize the possibility that your independent variable will have an effect on the dependent measure. You will also have to determine how to work within the limits of your budget and of the facilities available to you. And you will have to be sure that your experiment is ethical. You must decide on the types of control groups that will be used, how many subjects to choose, and how to select those subjects. You will need to analyze your results, and you will have to decide how to communicate those results to others. All of these aspects of conducting an experiment will be discussed in this and the following two chapters. **73**

The evolution of an idea from conception to publication is a long one, but it is an exciting process for the researcher who initiated the idea. This chapter gives you a detailed, behind-the-scenes look at the process of experimental research. We'll consider some of the general principles researchers use when they are planning the details of their experiments, so that you will be able to conduct your own research if you decide to do so.

MANIPULATING THE INDEPENDENT VARIABLE

To manipulate the independent variable, you have to turn a conceptual variable into a set of specific operations—that is, a set of specific instructions, events, and stimuli to be presented to subjects. In addition, the independent and dependent variables must be introduced within the context of the total experimental setting. This has been called "setting the stage" (Aronson & Carlsmith, 1968). It is always necessary that your procedures make sense to subjects.

Setting the stage

In setting the stage, you usually have to explain to subjects why the experiment is being conducted. Sometimes the rationale given is completely truthful, although rarely will you want to tell subjects the actual hypothesis. For example, subjects could be told you are conducting an experiment on learning when, in fact, you are studying a specific aspect of learning.

Sometimes the researcher conceals from the subjects the actual purpose of the experiment. The use of deception is common in social psychological research. Researchers often feel that subjects behave most naturally when they are unaware of the variable that is being manipulated. If subjects know what you are studying, they may try to confirm the hypothesis, or they may try to look good by behaving in a socially acceptable way.

Thus, deception may frequently be necessary if the experiment is to be conducted successfully. However, you must recognize that deception is an ethically questionable procedure and should be used only when necessary. Further, when subjects have been deceived during an experiment, it is very important that the researcher debrief the subjects after the experiment is completed.

There are no clear-cut rules for setting the stage, except that the total experi- mental setting must seem plausible to the subjects. And there are no clear-cut rules for translating conceptual variables into specific operations. Exactly how the variable is manipulated depends on the variable and on the cost, practicality, and ethics of the procedures you are considering using.

Types of manipulations

Straightforward manipulations Sometimes researchers can manipulate a variable with relative simplicity by presenting written or verbal material to the subjects. Consider an experiment on speaker credibility and attitude change. The researchers have decided to study whether speaker credibility influences attitudes about methadone treatment for drug addicts. They write a persuasive communication that is designed to change attitudes about methadone treatment. Then they tell the subjects that the communication was written by a person of low credibility or of high credibility and have the subjects read or listen to the communication. For example, a speech advocating increased methadone treatment for drug addicts could be attributed to either "George Klein, professor of neurosciences at Harvard Medical School" or "George Klein, biology major at a local college." The researchers would then compare the attitudes of the experimental and control groups toward this treatment.

Many of the experiments you will read about will be straightforward. It is impossible to detail all of the different procedures used in behavioral research. A few illustrations will suffice. Studying how people judge responsibility for an accident could involve having subjects read about a car accident. Specific aspects of the accident, such as its seriousness or the characteristics of the car driver, could be manipulated (Walster, 1966). In a study of how we form impressions of people, subjects could be asked to read about or to view people who vary on a particular characteristic, such as physical attractiveness (Dion, Berscheid, & Walster, 1972). Factors in learning could be studied by presenting subjects with material to learn. The difficulty of the material, subject motivation, or a variety of other factors could then be studied. There is an almost endless supply of behavior to be studied, and one way of studying behavior is to present subjects with a set of straightforward written or verbal stimuli.

Staged manipulations Other manipulations you may read about are less straightforward. Social psychologists often stage events that enable them to study various aspects of social behavior. Frequently these experiments involve a *confederate*—a person who poses as a subject but is actually part of the manipulation.

For example, a confederate is frequently used in experiments on aggression. The confederate and one subject both report to the experiment and are told to wait in a room before the experiment begins. During this waiting period, the confederate insults the subject in one condition but not the subject in the other condition. The experimenter then enters and informs the confederate and the subject that learning is being studied and that one of them will be a teacher while the other will be a learner. The assignments to the roles of teacher and learner appear to be random but are actually rigged by the experimenter—the confederate is always the learner and the subject is always the teacher. In the learning task, the subject is permitted to shock the confederate whenever an incorrect answer is given. The amount of shock chosen by the subject is the measure of aggression; the researcher compares the amount of shock given in the insult and no-insult conditions.

Staged manipulations demand a great deal of ingenuity and even some acting ability. They are used to involve subjects in an ongoing social situation. Thus, the subjects perceive the situation not as an experiment but as a real experience. Researchers assume that such procedures will result in natural behavior that truly reflects the feelings and intentions of subjects. However, such procedures allow for a great deal of subtle interpersonal communication that is hard to put into words. This may make it difficult for other researchers to replicate the experiment. Also, a complex manipulation is difficult to interpret. If many things happened to the subject, what *one* thing was responsible for the results? In general, it is easier to interpret results when the manipulation is relatively straightforward. However, sometimes the nature of the variable you are studying may demand complicated procedures.

Strength of the manipulation

In the simplest experimental design, there are two levels of the independent variable. In planning the experiment, the researcher has to choose these levels. A general principle to follow in choosing levels of the independent variable is that the manipulation should be as *strong* as possible. A strong manipulation is designed to maximize the differences between the two groups. A strong manipulation increases the chances that the independent variable will have an *effect*.

To illustrate, suppose you think that there is a positive linear relationship between attitude similarity and liking ("birds of a feather flock together"). In conducting the experiment, you could arrange for subjects to encounter another person, a confederate. In one group, the confederate and the subject would share similar attitudes, in the other group, the confederate and the subject would be dissimilar. Similarity, then, is the independent variable, and liking is the dependent variable. But you have to decide on the amount of similarity. Figure 6-1 shows the hypothesized relationship between attitude similarity and liking at ten different levels of similarity. Level 1 represents the least amount of similarity and level 10 the greatest similarity. To achieve the

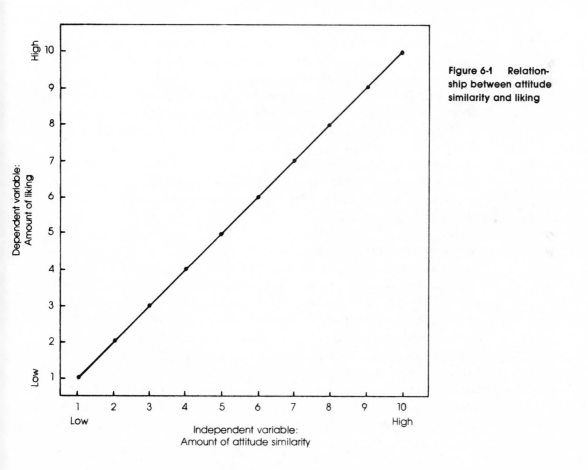

Figure 6-1   Relationship between attitude similarity and liking

strongest manipulation, the subjects in one group would encounter a confederate of level 1 similarity and the subjects in the other group would encounter a confederate of level 10 similarity. This would result in the greatest difference in the liking means. The strong manipulation would result in a 9-point difference in mean liking. A weaker manipulation—using levels 3 and 7, for example—would result in a smaller mean difference.

A strong manipulation is particularly important in the early stages of research, when the researcher is most interested in demonstrating that a relationship does in fact exist. If the early experiments are successful in finding a relationship between the variables, later research can systematically manipulate the other levels of the independent variable to provide a more detailed picture of the relationship.

The principle of using the strongest manipulation possible can be tempered by at least two considerations. First, the strongest possible manipulation may involve a situation that rarely if ever occurs in the real world. For example, an extremely strong crowding manipulation might involve placing so many people in a room that no one could move. Such a condition might result in a significant effect on a variety of behaviors. However, we wouldn't know if the results were similar to what occurs in more common situations that are less crowded—as in many classrooms or offices.

A second consideration is ethics. A manipulation should be as strong as possible within the bounds of ethics. A strong manipulation of punishment, for example, might not be possible because of the physical and psychological harm that might result.

Cost of the manipulation

Cost is another factor in the decision about how to manipulate the independent variable. When researchers have limited monetary resources, it is difficult for them to conduct research that involves expensive equipment or salaries for confederates or subjects in long-term experiments. Also, a manipulation in which subjects must be run individually is more costly of the researcher's time than a manipulation that allows running many subjects in a single setting. In this respect, a manipulation that uses straightforward presentation of written or verbal material is less costly than a complex, staged, experimental manipulation. The costs of research limit what a researcher can do. Some government and private agencies provide grants for research. A researcher can apply for such a grant for an expensive project. If the proposed research is judged to be important, funds may be provided to the researcher. Because much research is costly, continued public support of these agencies is very important.

MEASURING THE DEPENDENT VARIABLE

An investigator who is conducting an experiment must find a specific way to measure the dependent variable. We don't need to go into this topic in great detail—the same general considerations in measuring and observing behavior that were discussed earlier apply here as well.

The dependent variable in an experiment is usually in the form of a self-report or a direct behavioral observation. The measurement of either of these should be *reliable*. An unreliable measure contains a great deal of measurement error. Such error will be reflected in greater variability in scores. That is, scores on an unreliable measure will have greater variability about the group mean than scores on a reliable measure. When there is a large amount of error variance, it is difficult to obtain a significant difference between the means.

The dependent measure should also be *sensitive* enough to show a difference between groups. For example, a measure of liking that asks, "Do you like this person?" (answer yes or no) is probably less sensitive than one that asks "How much do you like this person?" (on a specific scale). The first measure allows only for a yes or no response—most subjects may be polite and say "yes" regardless of how they feel. The second measure allows for gradations of liking—a continuous scale ranging from "like extremely" through "neutral" to "dislike extremely" could be used. Such a scale makes it easier to detect differences between groups in terms of *amount* of liking. The main point is that the dependent measure should be able to detect the effect of the independent variable. It would be ridiculous, as Neale and Liebert (1973) have pointed out, to measure strength by asking subjects to lift a tiny thimble (everyone can do this) or a 500-pound weight (no one could do it)— it is impossible to find differences between groups with such measures.

When using self-report measures, it is often desirable to disguise the measures. One way to do this is to place the crucial question or questions among a number of *filler* items. For instance, measures of attitude toward increased methadone treatment could be placed among a series of attitude questions asking about a variety of other topics. This technique should divert the subjects' attention away from what you are really studying—attitude change. Another method of disguising the measure is to remove it from the primary experimental context. For instance, another experimenter might give the measure in the context of a separate experiment. Subjects are less likely to guess the true nature of the experiment and connect the experimental manipulation and dependent measure when the manipulation and measure are given in different contexts. Such procedures are particularly desirable in a pretest-posttest design. A disguised pretest should help prevent the subject from guessing the purpose of the experiment.

It is usually advisable to have multiple measures of the same dependent variable. There are usually several ways of actually measuring a variable. Confidence in the results is increased if the same results are found with a variety of operational definitions of the variable. It is usually possible to take multiple measurements in an experiment. (Performing multiple manipulations of the same independent variable is usually not possible in one experiment. We'll discuss this topic further in the chapter on generalizing results.) For example, the measurement of "liking" for someone can involve paper-and-pencil self-report measures, and behavioral measures. In addition, the relationship between the independent and dependent variable may not be a simple one. An independent variable such as attitude similarity or physical attractiveness might influence some aspects of liking (desirability as a work partner or a potential date) but not other aspects of liking (desirability as a roommate or potential spouse). Such differences are interesting and represent valuable information. If it is possible to collect multiple measures (and usually it is relatively easy and inexpensive to do this), such procedures are a good idea.

Finally, cost and ethics must be considered when you are choosing a dependent variable. Observational techniques that require several observers are more costly than self-report measures. Measurements made with expensive recording equipment present the same problem. Researchers require resources from the university or outside agencies to carry out such research. Ethical concerns are also crucial. Researchers must be extremely careful when invasion of privacy is a possibility. For instance, measures of sexual behavior require subject anonymity, and subjects should be free to refuse to divulge such information.

Our basic, simple experimental design contains two groups. In the simplest case, these may be an experimental group that receives the manipulation and a control group that does not. Use of a control group makes it possible to eliminate a variety of alternative explanations based on history, maturation, statistical regression, and so on.

Sometimes more than one control group may be necessary. The general purpose of a control group is to provide a basis for eliminating alternative explanations for the results. Different research problems may demand specific additional control groups. The need for such additional groups becomes a factor in planning the experiment.

In drug research, one specific control group is called a *placebo* group. Consider a drug experiment that is investigating whether a drug improves the behavior of a group of patients. One group receives the drug while the other group does not. Now suppose the drug group does show an improvement. The problem is that we don't know whether the improvement has been caused by the properties of the drug or whether it was caused by the placebo effect of the drug. In other words, just the administration of a pill or an injection may be enough to cause an observed improvement in behavior. To control for this possibility, a placebo group can be added. Subjects in the placebo group receive a pill or injection—for example, a sugar pill—but do not receive the drug given to subjects in the experimental group. If the improvement results from the active properties of the drug, the subjects in the experimental group should show greater improvement than those in the placebo group.

Another type of specific control is seen in brain lesion research. One way to study the relationship between brain and behavior is to surgically remove or destroy certain parts of the brain. The changes in behavior that result can then be observed. (Such research is conducted only on laboratory animals, of course). If your design had only two groups—one that receives the brain operation and one that does not—what is an alternative explanation for the results? The obvious one is that the change in behavior could be due to the effects of the operation procedure, rather than the actual lesion. The animal in the operation group is anesthetized, the scalp and skull is cut, and so on. Such procedures could cause a change in behavior even if the brain is left intact. To control for this possibility, a *sham operation* group can be added. Subjects in the sham operation group are treated exactly like subjects in the experimental group, *except* the brain is left alone. This group provides a basis for looking at the effect of the operation procedures as distinguished from the effects of the brain lesion.

Hypnosis research also provides an example of specific control groups. A basic hypnosis experiment might have two groups—one that receives the hypnotic induction procedure and one that does not. You could then see whether a behavior occurs under hypnosis but not under normal waking conditions. Let's say that subjects behave differently under hypnosis. A problem here is that we don't know whether their behavior is caused by the specific effects of the hypnotic state, or whether it occurs because subjects act as they think a hypnotized person would act. In other words, it may not be necessary to hypnotize subjects to produce certain behaviors. Simply motivating subjects to act hypnotized may be enough. One answer to this problem is to add a *simulator* control group. Simulators are not actually hypnotized but are asked to behave as they think a hypnotized person would. By comparing the hypnotized and simulator groups, you can see whether the hypnotic induction is necessary to produce a change in behavior. If the hypnotized subjects and the simulators behave alike, then the hypnotic state isn't necessary. If they behave differently, then you can conclude that hypnosis does have an effect. Hypnosis researchers such as Orne (1959) have successfully used the simulator technique to discover what effects hypnosis really has. For example, hypnosis does seem to aid in pain reduction. Hypnotized subjects can withstand levels of pain that are intolerable to simulators (Hilgard, 1969).

It is usually a good idea to think about your research procedure to see if there are alternative explanations such as these. If so, perhaps a specific control group can be added so that you can look at the alternative explanation.

THEORETICAL INTERNAL VALIDITY

If an experiment is well designed, the researcher can attribute the results to the effect of the independent variable manipulation. Often the researcher wants to do more than simply relate the independent and dependent variables. Instead, the researcher may want to explain the relationship by referring to an underlying psychological process as being responsible for the results. The specific manipulation might be said to create guilt, anxiety, cognitive dissonance, or some other psychological process that is operating in the situation. The use of such mediating processes is particularly common in personality and social psychological research.

The use of theoretical process variables, such as guilt, frequently leads to considerable controversy among researchers. Even though two researchers will readily agree that the results were due to the manipulation, they may disagree about the underlying process that was responsible for the results. The experimental design has internal validity, but there may be several theoretical explanations of *why* the results occurred.

Consider an experiment on the effect of harming someone on compliance by the person who did the harm with a request by the person harmed. The basic finding is that you are more likely to agree to perform a favor for someone if you have recently harmed that person. In an experiment by Carlsmith and Gross (1969), the subject was assigned to be the teacher in a learning task. In one condition, the learner received an electric shock (delivered by the teacher) whenever a mistake was made; in the other condition, the teacher sounded a buzzer for each mistake. You probably recognize this procedure now, and realize that the learner was really a confederate and did not actually receive electric shock. When the experiment was supposedly over, the confederate (the learner who was harmed) made a request of the subject (the teacher who administered the shock or buzz). The confederate, it seems, was trying to block plans for a freeway among the redwoods of Northern California. He requested that the teacher call people to get signatures for a petition against the freeway. The results showed greater compliance with the request when the subject had shocked the confederate than when he had merely buzzed him.

Carlsmith and Gross used guilt as a theoretical construct to explain their results. More guilt is generated when electric shock is delivered; the compliance with the favor represents an attempt by subjects to reduce their guilt feelings. No one doubts that delivering shock increases compliance. But is it really guilt that is responsible? Other researchers have offered alternative theoretical explanations. For instance, harming another person may reduce your self-esteem; compliance with a request to save the redwoods may be a way to restore your self-image (McMillen, 1971). Another explanation states that you comply to be consistent with the fact that you have controlled the other person's fate (Brock, 1969). The point is that the experiment lacks *theoretical* internal validity; there are a number of alternative theoretical explanations for the results.

Theoretical internal validity is important because researchers want to specify the correct theoretical explanation for the results, but it is not a problem if you simply wish to *use* the results. Thus, you now know that you can get someone to comply with your request more easily if they have previously harmed you. The theoretical explanation isn't that important. Explanation is, of course, important to the ultimate advance of a science, and further experiments are usually done to try to find the most plausible explanation.

In designing experiments, it is useful to try to directly measure the underlying process. Attempts could be made to directly measure guilt or self-esteem at various points in the experiment. Such measurements could provide support for the various theoretical explanations. Although it is easier to recommend such measurements than to make them, it is wise to consider them when planning an experiment. If at all possible, the researcher should try to directly measure the psychological processes that are presumably operating.

DEBUGGING THE EXPERIMENT

So far, we have discussed a number of the factors that a researcher considers when planning an experiment. Actually conducting the experiment and analyzing the results is a time-consuming process. Before actually doing the experiment, the researcher wants to be as sure as possible that everything will be done right. How can a researcher do this? There are a number of ways of eliminating the bugs from an experiment before you start.

Research proposals

After considerable thought has gone into the planning of the experiment, the researcher writes a research proposal. The proposal details why the research is being done—what questions the research is designed to answer—and discusses the variables being studied. The details of the specific procedures that will be used to test the idea are then given. A research proposal is quite similar to the introduction and method sections of a journal article.

Such proposals are required as part of applications for research grants. They are a useful part of the planning process for any type of research project. Just putting your thoughts into words helps you to organize and systematize your ideas. In addition, the proposal can be shown to friends, colleagues, professors, and other interested parties. These people can provide useful feedback about the adequacy of your procedures, and they may see problems that you didn't recognize. They may also be able to offer ways of improving the experiment.

Pilot studies

When the researcher has finally decided on all the specific aspects of the experimental procedure, it is possible to conduct a pilot study. A pilot study is a mini-experiment in which you test your procedures with a small number of subjects. Thus, the researcher can learn whether the planned procedures really work before efforts are expended on the full-blown experiment. The pilot study will reveal whether most subjects understand the instructions, whether the total experimental setting seems plausible, and so on. And a pilot study allows the experimenter (and confederates, if there are any) to practice, to become comfortable with their roles, and to standardize their procedures.

Manipulation checks

The pilot study also provides an opportunity for a *manipulation check*. A manipulation check is an attempt to directly measure whether the independent variable manipulation has the intended effect on subjects. If you were manipulating anxiety, a manipulation check could tell you whether subjects in the high anxiety group really were more anxious than subjects in the low anxiety condition. In the anxiety manipulation, the manipulation check might involve a self-report of anxiety, a behavioral measure (such as number of arm and hand movements), or a physiological measure. If the manipulation was the physical attractiveness of someone, the manipulation check could determine whether subjects do rate the high attractive person as more physically attractive. Manipulation checks can be included in the actual experiment, although you may want to avoid a check in the actual experiment if you are trying to disguise the purpose of the experiment.

A manipulation check has two advantages. First, if the check shows that your manipulation was not effective, you have saved the expense of running the actual experiment. You can turn your attention to changing the manipulation to make it more effective. For instance, if the manipulation check showed that neither the low nor the high anxiety group was very anxious, you could change your procedures to increase the anxiety in the high anxiety condition.

Second, a manipulation check is also advantageous if you get negative results—that is, if the results indicate that there is no relationship between the independent and dependent variables. A manipulation check can tell you whether the negative results are due to a problem in manipulating the independent variable. If your manipulation is not successful, then it is only reasonable that you will obtain negative results. If both groups are equally anxious after you manipulate anxiety, anxiety can't have any effect on the dependent measure. What if the check shows that the manipulation was successful, but you still get negative results? Then you know at least that the negative results were *not* due to a problem with the manipulation. The reason for not finding a relationship lies elsewhere. You may have had a poor dependent measure. Or possibly there really isn't a relationship between the variables.

DEBRIEFING

The final part of the experiment, if human subjects have participated in the research, is a debriefing session. During debriefing, the experimenter explains the purpose of the research and tells the subjects what kinds of results are expected. The practical implications of the research may also be discussed. This is the educational purpose of debriefing. Often subjects for research are recruited from introductory psychology classes. At the very least, participation should have some educational benefit.

If the subjects have been deceived in any way, debriefing is necessary for ethical reasons. The experimenter needs to explain why the deception was necessary and must assure the subjects that the particular research problem required the deception. If the research procedures altered the subjects' physical or psychological state in any way—for example, by lowering self-esteem or increasing anxiety—the subjects must be returned to their original condition. Debriefing, then, is an important part of the experiment. Hopefully, the subjects will leave the experiment without any ill feelings toward psychology. And they may leave with some new information about their own behavior.

The researcher may ask the subjects not to discuss the experiment with others. Such requests are made when an experiment has not been completed and more subjects will be participating. Subjects who have already participated are aware of the general purposes and procedures, and it is important that future subjects don't come to the experiment knowing everything that is going to happen.

After the data has been collected, the next step is to analyze the data. The scores on the dependent measure are tabulated and means are calculated. This data is subjected to a statistical analysis that provides a basis for interpreting the results. The statistical analysis helps the researcher to decide whether there really is a relationship between the independent and dependent variables. The logic underlying the use of statistical tests is discussed in Chapter 8. It is not the purpose of this book to teach you statistical methods. However, the calculations involved in several statistical tests are given in the Appendix.

WRITING THE RESEARCH REPORT

The last step is to write a report that details why you conducted the research, the procedures you used, and what was found. A description of how to write such reports is included in the Appendix. After a researcher has written the report, what does he or she do with it? How does the researcher communicate the findings to others?

Research findings are most likely to be communicated when the research was successful—when a significant relationship was obtained. Other researchers are primarily interested in knowing about relationships that do exist. They are not interested in knowing about all the relationships that don't exist, unless the absences of such relationships contradict common sense assumptions. This is definitely not the best of all possible worlds. Obviously, it would be useful to know about research that failed as well as about research that succeeded. However, we live in a hard world with lots of problems. The main problem here is that opportunities for publishing results are limited. Space in journals is limited, and even reports of studies that have found significant relationships are often rejected. Another problem is that negative results are very puzzling. Perhaps there really is no relationship between the variables. Or perhaps errors in the planning and execution of the specific experiment were responsible for the negative results. There may have been problems with the way the independent variable was manipulated or with the way the dependent variable was measured. Although negative results are sometimes published, usually the best you can do is to send your report to other researchers who are interested in your general topic. These people will be interested in your findings even if the report is not published in a journal.

There are a number of ways to communicate the findings of successful research. An important opportunity is provided by conventions. Each year professional associations hold conventions where scientists present reports of their research. In psychology, a national convention is held each fall, and regional and state conventions are also held each year. The regional and state conventions are usually close and easy to get to. They provide excellent opportunities for students to become involved with psychology as a profession. At conventions you can find out about recent research on topics you find interesting, you can hear and see major figures in the field, and you can see interesting films. Discussions of research on clinical problems are presented, and there are demonstrations and workshops on therapy techniques. Your professors can tell you more about these conventions. The locales and dates are different each year.

Many journals publish research findings. Most of the journals are specialized. For example, several journals publish research on personality and social psychology, some deal with clinical and abnormal psychology, and others specialize in physiological psychology. And so on. Because so many journal articles are published each year, you will find *Psychological Abstracts* a valuable aid in your efforts to keep abreast of psychological research in your particular field.

Because the number of journals is small compared to the number of reports written, it isn't easy to publish research. When a resarcher submits a paper to a journal, one or more reviewers read the paper and recommend that the paper be accepted or rejected. As many as 75 to 90 percent of the papers submitted to the more prestigious journals are rejected. Many of the rejected papers are eventually published in less prestigious journals, but much research is never published. This isn't necessarily bad. It simply means that selection processes separate high quality research from low quality research.

Now that you have a thorough understanding of how a research project is conducted, it is time to examine in more detail the various aspects of that process. Let us look next at how subjects are selected for research and how subjects are assigned to the various groups in an experiment.

STUDY QUESTIONS

1 *Discuss the considerations involved in deciding on how to manipulate an independent variable: straightforward vs. staged manipulations, strength of the manipulation, resemblance to the real world, ethics, and costs.*

2 *Discuss the considerations involved in deciding how to measure a dependent variable: reliability, sensitivity, disguising the measure, multiple measures, costs, and ethics.*

3 *What is the purpose of a control group? Why would a researcher need more than one control group?*

4 *What is the purpose of a placebo group?*

5 *Why do researchers worry about theoretical internal validity when an underlying theoretical process has been proposed to explain the results of an experiment?*

6 *What methods can be used to debug an experiment?*

7 *What is a manipulation check? How does it help the researcher interpret the results of an experiment?*

8 *What does a researcher do with the findings after completing a research project?*

7

CHOOSING AND ASSIGNING SUBJECTS

Subjects are an integral part of the research process. Whether the subjects are children, college students, schizophrenics, rats, pigeons, rabbits, or primates (even cockroaches and flatworms have been used), they must somehow be selected. The method used to select subjects has implications for generalizing the research results. I've already mentioned that subject assignment is important for the internal validity of the experiment. When the proper subject assignment procedures are used, the different groups in the experiment will be equivalent. Recall that when the groups are equivalent, the problem of selection differences is avoided.

SAMPLING TECHNIQUES

Most research projects involve *sampling* subjects from a population of interest. The population is composed of all of the individuals you are interested in. Thus, one population of interest to a pollster would be all people in the United States who are eligible to vote. This implies that the pollster's population of interest does *not* include people under the age of eighteen, people serving prison terms, visitors from other countries, and other ineligible people. With enough time and money, a pollster could, conceivably, contact everyone in the population who is eligible to vote. Fortunately, the pollster can avoid this massive undertaking by selecting a sample from the population of interest. With proper sampling, the pollster can use information obtained from the sample to determine what the population as a whole is like. Sampling is therefore very important in generalization of research results.

There are two basic types of sampling techniques—*probability sampling* and *nonprobability sampling*. In probability sampling, each member of the population has a specifiable probability of being chosen. In nonprobability sampling, we don't know the probability of any particular member of the population being chosen.

Nonprobability sampling

Haphazard sampling   Nonprobability sampling is quite arbitrary and sloppy. One form of nonprobability sampling is called *haphazard sampling*. Haphazard sampling could be called a "take 'em where you find them" method of obtaining subjects. For example, a representative of a television station might poll people who happen to walk past a particular street corner at a particular time of day *and* are willing to say a few words to the camera. The population of interest might be "people who live in this city," but the results of this poll could not really be generalized to this population. It would not be possible to specify the probability of a city resident being chosen as a participant in this poll. The probability would be quite high for some people (those who live or work near the street corner) and quite low for others. The haphazard sampling technique would exclude everyone who, for any reason, wasn't present at that location at that particular time. Thus, any generalization of the results to the entire city would probably be inaccurate.

Quota sampling   Another form of nonprobability sampling is called *quota sampling*. A researcher who used this technique chooses a sample that reflects the numerical composition of various subgroups in the population. For instance, suppose you know that your city has the following composition: 60 percent white, 20 percent black, 10 percent Chicano, 5 percent Asian, and 5 percent Native American. A quota sampling technique that uses nationality and ethnic subgroups would produce a sample that numerically reflects these percentages. Thus, a sample of one hundred people from your city would have sixty whites, twenty blacks, ten Chicanos, five Asians, and five Native Americans. Similarly, subgroups might be based on age, sex, socioeconomic class, the number of people in each major at your school, and so on. Quota sampling is a bit more elegant than haphazard sampling. However, we still have problems because no restrictions are placed on how individuals in the various subgroups are chosen. Although the sample reflects the numerical composition of the whole population of interest, subjects within each subgroup are selected in a haphazard manner.

Much of the research in psychology and the behavioral sciences uses nonprobability sampling techniques. The advantage of these techniques is that they are cheap and easy methods of obtaining subjects. It is, for example, common practice to select subjects from students in introductory psychology classes. Often these students are required to participate in experiments; they can then choose which experiments they wish to participate in. With this kind of sampling technique, it is difficult to even define the population of interest. Usually, we want to generalize to "people in general" or at least to "adults who live in the United States." Obviously, generalizing to these populations is risky when the haphazard sample is composed of students at a particular college who have decided to take intro psych and have volunteered for a particular experiment.

If generalization is such a problem, why do researchers use these techniques? First, they are cheap and practical. The researcher usually decides to spend the limited resources he has on the experiment rather than on obtaining a representative sample. Also, it would be difficult to find a sample of the general population willing to come into the lab for an experiment. Second, the researcher is mainly interested in finding a relationship between variables. The purpose of the research is to test a hypothesis that certain variables are related; generalization is usually not the immediate goal. If a relationship is found, generalization research can come later. When generalization is the main goal of the research, probability sampling techniques must be used. For example, research that is aimed at determining how many people will vote for a particular political candidate, or how many people use the parks in a city, must use a truly representative sample. Let's examine three general types of probability sampling—simple random sampling, stratified random sampling, and area sampling.

Probability sampling

Simple random sampling   With *simple random sampling,* every member of the population has an *equal* probability of being selected for the sample. If the population has one thousand members, each has one chance out of a thousand of being selected. As an example of a simple random sampling procedure, suppose you want to sample students who attend your school. A list of all students would be needed. From that list, students would be chosen at random to form the sample. Notice that this procedure doesn't introduce any *biases* in who gets chosen. A haphazard procedure in which you sampled from students walking by a certain location at 9 a.m. would involve all sorts of biases. For example, that procedure would eliminate students who don't frequent this location, and also afternoon and evening students.

Stratified random sampling   A somewhat more complicated procedure is called *stratified random sampling.* Stratified random sampling is analogous to quota sampling in that the population is divided up into subgroups (or *strata*). Random sampling techniques are then used to select sample members from each stratum. A number of dimensions could be used to divide the population. Usually the dimension (or dimensions) used are relevant to the problem you are studying. For instance, a survey of sexual attitudes might stratify on the basis of age, sex, and amount of education, because these factors are related to sexual attitudes. Stratification on the basis of height or hair color would be ridiculous. Stratified random sampling has the advantage of a built-in assurance that the sample will accurately reflect the numerical composition of the various subgroups. This kind of accuracy is particularly important when some subgroups comprise very small percentages of the population. For instance, if blacks comprise 5 percent of a city of one hundred thousand population, a simple random sample of one hundred people might not include any blacks. But a stratified random sample would include five blacks chosen randomly from the blacks in the population.

Area sampling   It may have occurred to you that obtaining a list of all members of a very large population (for instance, the residents of an entire city) might be very difficult. In such situations, a technique called *area sampling* can be used. Rather than random sampling from a list of individuals, the researcher can sample from a list of geographical areas. For instance, a city could be described by a list of city blocks. The researcher could then take a random sample of the city blocks and survey all the people who live on the blocks that are chosen.

All of these attempts to form a representative sample of the population can be fouled up in the data collection phase. Biases are still possible if some people in the sample are not contacted. It is easy to see how foul-ups could occur. For example, consider what would happen if the researcher were to bypass dilapidated houses. Low income individuals would be systematically excluded from the sample. A similar bias would develop if an interviewer didn't follow up on people who weren't home but only did this in the slum areas of town. A random sample can quickly become nonrandom unless care is taken to collect data from the entire sample.

ASSIGNING SUBJECTS

The technique used to choose research participants affects the researcher's ability to generalize. The procedure used to assign subjects to the various groups in an experiment involves other considerations. As I have noted several times before, in a good experimental design the groups must be equivalent prior to the introduction of the independent variable. This is necessary even if the most haphazard sampling procedures have been used.

There are two basic ways of assigning subjects to groups. One way is to randomly assign subjects to the various conditions. In this situation, each subject participates in only one group. This is called an *independent groups* experimental design. A second subject assignment procedure involves participation by subjects in more than one group. In the simplest experiment, each subject would be assigned to both levels of the independent variable. This is called a *repeated measures* design, because each subject is measured after receiving each level of the independent variable.

Independent groups designs

Simple random assignment   The simplest method for assigning subjects to different groups is the *simple random assignment* procedure. If there are two groups in the experiment, a possible randomization procedure would be to flip a coin. If the coin comes up heads, the subject would be assigned to one group; if it came up tails, the subject would be assigned to the other group. If there are more than two groups, the researcher would need to use a table of *random numbers* to assign subjects. (A table of random numbers is printed in Table C-1 of the Appendix at the end of the book. The table is made up of a series of the digits 0 through 99. The arrangement of the digits is entirely random—they were generated by a computer. Instructions for using the random number table are also given in Table C-1. The researcher can use the arrangement of the numbers in the table to determine which group each subject will be assigned to.) Random assignment will prevent any biases. The various groups will be equivalent in terms of subject characteristics, such as social class, intelligence, age, and political attitudes.

Matched random assignment   A somewhat more complicated method of assigning subjects to the different groups is called *matched random assignment*. Matching procedures are sometimes used when the researcher wants to make sure that the groups are equivalent on some subject characteristic. Typically, the matching variable will be some subject characteristic that is strongly related to the dependent variable. For example, in a learning experiment, subjects might be matched on the basis of IQ scores. However, if intelligence is not related to the dependent measure, matching on the basis of intelligence would be a waste of time.

When matched random assignment procedures are used, the first step is to obtain a measure of the matching variable from each subject. The subjects are then rank-ordered from highest to lowest on the basis of their scores on the matching variable. Now the researcher can form subject pairs that are approximately equal on the characteristic (the highest two subjects form the first pair, the next two would form the second pair, and so on). Finally, the members of each pair are randomly assigned to the conditions in experiment.

Use of matched random assignment assures that the groups are equivalent (on the matching variable) prior to introduction of the independent variable manipulation. This assurance could be particularly important with small sample sizes—recall that random assignment procedures are more likely to produce equivalent groups as the sample size increases. The matched random assignment procedure described will also reduce *error variance*. Reduction of error variance increases the chances that a significant effect of the independent variable will be obtained. Of course, such reductions in error variance occur only to the extent that the matching variable and the dependent variable are related. Matching procedures can be costly and time-consuming. They require that subjects be measured on the matching variable in a testing session prior to the experiment. Such efforts are worthwhile only when the matching variable is very strongly related to the dependent measure. Match- ing procedures are rarely used in psychology research. An exception is animal research, in which litter mates are randomly assigned to the various conditions in the experiment.

In both the simple and matched random assignment procedures, each subject participates in only one of the groups in the experiment. An alternative procedure is to have the *same* subjects participate in all of the groups. This is called a repeated measures experimental design.

Repeated Measures Designs

A rather ridiculous example of a repeated measures design was recently provided by a television commercial for an underarm deodorant. The man in the commercial challenges us to try his brand (A) under our left arms while spraying our own brand (B) under our right arms. Presumably, his brand would result in greater dryness. If we translate this commercial into the terminology of research methods, the independent variable is the type of deodorant and the dependent variable is amount of dryness. We've already got some problems, since the second brand of deodorant isn't specified and the commercial doesn't indicate how to measure dryness. But for the sake of illustration, let's ignore such difficulties.

An independent groups design could have been used in which some people receive deodorant A under their (right or left) arms while others receive deodorant B. The commercial, however, asks us to use a repeated measures design since each person receives both deodorants, one under each arm. We now confront our first major problem with the repeated measures design: The brand of deodorant is confounded with side of the body. That is, the commercial specifies that one brand is to be used with the right arm while the other brand is to be used with the left arm. It is possible that the arms are not equivalent in dryness prior to the introduction of the independent variable. In other words, maybe left arms are dryer anyway. If so, whichever brand I spray under my left arm will seem more effective—the brand of deodorant doesn't really matter. To do this experiment properly, we would need to counterbalance the order of presenting the deodorants. People in one group would receive brand A under the left arm and brand B under the right; another group of people would receive the opposite (right–left) order.

Counterbalancing and order effects   For a more mundane example of a repeated measures design, consider an experiment on the meaningfulness of material and the learning of that material. In a repeated measures design, subjects might first read "low meaningful" material and take a test of recall to measure learning. The same subjects would then read "high meaningful" material and take a recall test. Suppose now that there is greater recall in the high meaningful condition. Such a result could be due to the manipulation of the meaningfulness variable. However, it could also be attributed to the fact that the high meaningful task came second in the order of presentation of the conditions. Performance on the second task might increase simply because of the practice received on the first task. Again, *counterbalancing* is necessary in a repeated measures design to control for *order effects*. In the above example, half of the subjects would be randomly assigned to the low–high order while the other half would be assigned to the high–low order. Counterbalancing principles can be extended to experiments with three or more groups; with three groups, there would be six possible orders. In practice, with four or more groups, the order of presentation is randomized across subjects. Complete counterbalancing with all orders represented is usually not feasible with many groups.

Advantages of repeated measures designs   The repeated measures design has several advantages. An obvious advantage is that fewer subjects are necessary, because each subject participates in all conditions. When subjects are scarce or when it is costly to run subjects, a repeated measures design may be preferred. In much research on perception, for instance, extensive training of subjects is necessary before the actual experiment is begun. Such research often involves only a few subjects who participate in all conditions of the experiment.

An additional advantage of repeated measures designs is that they are extremely sensitive to finding differences between groups. Because subjects in the various groups are identical in *every* respect (they are the same people), error variability due to subject differences is minimized. The principle is the same as with matching designs. Note that we've gone beyond matching, however. Subjects are not just matched on a single characteristic—they are identical on all characteristics. The end result is that you are much more likely to detect an effect of the independent variable if a repeated measures design is used. Despite these advantages, repeated measures designs do have drawbacks and limitations.

Carry-over effects   The major drawback occurs when there is a possibility of *carry-over effects*. Carry-over effects occur when the effects of one
treatment are still present when the next treatment is given. Consider an experiment on marijuana and driving performance. Whenever the marijuana
treatment precedes the control (no marijuana) condition, there is the possibility that the effect of the marijuana will carry over and influence how the subject
behaves in the control condition. Notice that this won't be a problem when
the treatment order is from control to marijuana. Counterbalancing is necessary to control for order effects. The problem of carry-over effects is present
in almost any repeated measures design in which the effect of a drug is being
studied. In such situations, the interval between conditions must be long
enough to allow the drugs to wear off. An alternative, of course, is to use an
independent groups design.

Carry-over effects can also occur in research that does not involve drugs.
For example, the effects of heightened anxiety might carry over to the other
treatments. In an extreme example, consider the carry-over effect of a brain
lesion. Since the brain lesion is irreversible, the use of a repeated measures
design would not be possible.

Demand characteristics   Another problem stems from the fact that subjects
have knowledge of all of the conditions in a repeated measures design. When
subjects participate in all of the groups, they may quickly figure out the true
purpose of the experiment. If this happens, subjects may behave differently
than they would if they were unaware of the hypothesis. Usually it is more
difficult for subjects to discern the true purpose of the experiment in an independent groups design. The general problem here is one of *demand characteristics* —various aspects of the experiment provide cues that enable the subject
to discover the researcher's hypothesis.

So, repeated measures designs have both advantages and disadvantages.
The advantages are (1) a savings in the number of subjects required to run the
experiment, and (2) greater control over subject differences and thus greater
ability to detect an effect of the independent variable. Obviously, the advantages are worthwhile only if the problems of carry-over effects and demand
characteristics seem minimal.

A variation on the repeated measures design that has been used with increasing frequency in recent years involves research with only one subject.
We'll now turn to a brief discussion of single-subject research.

SINGLE-SUBJECT EXPERIMENTS

Single-subject experiments frequently take place within the context of research on reinforcement. This research tradition can be traced back to the work of B. F. Skinner (1953) on reinforcement schedules and is often seen in applied and clinical settings when behavior modification techniques are used. The techniques and logic of the single-subject procedures can be readily applied to other research areas, however.

Reversal designs

The basic issue in single-subject experiments is how to determine that the manipulation of the independent variable has had an effect. One method is to demonstrate the reversibility of the manipulation. A single-subject reversal design takes the following form:

A (control condition) – B (experimental manipulation) – A (control condition)

This design, frequently called an *ABA design,* involves measuring the subject to obtain a baseline of behavior during a control period, then introducing the manipulation and measuring behavior during this period, and finally measuring the subject during a second control period. For example, a subject's smoking behavior could be observed during the first control period. The researcher would obtain a measure of the number of cigarettes smoked per day. Then the experimental manipulation would be introduced—the subject might be supplied with sugarless gum and told to take a piece whenever there was an urge to smoke. Smoking behavior during the experimental period would be measured. Finally, the gum would be taken away and smoking would again be observed. If the experimental manipulation is effective, we would expect to see the number of cigarettes smoked during the first control period decrease during the experimental period; then there would be an increase, or reversal, of smoking behavior in the final control period. The ABA sequence of number of cigarettes might be 40-15-37. Such results indicate the effectiveness of the manipulation by demonstrating a reversal of the behavior.

The ABA design can be greatly improved by extending it to an ABAB design in which the experimental manipulation is introduced a second time. When an ABA design is used, it is possible to argue that various other factors are responsible for the reversal. For example, outside historical events that happen to coincide with the experimental manipulation could cause the results. If a friend of the subject dies of lung cancer, it could be argued that that death caused a temporary reduction in the number of cigarettes smoked by the subject. Or possibly the manipulation coincides with a yearly check-up, which always results in a drop in smoking. If an ABAB design is used, such arguments could be easily rejected. It seems unlikely that coincidental factors could be responsible for *both* reversals in behavior. Thus, evidence from an ABAB design experiment is extremely convincing.

Random time series design

It may have occurred to you that a reversal of some behaviors may be impossible or unethical. For example, it would be unethical to reverse treatment that reduces undesirable or illegal behaviors, such as heroin use, indecent exposure, or alcoholism. In such cases, multiple measures over time can be made before and after the manipulation. A number of measures of the behavior to be changed are made prior to the manipulation. At a randomly determined time, the manipulation is introduced. If the manipulation is effective, the behavior will now change, and this change will continue to be reflected in further measures of the behavior. This procedure is called a *random time series* design, because the manipulation is introduced randomly during a series of measures that are made over time.

Figure 7-1 shows how a random time series design might operate in the smoking reduction experiment. The subject's smoking behavior is recorded for eight days before the manipulation is introduced (remember that the specific day for introducing the manipulation is chosen at random). Further measures are made on successive days. The fact that there was a reduction in smoking following the manipulation and that this reduction was maintained over time is evidence for the effectiveness of the manipulation. Of course, it is still possible that the reduction in smoking could be due to some other event that happened to coincide with the manipulation. To be entirely confident that the manipulation is effective, we would need to replicate the random time series experiment with other subjects.

Single-subject design with replications

These procedures for use with a single subject can be replicated with other subjects. Such replications greatly add to the generalizability of the results. Usually reports of research that employs single-subject experimental procedures do present the results from several subjects. Typically, the data from each subject is presented separately, however. In some clinical research, this is

Figure 7-1   Hypothetical data from random time series design examining the effectiveness of a smoking reduction manipulation

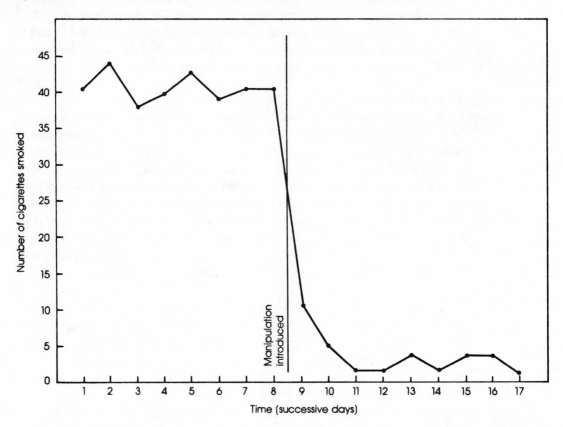

done because the behavior change technique was individually programmed for each individual subject. In other research, however, data from individual subjects rather than group means are often presented because of a tradition that stresses understanding of responses to the manipulation at the level of the individual. Sidman (1960), a leading spokesman for this tradition, has pointed out that grouping the data from a number of subjects by using group means can sometimes give a misleading picture of individual responses to the manipulation of the independent variable. One problem, for example, is that the manipulation may be effective in changing the behavior of some subjects but not others. An emphasis on the individual subject will quickly reveal this, and steps can be taken to find out why the manipulation wasn't effective for these particular subjects.

I should point out that most research in the behavioral sciences involves large samples rather than the single-subject research. One reason for this is the relative lack of generalizability of single-subject research. Another reason is that not all variables can be studied with the reversal and random time series procedures used in single-subject experiments. Specifically, these procedures are useful only when the behavior is reversible or when you can expect a relatively dramatic shift in behavior after the manipulation.

I have mentioned the use of statistical significance tests several times. Now that you have a basic understanding of the principles of experimental design, we can turn to a consideration of the role of statistics in testing research hypotheses. In the next chapter, we'll examine how researchers use statistics in evaluating the outcomes of their research.

STUDY QUESTIONS

1 *Distinguish between probability and nonprobability sampling techniques. What are the implications of each?*

2 *Why do researchers use nonprobability sampling?*

3 *Distinguish between the types of independent groups designs.*

4 *What is a repeated measures design? Why is counterbalancing necessary in this design?*

5 *What is the problem of carry-over effects in a repeated measures design?*

6 *Why would a researcher use a repeated measures design instead of an independent groups design?*

7 *What is a reversal design? Why is an ABAB reversal design superior to an ABA design?*

8 *What is the difference between a reversal design and a random time series design? How does the researcher determine whether the independent variable has an effect when these designs are used?*

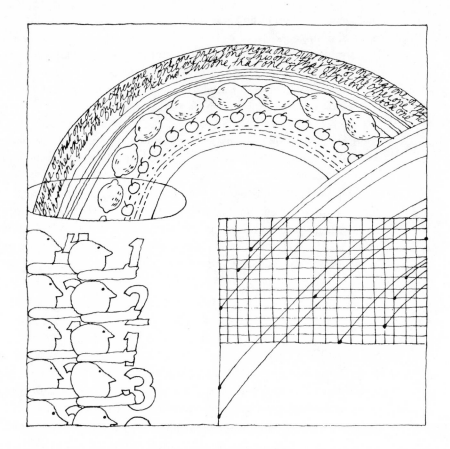

8

ANALYSIS OF RESEARCH RESULTS

Now that you understand the major concepts in designing and conducting experiments, you are ready to study the analysis and evaluation of the results. The analysis of research data involves the use of statistics. There are two reasons for using statistics. First, statistics are used to describe the data collected in the study. Second, statistics are used to make inferences, on the basis of sample data, about the population of interest. In this chapter, we are concerned with the use of descriptive and inferential statistics. The discussion here is quite general. Specific calculations are in Appendix B.

Let's start with some fictitious data from a hypothetical experiment on modeling and aggression. The twenty subjects were six-year-old children selected from the students at an elementary school. The children were randomly assigned to one of two groups. The experimental group witnessed an aggressive adult (a *model*); the control group was not exposed to the model. The children then played alone in room that contained a number of toys. Observers watched each child and rated the child on the dependent variable, aggression. The children's scores on the aggression measure are shown in Table 8-1. We'll use these data in discussing the analysis of research results.

Table 8–1   Scores on aggression measure in a hypothetical
experiment on modeling and aggression

No-model group	Model group
1	3
2	4
2	5
3	5
3	5
3	5
4	6
4	6
4	6
5	7
$\Sigma X = 31$	$\Sigma X = 52$
$\overline{X} = 3.10$	$\overline{X} = 5.20$
$s^2 = 1.29$	$s^2 = 1.16$
$s = 1.14$	$s = 1.08$
$n = 10$	$n = 10$

SAMPLES AND POPULATIONS

The first thing to note about the results of the experiment is that they are based on data obtained from samples of subjects. It is important to remember that there is a population of children who either witness or do not witness the aggressive model. Researchers rarely if ever study entire populations. Their findings are based on sample data.

Descriptive statistics provide a description of the sample. However, we are usually not interested in simply describing the sample. Instead, we want to make statements about the population (for example, other six-year-olds at other schools who receive the independent variable manipulation of witnessing a model). *Inferential statistics* are used to determine whether we can, in fact, make such generalization statements.

When analyzing results it is useful to start by constructing a frequency distribution from the data. A *frequency distribution* indicates the number of subjects who receive each possible score on a variable. You are probably familiar with frequency distributions of exam scores—they tell how many students received each score on an exam.

Frequency distributions can be depicted in a graph such as Figure 8-1, which presents the data from the modeling experiment. These two *frequency polygons*—one for each group—show us how many people received each score on the aggression measure. The solid line represents the no-model group, and the dotted line stands for the model group.

You can see that the frequency distributions for the two groups in the experiment are not identical. However, a researcher wants to make precise statements about the data. Two statistics are needed to describe the data. A single number can be used to describe the *central tendency*, or how subjects scored overall. Another number describes how much *variability* there is in the scores, or how widely the distribution of scores is spread. These two numbers summarize the information contained in a frequency distribution.

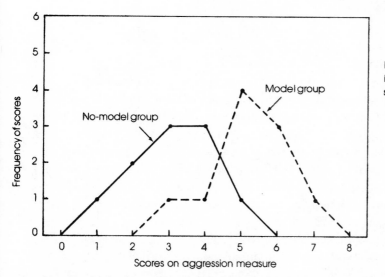

Figure 8-1   Frequency polygons illustrating the distributions of scores in Table 8-1

Note: Each frequency polygon is anchored at scores that were not obtained by anyone (0 and 6 in the No-Model group; 2 and 8 in the Model group).

DESCRIPTIVE STATISTICS
Central tendency

A central tendency statistic tells us what the sample as a whole, or on the average, is like. The most common central tendency statistic is the *mean,* which is symbolized as $\bar{X}$. The mean of a set of scores is obtained by taking the sum of all scores and dividing by the number of scores. In Table 8-1, you can see that the mean score in the no-model group is 3.10, and the mean of the model group is 5.20.

Variability

We can also determine how much variability exists in a set of scores. A measure of variability is a number that characterizes the amount of spread in a distribution of scores. One such measure is the variance, which is symbolized as s^2. The variance indicates the extent to which the scores deviate from the group mean. The greater the spread about the group mean, the higher the variance. The variance and a related statistic, the *standard deviation*—abbreviated as *s*—have been calculated for the aggression data and are presented in Table 8-1. (The standard deviation is simply the square root of the variance.) The variance in the no-model group is 1.29, and the variance in the model group is 1.16.

INFERENTIAL STATISTICS

We now know that the no-model mean score is 3.10 and the model group mean is 5.20. What does this say about the effect of the independent variable? The independent variable seems to have had an effect on aggression. Children who viewed the aggressive model were more aggressive than children who didn't witness the model. We have to remember that these statements are based on sample data. Can we infer, on the basis of this information, that this difference between groups holds true in the population?

   You may be wondering why we have to worry about making such inferences. Much of the previous discussion of experimental design has centered on the importance of making sure that the groups are equivalent in every way *except* the independent variable manipulation. Equivalency of groups is achieved by experimentally controlling all other variables or by randomization. The assumption is that if the groups are equivalent, any differences in the dependent variable must be due to the effect of the independent variable.

This assumption is usually valid. However, it is also true that the differ- ence between any two groups will almost never be zero. In other words, there will be some difference in the sample means, even when all of the principles of experimental design are utilized. This is true because we are dealing with samples rather than populations. Random or chance error may affect the results. For example, random assignment to groups is not absolutely perfect in ensuring equivalency of groups. It is possible that, as a result of the way we obtained our no-model and model group samples, the groups in the experiment were not equivalent to begin with.

The point here is that the difference in the sample means reflects a true difference in the population plus any random error. Inferential statistics allow us to make inferences about the true difference in the population on the basis of the sample data. Specifically, inferential statistics tell us the probability that the difference between means reflects random error rather than a real difference.

NULL HYPOTHESIS

When a researcher uses inferential statistics, he or she begins by stating a *null hypothesis* and a *research* (or *alternative*) *hypothesis*. The null hypothesis is simply that the population means are equal—the observed difference is due to random error. The research hypothesis is that the population means are in fact not equal. The null hypothesis states that the independent variable had *no effect;* the research hypothesis states that the independent variable did have an effect. In the modeling experiment, the null and research hypotheses are:

H_0 (null hypothesis):	The population mean of the no-model group is equal to the population mean of the model group.
H_1 (research hypothesis):	The population mean of the no-model group is not equal to the population mean of the model group.

The logic of the null hypothesis is this: If we can reject the null hypothesis as incorrect, then we accept the research hypothesis as correct. Acceptance of the research hypothesis means that the independent variable had an effect on the dependent variable.

The null hypothesis is used because it is a very exact statement—the population means are exactly equal. This permits us to know precisely the probability of the outcome of the study occurring if the null hypothesis is correct. Such precision isn't possible with the research hypothesis, so we infer that the research hypothesis is correct only by rejecting the null hypothesis. The null hypothesis is rejected when there is a very low probability that the obtained results could be due to random error. This is what is meant by *statistical significance*: A significant result is one that has a very low probability of occurring if the population means are actually equal. More simply, significance indicates that there is a low probability that the difference between the obtained sample means was due to random error. Significance, then, is a matter of probability.

PROBABILITY AND RARE EVENTS

Probability is the likelihood of the occurrence of some event or outcome. All of us use probabilities frequently in everyday life. If you say that there is a high probability that you will get an "A" in this course, you mean that it is likely that that will happen. Your probability statement is based on specific information, such as your grades on examinations. The weatherman states that there is a 10 percent chance of rain today: This means that the likelihood of rain is very low. A gambler gauges the probability that a particular horse will win a race on the basis of the past records of that horse.

We use probability in statistical inference in much the same way. We want to specify the probability of an event (a difference between means in the sample) occurring if there is no difference in the population. The question is, "What is the probability of obtaining this result if only random error is operating?" If this probability is very low, we reject the possibility that only random or chance error is responsible for the obtained difference in means.

The use of probability in statistical inference can be understood intuitively from a simple example. Let's say that a friend claims to have ESP (extrasensory perception) ability. You decide to test your friend by using a set of five cards that have been used in ESP research. A different symbol is presented on each card. In the ESP test, you look at each card and think about the symbol. Your friend, the subject, tells you which symbol you are thinking about. In your actual experiment, you have ten trials; each of the five cards is presented

two times in a random order. Your task is to know whether your friend's answers reflect random error (guessing) or whether the answers indicate that
something more than random error is occurring.

The null hypothesis in your study is that only random error is operating.
The research hypothesis is that the number of correct answers shows more
than just random or chance guessing. (Note, however, that accepting the research hypothesis could mean that your friend has ESP ability, but it could
also mean that the cards were marked, that you had somehow cued your
friend when thinking about the symbols, and so on.)

You can easily determine the number of correct answers to expect if the
null hypothesis is correct. Just by guessing, the subject should get one out of
five correct (20 percent). On ten trials, two correct answers are expected under
the null hypothesis. If, in the actual experiment, more (or less) than two correct answers are obtained, would you conclude that the obtained data reflect
random error, or would you conclude that the data reflect something more
than just random guessing?

Let's say that your subject gets three correct. Then you would probably
conclude that only guessing is involved, because you would recognize that
there is a high probability that the subject would get three correct *even though
only two correct are expected under the null hypothesis.* You expect that exactly two out of ten answers would be correct in the long run, if you conducted
this experiment with this subject over and over again. However, small deviations away from the expected two are highly likely in a sample of ten trials.

Suppose, though, that your subject gets seven correct—you would probably conclude that the results indicate more than random error. This conclusion
would be based on the very low probability of the subject getting seven correct
by simply guessing. This outcome of the experiment would be a *rare event,*
and you would say that the result is significant. A significant result is one that
would occur rarely if the null hypothesis is correct.

How rare does an event have to be before we say that it is significant? The
most commonly used probability is .05. The outcome of an experiment is
considered rare when there is a .05 probability or less of obtaining the results—
that is, when there are only five chances out of one hundred that the results
would be obtained on the basis of random error. If it is very unlikely that random error is responsible for the results, the null hypothesis is rejected.

I hope that you can see intuitively why obtaining seven correct on the ten
trials is a rare event. Fortunately, we don't have to rely on intuition to deter-

mine the probability of our results occurring by random error. Table 8-2 shows the probability of actually obtaining each of the possible outcomes in the ESP experiment.[1] Notice that an outcome of two correct answers has the highest probability of occurrence. Also, as your intuition told you, an outcome of three correct is highly probable, but an outcome of seven correct has a low probability of occurrence and so can be considered a rare event.

Table 8–2   Exact probability of each possible outcome of the ESP experiment with ten trials

Number of correct answers	Probability
10	.00000+
9	.00000+
8	.00007
7	.00079
6	.00551
5	.02642
4	.08808
3	.20133
2	.30199
1	.26844
0	.10737

THE *F* TEST

A number of different statistical tests allow us to use probability in deciding whether to reject the null hypothesis. (Appendix B contains a discussion of the rationale underlying use of the various tests, as well as calculating formulas.) A statistic that is frequently used to evaluate the difference between means is the *F* test. The letter *F* stands for the person who developed much of the theory of statistical tests, Sir Ronald Fisher.

---

1   These exact probabilities were obtained through the use of a probability distribution called the *binomial distribution*. All of our statistical significance decisions are based on probability distributions such as this one. For a discussion of the binomial distribution and other probability distributions, see W. L. Hayes, *Statistics for psychologists*. New York: Holt, Rinehart & Winston, 1963.

A value of F is calculated from the obtained data and is then evaluated in terms of the probability of obtaining the F if the null hypothesis is true. If the obtained F has a low probability of occurrence, then the null hypothesis is rejected. As a general rule, researchers use a *significance level* of .05 in deciding to reject the null hypothesis. The results are said to be significant when the probability of obtaining the results is .05 or less, *if the null hypothesis is correct.*

The F statistic is a ratio of two aspects of the data—the difference between the group means, and the variability within groups. Formally, F is described as:

$$F = \frac{\text{systematic variance}}{\text{error variance}}$$

Systematic variance refers to how much the group means vary from one another—the size of the difference between means. *Error variance* refers to how much the scores within each group vary about the group mean (recall the earlier discussion of variability in a group of scores).

A large F value is one that has a large systematic variance relative to the amount of error variance. The greater the systematic variance (the greater the difference between the group means), the more likely it is that there is a real difference in the population. The lower the error variance, the less random error there is in the scores. The error variance indicates the extent to which random error is responsible for the difference between means. Thus, we are more confident that the difference between means reflects a true population difference when the systematic variance is greater than the error variance.

To illustrate, let's again consider the data from the modeling and aggression experiment (Table 8-1). We can summarize the results of the F test as follows:

$$F = \frac{\text{systematic variance}}{\text{erorr variance}} = \frac{22.05}{1.36} = 16.21$$

Thus, the F value calculated from the data is 16.21. Is this a significant result? The probability of finding an F of 16.21, if in fact the population means are equal, is less than .05. In other words, there is a .05 probability that we would get an F value of 16.21 if the null hypothesis is correct. Obtaining an F this large is a rare event. And so we conclude that the means obtained in the no-model and model groups reflect a real population difference and that the results are significant.

TYPE I AND TYPE II ERRORS

The decision to reject the null hypothesis is based on probabilities rather than on certainties. The decision is made without direct knowledge of the true state of affairs in the population. Thus, the decision may or may not be correct; there may be errors resulting from the use of inferential statistics.

A *decision matrix* is shown in Table 8-3. Notice that there are two possible decisions. We can (1) reject the null hypothesis, or (2) accept the null hypothesis. There are also two possibilities that may be true in the population: (1) the null hypothesis is true, or (2) the research hypothesis is true. You can see from this decision matrix that there are two kinds of correct decisions and two types of errors.

Table 8–3   Decision matrix: Type I and Type II errors

		Population	
		Null hypothesis is true	Research hypothesis is true
Decision	Reject the null hypothesis	Type I error	Correct decision
	Accept the null hypothesis	Correct decision	Type II error

Correct decisions

One correct decision occurs when we reject the null hypothesis and the research hypothesis is true in the population. Our decision is to say that the population means are not equal, and in fact this is true in the population. The other correct decision is to accept the null hypothesis and the null hypothesis is true in the population. The population means are in fact equal.

Type I errors

A *Type I error* is made when we reject the null hypothesis but the null hypothesis is actually true. Our decision is that the population means are *not* equal when they actually are equal. Type I errors occur when, just by chance, we obtain a large F value. For example, even though an F value of 16.21 is highly improbable if in fact the population means are equal (less than five chances out of one hundred), it *can* happen. When we do obtain an *F* value this large by chance, we *incorrectly* decide that the independent variable had an effect.

The probability of making a Type I error is determined by the choice of significance level. When the significance level for deciding whether to reject the null hypothesis is .05, the probability of a Type I error is .05. If the null hypothesis is rejected, there are five chances out of one hundred that the decision is wrong. The probability of making a Type I error can be changed by changing the significance level. If we use a significance level of .01, there is less chance of making a Type I error. With a .01 significance level, the null hypothesis is rejected only when the probability of obtaining the results is .01 or less if the null hypothesis is correct.

Type II errors

A *Type II error* occurs when the null hypothesis is accepted although in the population the research hypothesis is true. The population means are not equal, but the results of the experiment do not lead to a decision to reject the null hypothesis.

The probability of making a Type II error is not directly specifiable, although the significance level is an important factor. If we set a very low significance level in order to decrease the chances of a Type I error, we *increase* the chances of a Type II error. In other words, if we make it very difficult to reject the null hypothesis, the probability of incorrectly accepting the null hypothethis goes up.

INTERPRETING NEGATIVE RESULTS

I have been talking about "accepting the null hypothesis." Although this is convenient terminology, it is important to recognize that researchers are not generally interested in accepting the null hypothesis. Research is designed to show that a relationship between variables does exist, rather than to demonstrate that variables are unrelated.

More important, there are problems with a decision to actually accept the null hypothesis when the study doesn't show significant results. As noted in Chapter 6, negative or nonsignificant results are difficult to interpret. First, it isn't possible to specify the probability that you could be wrong in the decision to accept the null hypothesis. Also, there are a number of reasons why a single study might not show significant results, even when there is a relationship between the variables in the population. For example, an incompetent researcher might obtain nonsignificant results by making the instructions to subjects incomprehensible, by having a very weak manipulation of the independent variable, or by using a dependent measure that is unreliable and insensitive.

Nonsignificant results can also be obtained by using a very low significance level. If the researcher uses a significance level of .001 in deciding whether to reject the null hypothesis, there isn't much chance of a Type I error. However, a Type II error is possible, because the researcher has decreased the chances of wrongly rejecting the null hypothesis. In other words, a meaningful result is more likely to be overlooked when the significance level is very low.

A small sample size also might cause a researcher to be wrong in accepting the null hypothesis. A general principle is that the larger the sample size, the greater the likelihood of obtaining a significant result. This is because large sample sizes give more accurate estimates of the actual population than do small sample sizes. It is possible, in any given study, that the sample size is too small to permit detection of a significant result.

I do not mean to imply that researchers should always use huge samples. A very large sample size (for example, one hundred or two hundred subjects in each group) might enable the researcher to find a significant difference between means. However, this difference, even though it is statistically significant, might have very little *practical* significance. For example, if an expensive new psychiatric treatment technique significantly reduces hospital stay from sixty days to fifty-eight days, it might not be practical to use the technique even though there is evidence for its effectiveness.

The general point of this discussion is that we should *not always accept the null hypothesis* just because the results are nonsignificant. Before a researcher accepts the null hypothesis, the experiment must be conducted again with refined procedures and possibly a larger sample. But if repeated evidence from well-designed studies with adequate sample sizes shows no relationship between the variables, then the researcher is justified in concluding that there is no relationship in the population.

CHOOSING A SIGNIFICANCE LEVEL

Researchers have traditionally used either a .05 or a .01 significance level in the decision to reject the null hypothesis. If there is less than a .05 or a .01 probability that the results occurred because of random error, the results are said to be significant. It is important to recognize, however, that there is nothing magical about a .05 or a .01 significance level. The significance level chosen merely specifies the probability of a Type I error if the null hypothesis is rejected. The significance level chosen by the researcher is usually dependent on the consequences of making a Type I versus a Type II error.

Researchers usually feel that the consequences of making a Type I error are more serious than the consequences of a Type II error. If the null hypothesis is rejected, the researcher may publish the results in a journal and the results might be reported by others in textbooks or in newspaper or magazine articles. Researchers don't want to mislead others or risk damaging their reputations by publishing results that aren't true in the population. Thus, they want to guard against the possibility of making a Type I error by using a very low significance level (.05 or .01). In contrast to the consequences of publishing false results, the consequences of a Type II error are not seen as being very serious.

Thus, researchers want to be very careful to avoid Type I errors when their results may be published. However, there are circumstances when a Type I error is not serious. For example, if you are engaged in pilot or exploratory research, your results are used primarily to decide whether it is worthwhile to pursue your research ideas. In this situation, it would be a mistake to overlook potentially important data by using a very conservative significance level. In exploratory research, you might want to use a significance level of .25 in deciding whether to do more research. Remember, the significance level chosen and the consequences of a Type I or a Type II error are determined by what the results are going to be used for.

We have now considered all aspects of conducting and interpreting experimental research. In the next chapter we will examine the methods of correlational research. Both experimental and correlational research are necessary for a complete understanding of behavior.

STUDY QUESTIONS

1 *What is a frequency distribution? What statistics are needed to describe a frequency distribution?*

2 *Why are inferential statistics necessary—that is, why can't a researcher simply assume that any differences between groups on the dependent measure shows that the independent variable had an effect?*

3 *Distinguish between the null hypothesis and the research hypothesis. When does the researcher decide to reject the null hypothesis?*

4 *What is meant by statistical significance?*

5 *What is meant by systematic variance and error variance?*

6 *Distinguish between a Type I error and a Type II error. What determines the probability of each type of error?*

7 *What is the difference between statistical significance and practical significance?*

8 *What factors are involved in choosing a significance level?*

9 *Discuss the reasons a researcher might obtain negative (nonsignificant) results.*

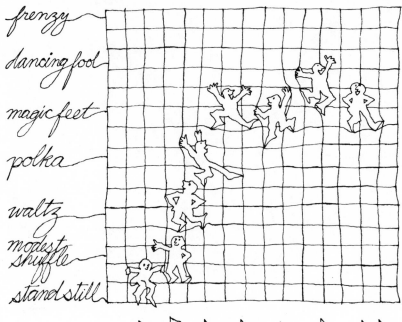

9

CORRELATIONAL RESEARCH TECHNIQUES

The correlational method involves observation rather than manipulation of variables. We have already examined the basic distinctions between the correlational and experimental methods as well as techniques of measuring behavior. This chapter discusses the use of *correlation coefficients* in behavioral research. A correlation coefficient is a statistic that indicates how strongly two variables are related.

FUNDAMENTAL PROCEDURES

Data collection procedures must involve making pairs of observations on each subject. Thus, each subject has two scores, one on each of the variables. Table 9-1 shows fictitious data for ten subjects who were measured on the variables of classroom seating pattern and exam grade. Students in the first row receive a seating score of 1, those in the second row receive a 2, and so on. Once we have made our observations, we can see if the two variables are related. Do the variables go together in a systematic fashion?

Table 9–1   Pairs of scores for ten subjects on seating
pattern and exam score (fictitous data)

Subject identification number	Seating	Exam score
01	2	95
02	5	50
03	1	85
04	4	75
05	3	75
06	5	60
07	2	80
08	3	70
09	1	90
10	4	70

INDEXING THE STRENGTH OF A RELATIONSHIP

To determine whether two variables are related, a descriptive statistic called a correlation coefficient is used. There are a number of different types of correlation coefficients (see Appendix B). One of the most frequently used is the *Pearson product-moment* correlation coefficient, which is referred to as *r*.

The values of *r* can range from +1.00 to −1.00. The plus and minus signs indicate whether there is a positive linear or negative linear relationship between the two variables. The absolute size or *r* is an index of the strength of the relationship. The nearer *r* is to 1.00 (plus *or* minus), the stronger the relationship. Indeed, a 1.00 correlation is sometimes called a perfect relationship, because the two variables go together in a perfect fashion.

Correlation coefficients can be visualized in scatterplots in which each subject's pair of scores is plotted as a single point in a diagram. Figure 9-1 shows such scatterplots for a perfect positive relationship (+1.00) and for a perfect negative relationship (−1.00). Look carefully, for you will probably never see such relationships in actual research. You can easily see why these are perfect relationships. For all subjects, the scores on the two variables fall on a straight line that is on the diagonal of the diagram. Each subject's score on one variable goes perfectly with his or her score on the other variable. If we know a subject's score on one of the variables, we can predict perfectly what his or her score will be on the other variable.

The diagrams in Figure 9-2 show patterns of correlation you are likely to **123** encounter in exploring research findings. The first diagram shows data that yields a correlation of +.65. The second diagram shows a negative relationship of −.77. The data points in these two scatterplots show a general pattern of either a positive or negative relationship, but the relationships are not perfect. You can make a general prediction in the first diagram, for instance, that the higher the score on one variable, the higher the score on the second variable. However, if you know a subject's score on the first variable, you can't *perfectly* predict what that person's score will be on the second variable. To confirm this, take a look at value 1 on variable X (the horizontal axis) in the positive scatterplot. Looking up, you will see that two subjects had a score of 1. One of these subjects had a score of 1 on variable Y (the vertical axis), and the other subject had a score of 3. The data points do not fall on the perfect diagonal (as in Figure 9-2). Instead, there is variation *(scatter)* from the perfect diagonal line.

The third diagram shows a scatterplot in which there is absolutely no correlation (*r* = 0.00). The points fall all over the diagram, and there is no pattern. Scores on variable X are not related to scores on variable Y.

The fourth diagram has been left blank, so that you can plot the scores from the data given in Table 9-1. The X (horizontal) axis has been labeled for the

Figure 9-1   Perfect (±1.00) relationships

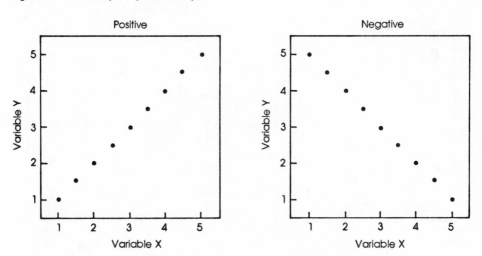

seating pattern variable, and the Y (vertical) axis has been labeled for the exam score variable. To complete the scatterplot, you will need to plot the scores for each of the ten subjects. For each subject, find the score on the seating pattern variable. Then go up until you reach that subject's exam score. A point there will describe the subject's score on both variables. There will be ten points on the finished scatterplot.

Figure 9-2   Scatterplots

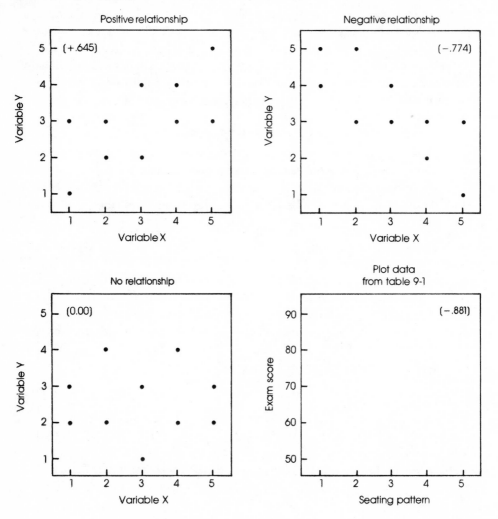

The correlation coefficient calculated from this data shows that there is a negative relationship between the variables ($r = -.88$). As the seating distance from the front of the class increases, the exam score decreases.

It is always important to remember that results based on the correlational method have the problems of direction of cause-and-effect and of uncontrolled third variables. It is possible that sitting close to the front *causes* good grades, but it is also possible that good exam scores received earlier *cause* people to sit at the front of the class. Uncontrolled third variables may also be responsible for the correlation. Being highly motivated may cause students to arrive early to get front seats *and* may also cause them to study to get good grades. If this is true, seating pattern and grades are not directly related. Instead, the third variable is actually responsible for the apparent correlation.

IMPORTANT CONSIDERATIONS
Restriction of range
It is important that the researcher sample from the full range of possible values of both variables. If the range of possible values is restricted, the magnitude of the correlation coefficient is reduced. For example, if the range of seating pattern scores had been restricted to the first two rows, you would not get an accurate picture of the relationship between seating pattern and exam score. In fact, the correlation between the two variables when *only* scores of subjects sitting in the first two rows are considered is exactly 0.00.

The restriction of range concept is similar to the strength of manipulation concept discussed in Chapter 6. Just as a weak independent variable manipulation reduces the magnitude of the relationship between the variables in an experimental study, restriction of range of one of the variables reduces the magnitude of the relationship in a correlational study.

Curvilinear relationships
The Pearson product-moment correlation coefficient (r) is designed only to detect linear relationships. If the relationship is actually curvilinear, as in the scatterplot shown in Figure 9-3, the correlation coefficient will not indicate that there is a relationship. The correlation coefficient (r) calculated from the data in Figure 9-3 shows an r of 0.00, although it is clear that the two variables are related.

When the relationship is curvilinear, special correlational techniques are necessary to determine the strength of the relationship. Because a relationship may be curvilinear, it is important to construct a scatterplot in addition to looking at the magnitude of the correlation coefficient. The scatterplot is valuable because it gives a visual indication of the shape of the relationship.

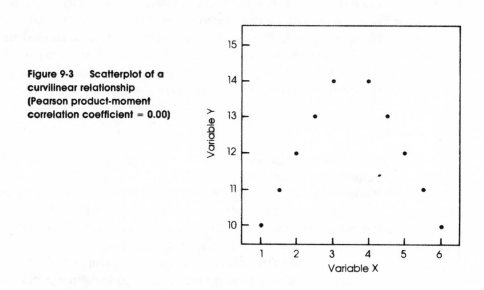

Figure 9-3   Scatterplot of a curvilinear relationship (Pearson product-moment correlation coefficient = 0.00)

Significance of a correlation coefficient

The correlation coefficient is a descriptive statistic—it describes the strength of the relationship between the variables in the sample of subjects studied. Researchers are also interested in learning whether the obtained correlation coefficient is large enough to infer that there is a relationship between the variables in the population. Thus, null hypothesis testing procedures can be used to see whether the correlation coefficient in the population is 0.00. Table C-6 in Appendix C shows the size of the obtained r that is necessary for rejection of the null hypothesis at the .05 level. By rejecting the null hypothesis, we infer that the population correlation is *not* 0.00.

The importance of sample size in making inferences from the sample to the population can be seen in Table C-6 of Appendix C. When the sample size is 4, an obtained r of at least .950 (plus or minus) is necessary to reject

the null hypothesis of the .05 level. However, the obtained r must be .444 **127**
(plus or minus) or larger when the sample size is 20. For much research in the
behavioral sciences, a sample size of between 50 and 100 is necessary to reach
a .05 significance level.

RELIABILITY AND CORRELATION COEFFICIENTS

The concept of reliability was discussed briefly in Chapter 4. Recall that any
measurement contains two components, a true score component and a measurement error component. A reliable measure contains little measurement
error. We cannot directly observe the true score and error components of an
actual score on the measure, however. Instead, correlational techniques are
used to give an estimate of the extent to which the measure reflects true score
rather than measurement error. There are several ways of estimating reliability, each involving correlation coefficients.

Test-retest and alternate forms reliability

Test-retest and *alternate forms reliability* involve measuring the same individuals at two points in time. For example, the reliability of a test of intelligence
could be assessed by giving the measure to a group of subjects on one day
and then again a week later. We would then have two scores for each subject,
and a correlation coefficient could be calculated to determine whether there
is a relationship between the test score and the retest score. High reliability
is indicated by a high correlation coefficient. It is difficult to say how high the
correlation should be before accepting the measure as reliable but for most
measures the correlation would probably be at least +.80.

Test-retest reliability involves giving the *same* test twice, and this could create a problem—the correlation might be artificially high because the subjects
might remember how they responded the first time. Alternate forms reliability
is sometimes used to avoid this problem. Alternate forms reliability involves
administering two different forms of the same test to the same subjects at two
points in time.

Intelligence is a variable that can be expected to stay relatively constant
over time. Thus, we expect the test-retest reliability for intelligence to be very
high. Test-retest and alternate forms reliability should be used for variables
that remain stable over time, such as intelligence and achievement. However,

some variables may be expected to change from one test period to the next. A mood scale designed to measure a person's current mood state is an example of a measure that might easily change from one test period to another. When examining such variables, the split-half method or odd-even method would be better for assessing reliability.

Split-half and odd-even reliability

It is possible to assess reliability by measuring the subjects at only one point in time. We can do this because most psychological measures are made up of a number of different items. For example, an intelligence test might have 100 items; a subject's test score would be based on the total of his or her scores on all items. *Split-half reliability* is the correlation between the subject's total score on the first half of the test and his or her total score on the second half of the test. *Odd-even reliability* involves finding the correlation between total score on the odd numbered items and total score on the even numbered items. If the test is reliable, then the correlation coefficients will be high.

Inter-rater reliability

Inter-rater reliability is used when observers serve as raters of subjects' behavior. For example, observers might be used to rate the aggressiveness of each child in a class during a play period. Reliability can be assessed because two raters provide a pair of observations for each subject. The inter-rater reliability is the correlation between the ratings given by Rater 1 and those given by Rater 2.

MULTIPLE CORRELATION

In Chapter 3, I noted that the correlational method is used when the researcher is only interested in making successful predictions about people. This technique is applied, for example, when a college wishes to predict which applicants will successfully complete a degree, when an employer wants to predict which applicants will become the best workers, and so on. These are applied problems for which researchers design tests that can be used to predict future performance. Tests have been devised that allow prediction of future performance in school, on the job, and so on. Scores on these tests are used in deciding who to admit or hire (see the discussion of criterion validity in Chapter 4).

When researchers are interested in predicting future behavior (the *criterion variable*), they often recognize that there may be a number of different variables that allow prediction of the behavior. Variables that are used to predict future behavior are called *predictor variables.* A technique, called *multiple correlation,* is used to combine a number of predictor variables to increase the accuracy of prediction.

A multiple correlation is the correlation between a combined set of predictor variables and a single criterion variable. When all of the predictor variables are taken into account, it is usually possible to achieve greater accuracy of prediction than if any single predictor is considered alone. For example, applicants to graduate school in psychology could be evaluated on a combined set of predictor variables using multiple correlation. The predictor variables might be: (1) college grades, (2) scores on Graduate Record Exam Aptitude Test, (3) score on Graduate Record Exam Psychology Test, and (4) favorability of letter of recommendation. No one of these factors is a perfect predictor of success in graduate school. But a prediction based on this combination of variables can be more accurate than a prediction based on just one of them. The multiple correlation is usually higher than the correlation between any one of the predictor variables and the criterion variable.[1]

PARTIAL CORRELATION AND THE THIRD VARIABLE PROBLEM

Researchers face the third variable problem in correlational research when it is possible that some uncontrolled third variable is responsible for the relationship between the two variables of interest. The problem doesn't exist in experimental research, because all extraneous variables are controlled either by keeping the variables constant or by the use of randomization. A technique called *partial correlation* provides a way of statistically controlling third variables. A partial correlation is a correlation between the two variables of interest, with the influence of the third variable removed, or *partialled out,* of the original correlation.

Suppose that a researcher finds that the correlation between residential crowding and performance on a test is −.50. However, the researcher sus-

---

1 For a more complete discussion of the use and interpretation of multiple correlation, see J. P. Guilford, *Fundamental statistics in psychology and education.* New York: McGraw-Hill, 1965.

pects that a third variable may be operating. The third variable of social class could influence both crowding and performance. The use of partial correlations involves measuring subjects on the third variable in addition to the two primary variables. Thus, the researcher has to measure subjects on all of the variables—crowding, performance, and social class.

When a partial correlation between crowding and performance, with social class partialled out, is calculated,[2] we can determine whether the original correlation is substantially reduced. Is our original correlation of −.50 lowered very much when the influence of social class is removed? Figure 9-4 shows two different partial correlations. In both, there is a −.50 correlation between crowding and performance. However, the first partial correlation drops to −.09

Figure 9-4   Two partial correlations between crowding and performance

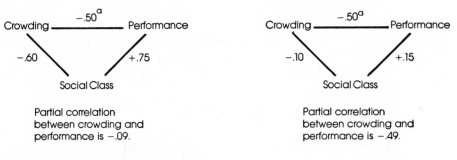

Partial correlation between crowding and performance is −.09.

Partial correlation between crowding and performance is −.49.

[a]The original correlation in both cases is −.50.

when social class is statistically controlled, and the second partial correlation remains high even when the influence of social class is removed. The outcome of the partial correlation depends on the magnitude of the correlations between the third variable and the two variables of primary interest.

TIME-LAGGED CORRELATIONS AND THE CAUSE-EFFECT PROBLEM
One potential solution to the direction of cause-and-effect problem in correlational research is to look at the pattern of correlation between the two vari-

---

2   A statistics text such as Guilford (see note 1) will give a more complete discussion of partial correlations.

ables *over time*. In a time-lagged correlation, the two variables are measured
at two different times.

The use of time-lagged correlations is nicely illustrated by a study (Eron, Huesmann, Lefkowitz, & Walder, 1972) on the relationship between agression and watching violence on television. The original finding was a significant correlation of +.21 for a group of third grade males. This correlation doesn't tell us anything about the direction of cause-and-effect: Does watching violence on television cause aggression, or does being aggressive cause a preference for watching violence on television? We can get a possible answer to this question by measuring the same subjects on the same variables at a later time. The researchers did this by measuring the same subjects ten years later.

With a time-lagged correlation, we are interested in the correlation between each variable at time one with the other variable at time two. We see these two correlations in Table 9-2. The assumption in time-lagged correlations is that we can infer direction of cause-and-effect because the cause comes first with effect coming later (Neale & Liebert, 1973). If there is a relationship between television violence at time one and aggression at time two, then we infer that television violence causes aggression. However, if aggression at time one is related to television violence at time two, then it is aggression that causes television violence watching. From Table 9-2, you can see that it is television violence that appears to be the causal factor.

A future trend in research methods is the use of complex methods of inferring cause-and-effect from correlational data. Such methods are valuable

Table 9–2   Time-lagged correlations between television violence and aggression in third grade and ten years later

Variable at time one	Correlation coefficient	Variable at time two
Watching TV violence (third grade)	+.31	Aggression (ten years later)
Aggression (third grade)	+.01	TV violence (ten years later)

tools in the study of variables in naturalistic settings, because they increase our understanding of the nature of the relationship between variables.[3]

This chapter has explored a number of aspects of correlational research. It is important to keep in mind that use of the correlational method is separate from the use of any particular statistic, such as the product-moment correlation coefficient. Remember, when the correlational method is used, there is no manipulation of the variables. The exact statistical analysis of the data is not determined by whether the research employed the correlational or experimental method. We'll see this in the next chapter, when we discuss research that uses both the experimental and correlational methods in the same design and uses the same statistical treatment for both types of data.

Chapter 10 considers some complex designs that are frequently used in research.

---

3 A detailed discussion of time-lagged correlations and other techniques of inferring cause-and-effect from correlational data is beyond the scope of this book. The statistical analysis and interpretation of such correlations are quite complex. See D. A. Kenney, Cross-lagged panel correlation: A test for spuriousness. *Psychological Bulletin*, 1975, *82*, 887–903.

STUDY QUESTIONS

1 *What is a correlation coefficient? What do the size and sign of the correlation coefficient tell us about the relationship between variables?*

2 *What is a scatterplot? Be able to construct a scatterplot like the ones in Figures 9-1 and 9-2. What happens if the scatterplot shows the relationship to be curvilinear?*

3 *What is meant by restriction of range?*

4 *Distinguish between the types of reliability that are described: (a) test-retest and alternate forms; (b) split-half and odd-even; (c) interrater reliability.*

5 *What is a multiple correlation? Why would a multiple correlation be higher than single correlation coefficients?*

6 *What is a partial correlation, and what is its purpose?*

7 *What is a time-lagged correlation, and what is its purpose?*

10

COMPLEX EXPERIMENTAL DESIGNS

Only the simplest experimental design has been discussed so far. This design contains one independent variable with two levels and one dependent variable. This simple design has allowed us to examine important aspects of research, such as internal validity and the procedures used in conducting an experiment. These considerations are common to all experimental research. However, the very simple design has its limitations, and researchers often investigate problems that demand more complicated experimental designs. These complex experimental designs are the subject of this chapter.

INCREASING THE NUMBER OF DEPENDENT VARIABLES

The first addition we can make to the simple design is to increase the number of dependent variables. A researcher can measure more than one aspect of a subject's behavior.

We have already seen one reason for increasing the number of dependent variables. In Chapter 4, we noted that there is no single, best way of measuring **135** behavior. Thus, the researcher may wish to measure the dependent variable in several different ways in the same experiment. A researcher interested in "liking," for example, could measure this variable by asking how much you like another person, how willing you are to work with the other, and how interested you are in dating or friendship with the other. And the researcher could also make behavioral observations of physical distance and eye contact. These multiple measures of the liking variable would provide a more accurate description of the relationship between the independent variable and liking.

A second reason for using several dependent variables is that any independent variable will have an effect on a number of different behaviors. For example, a researcher interested in studying the effects of marijuana might want to know how marijuana affects simple and complex motor skills, verbal ability, creativity, time perception, and so on. The marijuana researcher would probably try to measure as many of these dependent variables as possible in a single experiment.

INCREASING THE NUMBER OF LEVELS OF AN INDEPENDENT VARIABLE

In the simplest experimental design, there are two levels of the independent variable. There are several reasons why a researcher would want to design an experiment with more than two levels. First, when the design includes only two levels, the research does not produce a completely accurate description of the nature of the relationship between the independent and dependent variables. If there are only two levels of the independent variable, it is possible to show only linear relationships. For example, Figure 10-1 shows the outcome of a hypothetical experiment on the relationship between motivation and performance on a motor task. The solid line describes the results when there are only two levels—no reward promised for good performance, and $1 offered as a reward for high performance. Because there are only two levels, the relationship can only be described with a straight line. We don't know what the relationship would look like if promise of more or less reward were used. The dotted line in Figure 10-1 shows the results when 25¢, 50¢, and 75¢ were included as additional levels of the independent variable. This result is a much more accurate description of the relationship between promised reward and performance. In the hypothetical experiment, increasing the amount of reward is effective up to a point (50¢); further increases in reward do not increase performance. The experiment with two levels cannot yield such exact information. An experiment that is designed to map out the exact relationship between variables is called a *functional design*. It is intended to show how scores on the dependent variable change as a function of changes in the independent variable.

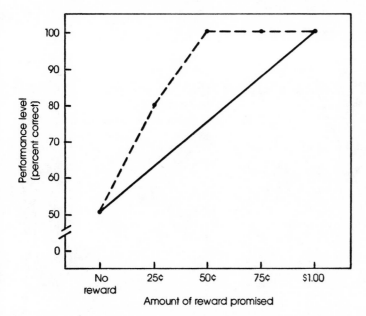

Figure 10-1   Comparison of results of a hypothetical experiment

An experimental design with only two levels of the independent variable also cannot detect curvilinear relationships between variables. If a researcher predicts a curvilinear relationship, such as the one illustrated in Figure 10-2, then at least three levels must be used. Looking at Figure 10-2, you can see that if only levels 1 and 3 of the independent variable had been used, there would appear to be no relationship between the independent and dependent variables.

Finally, a researcher may find that more than two levels of the independent variable are of interest. For example, researchers at Stanford University (Lieberman, Yalom, & Miles, 1973) wanted to compare a number of different types of encounter groups. Ten different types of groups were created, including T-groups, Gestalt therapy groups, transactional analysis groups, marathon groups, and psychodrama groups. The nature of the research problem required the investigators to have many more than two levels of the type of group variable. The researchers concluded from their results that encounter groups in general have a somewhat positive impact on participants, but that the particular type of group doesn't seem to matter.

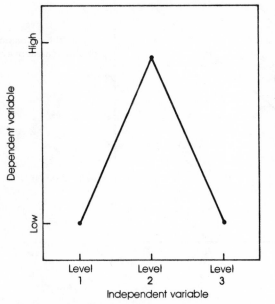

Figure 10.2
An inverted-U relationship

Note: At least three levels of the independent variable are required to show curvilinear relationships.

INCREASING THE NUMBER OF INDEPENDENT VARIABLES: FACTORIAL DESIGNS
Researchers often manipulate more than one independent variable in a single experiment. Typically, two or three independent variables are considered simultaneously. This type of design results in a greater approximation of real-world conditions in which independent variables do not exist by themselves. Researchers recognize that in any given situation a number of variables are operating to affect behavior, and so they design experiments with more than one independent variable.

Factorial designs are designs with more than one independent variable (or *factor*). In a factorial design, all levels of each independent variable are combined with all levels of the other independent variables. To illustrate, let's consider the simplest factorial design—two independent variables, each having two levels.

The Aronson blunder experiment (Aronson et al., 1966) described in Chapter 2 is an example of such a design. Recall that Aronson was investigating the effect of committing a blunder on liking for a person. Aronson had two independent variables: (1) committing a blunder—no blunder or blunder present, and (2) type of person who commits the blunder—average or superior. When the two levels of the two independent variables are combined, a total of four groups—or conditions—is produced: (1) no blunder—average person, (2) no blunder—superior person, (3) blunder—average person, and (4) blunder—superior person. This particular design is called a 2 × 2 (two by two) factorial design, because there are two independent variables, each with two levels. The general format for describing factorial designs is:

$$\begin{bmatrix} \text{Number of levels} \\ \text{of first IV} \end{bmatrix} \times \begin{bmatrix} \text{Number of levels} \\ \text{of second IV} \end{bmatrix} \times \begin{bmatrix} \text{Number of levels} \\ \text{of third IV} \end{bmatrix}$$

and so on.

Thus, a design with two independent variables, each with three levels, would be a 3 × 3 factorial design. A 3 × 3 design would have nine conditions.

Interpretation of factorial designs

Factorial designs yield two kinds of information. One is information about the effect of each independent variable taken by itself. This is called the *main effect* of an independent variable. In a design with two independent variables, there are two main effects—one for each independent variable. The second type of information is called an *interaction*. If there is an interaction between two independent variables, the effect of one variable depends on the particular level of the other variable. In other words, the effect that an independent variable has on the dependent variable depends on the level of the other independent variable. Interactions are a new source of information that cannot be obtained in a simple experimental design in which only one independent variable is manipulated.

To illustrate main effects and interactions, we can consider the results of the Aronson blunder experiment. Table 10-1 illustrates a common method of presenting the means for the various groups in a factorial design. The numbers in each cell represent the *mean* amount of liking for each of the stimulus persons in the four conditions.

Table 10-1   Results of the blunder experiment

Blunder condition (independent variable A)	Type of person (independent variable B)		
	Average	Superior	Overall means (Main effect) of A
No blunder	17.8	20.8	19.30
Blunder	−2.5	30.2	13.85
Overall means (Main effect) of B	7.65	25.50	

Main effects   A *main effect* is the effect each independent variable has by itself. The main effect of independent variable A, the blunder, is the effect committing a blunder does or does not have on liking. Similarly, the main effect of independent variable B, type of person, is the effect type of person has on liking.

The main effect of each independent variable is the *overall* relationship between the independent variable and the dependent variable. For independent variable A, is there a relationship between committing a blunder and liking? We can find out by looking at the overall means in the no-blunder and blunder conditions. These means are shown in the margins of the table. The overall mean liking in the no-blunder condition is 19.30, while the mean liking in the blunder condition is 13.85. These means are obtained by averaging across all subjects in the no-blunder and blunder conditions, whether the subjects were in the average or in the superior person condition. For example, the mean of 19.30 in the no-blunder condition is the average of 17.8 in the no-blunder—average person group and 20.8 in the no-blunder—superior person group. Thus, the calculations of means for the main effect of the blunder manipulation are as follows:

$$\overline{X}_{\text{No blunder}} = \frac{17.8 + 20.8}{2} = \frac{38.6}{2} = 19.30$$

$$\overline{X}_{\text{Blunder}} = \frac{-2.5 + 30.2}{2} = \frac{27.7}{2} = 13.85$$

It can be seen that, *overall,* subjects like the no-blunder person more than the person who committed a blunder. Statistical tests would enable us to determine whether this is a *significant* main effect.

The main effect for variable B (type of person) is the overall relationship between the independent variable, by itself, and the dependent variable. The calculations of the overall means for the average and superior persons are as follows:

$$\overline{X}_{\text{Average}} = \frac{17.8 + (-2.5)}{2} = \frac{15.3}{2} = 7.65$$

$$\overline{X}_{\text{Superior}} = \frac{20.8 + 30.2}{2} = \frac{51.0}{2} = 25.50$$

The overall means of 7.65 in the average condition and 25.50 in the superior conditon show that, in general, subjects like a superior person more, whether or not a blunder is committed.

Interaction An interaction between independent variables indicates that the effect of one independent variable is different at different levels (values) of the other independent variable. We can see an interaction in the results of the blunder study. The effect of committing a blunder is different, depending on whether the person is average or superior. Liking for the average person decreases when a blunder is committed, while liking for the superior person increases when a blunder is committed. The relationship between the blunder variable and liking can be best understood by considering both independent variables: We must consider whether there is a blunder *and* whether the person is average or superior.

Interactions can be easily seen when the means for all conditions are represented in a graph. Figure 10-3 is a graph of the results of the blunder experiment. Note that all four means have been graphed and that there are two lines to describe the relationship between a blunder and liking. One line represents this relationship for the average person, and the other line shows the relationship for the superior person. The fact that the relationship between the blunder variable and liking is different, depending on whether the person is average or superior, shows that there is an interaction. The relationship is positive when the person is superior and negative when the person is average.

The concept of interaction is a relatively simple one that you probably use all the time. When you say "it depends," you are usually indicating that

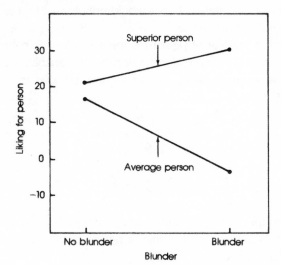

Figure 10-3   Interaction between committing a blunder and type of person

some sort of interaction is operating—it depends on some other variable. For example, a decision about whether to go to a party may reflect an interaction between two variables: (1) do you have an exam coming up, and (2) is a particular person of the opposite sex going to be there. If you have an exam coming up, you can't go under any circumstances. If you do not have an exam coming up, your decision will depend on the presence of the other person. That is, you will go only if he or she will be there.

You might try graphing the party example in the same way we graphed the blunder experiment in Figure 10-3. The dependent variable (going or not going to the party) is always placed on the vertical axis. Independent variable A is placed on the horizontal axis. The results for the first level of independent variable B are then placed on the graph and a line is drawn to connect the points. The same thing is then done for the second level of B.

Outcomes of a 2 × 2 factorial design

A 2 × 2 factorial design has two independent variables, each with two levels. When analyzing the results, there are several possibilities: (1) there may or may not be a significant main effect for independent variable A; (2) there may or may not be a significant main effect for independent variable B; (3) there may or may not be a significant interaction between the independent variables. Statistical significance is determined by the F test.

Figure 10-4 illustrates the eight possible outcomes in a 2 × 2 factorial design. For each outcome, the means are given and then graphed. Note on each graph that the dependent variable is placed on the vertical axis, and independent variable A is placed on the horizontal axis. The two means for B_1 are plotted and a line is drawn to represent this level of B. Similarly, the B_2 means are plotted and a second line is drawn to represent this level. In the first two graphs, the lines representing B_1 and B_2 coincide, so only one line is seen.

The means that are given in the figure are idealized examples. Such perfect outcomes rarely occur in actual research. Nevertheless, you should study the graphs to determine for yourself why, in each case, there is or isn't a main effect for A, a main effect for B, and an A × B interaction.

The first four graphs illustrate outcomes in which there is no A × B interaction effect. The last four graphs are outcomes in which there is an interaction. When there is no interaction, the lines for B_1 and B_2 are *parallel.* The parallel lines indicate that the nature of the relationship between independent variable A and the dependent variable is the same at B_1 as it is at B_2. In the first graph, there is no relationship between A and the dependent variable at either level of B. In each of the first four graphs, the lines are parallel, indicating *no interaction.*

When the lines are *not* parallel, an interaction is present. Such outcomes indicate that the nature of the relationship is different, depending on the particular level of B. In the last four graphs, the two lines are not parallel. In the last graph, there is a positive relationship between A and the dependent variable at B_1, and a negative relationship exists at B_2. An interesting feature of this last graph is that neither independent variable has an effect *by itself.* However,

Figure 10-4   Outcomes of a factorial design with two independent variables

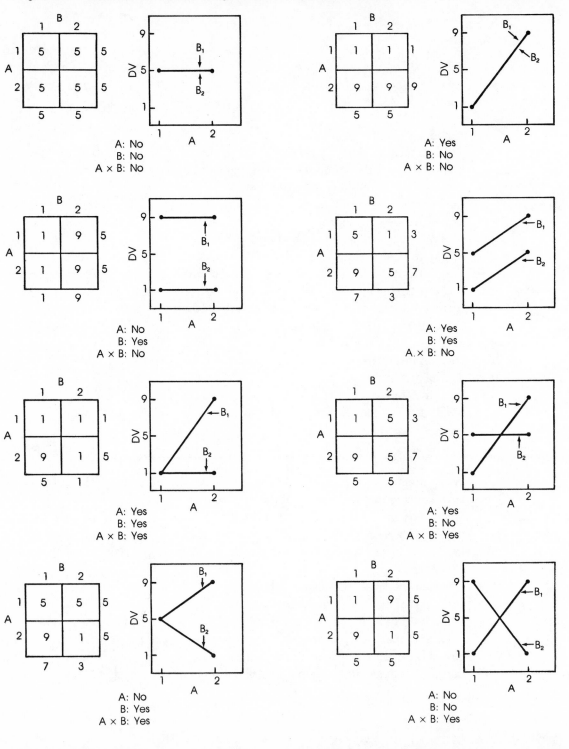

the interaction shows that A has strong (but opposite) effects, depending on the particular level of B. The interaction means that both independent variables must be considered if the relationships involved are to be understood. To make sure that you fully understand these graphs, you might test yourself. Cover the answers or draw a new set of graphs; see if you can say whether or not there are main effects or an interaction.

Mixed factorial designs

One common type of factorial design is a mixed factorial design that includes a mix of both experimental and correlational variables. For example, in a 2×2 mixed design, one variable is manipulated, and the other is a nonmanipulated variable. Thus, mixed factorial designs use both the experimental and correlational methods.

Mixed designs enable researchers to investigate how different types of subjects respond to the same manipulated independent variable. The kinds of subject variables studied would include such characteristics as sex, age, ethnic group, personality characteristics, or clinical diagnostic category.

An example of the use of a mixed design in clinical research is provided by a recent study on self-disclosure. The researchers (Chaikin, Derlega, Bayma, & Shaw, 1975) showed that normals and neurotics respond differently when another person discloses information to them. The results of this study are shown in Figure 10-5. The manipulated variable was the amount of information that a person (a confederate) disclosed to subjects. The correlational variable was neuroticism as measured by a personality test—subjects were classified as normal or as neurotic. The dependent variable was the amount of disclosure that the subjects returned to the confederate. It is obvious that an interaction between the manipulated and nonmanipulated variables was found. The normals disclosed more when the confederate disclosed at high levels; the neurotic subjects disclosed at almost identical levels in both conditions.

The basic distinctions between the experimental and correlational methods apply when interpreting the results of a mixed factorial design. The direction of cause-and-effect problem and the third variable problem discussed in Chapter 3 are relevant to the correlational variable used in a mixed design. You cannot say that the correlational variable *caused* the results. For example, in the self-disclosure study, you don't know whether being neurotic causes disclosing behavior or the self-disclosing behavior causes neuroticism. Further, some third variable may be responsible for both the neuroticism and the disclosing behavior.

Mixed designs offer a very appealing method for investigating many problems in the behavioral sciences. Mixed designs recognize that full understanding of behavior requires knowledge of both situational variables and the personality and background characteristics of the individuals in the situations.

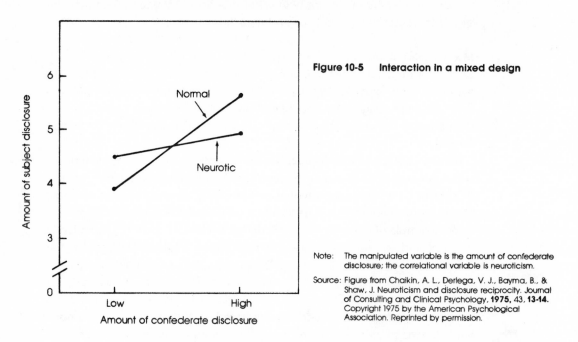

Figure 10-5   Interaction in a mixed design

Note: The manipulated variable is the amount of confederate disclosure; the correlational variable is neuroticism.

Source: Figure from Chaikin, A. L., Derlega, V. J., Bayma, B., & Shaw, J. Neuroticism and disclosure reciprocity. Journal of Consulting and Clinical Psychology, **1975**, 43, **13-14.** Copyright 1975 by the American Psychological Association. Reprinted by permission.

Subject assignment and factorial designs

The considerations of subject assignment discussed in Chapter 7 can be generalized to factorial designs. There are two basic ways of assigning subjects to groups. In an independent groups design, different subjects are assigned to each of the conditions in the study. In a repeated measures design, the same subjects participate in all conditions in the study. These two types of subject assignment procedures have implications for the number of subjects necessary to complete the experiment. We can illustrate these implications by looking at a 2 × 2 factorial design. The design can be completely independent groups, completely repeated measures, or a combination of the two.

Independent groups   In a 2 × 2 factorial design, there are four conditions. If we want a completely independent groups design, a different group of subjects will be assigned to each of the four conditions. If we want to have ten subjects in each condition, a total of forty subjects will be needed. You can visualize this by looking at the first table in Figure 10-6. Forty *different* subjects are shown in the four conditions.

Repeated measures   In a completely repeated measures procedure, the same subjects will participate in *all* conditions. The second table in Figure 10-6 shows that we need a total of ten subjects, because the same ten subjects participate in each condition. This design offers considerable savings in the number of subjects required. However, in deciding whether to use a completely repeated measures assignment procedure, the researcher would have to consider the disadvantages of repeated measures designs.

Combined assignment procedures   The third table in Figure 10-6 illustrates the use of both independent groups and repeated measures procedures in the same design. Independent variable A is an independent groups variable. Ten subjects are assigned to level one of this independent variable, and another ten subjects are assigned to level two. Independent variable B is a repeated measures variable, however. The ten subjects who are assigned to A_1 receive both levels of independent variable B. Similarly, the other ten subjects assigned to A_2 receive both levels of the B variable. Thus, a total of twenty subjects is required.

Figure 10-6   Number of subjects required to have ten subjects in each condition

Table I — Independent groups design

		B 1		B 2	
A	1	S_1 S_6		S_{11} S_{16}	
		S_2 S_7		S_{12} S_{17}	
		S_3 S_8		S_{13} S_{18}	
		S_4 S_9		14 S_{19}	
		S_5 S_{10}		S_{15} S_{20}	
	2	S_{21} S_{26}		S_{31} S_{36}	
		S_{22} S_{27}		S_{32} S_{37}	
		S_{23} S_{28}		S_{33} S_{38}	
		S_{24} S_{29}		S_{34} S_{39}	
		S_{25} S_{30}		S_{35} S_{40}	

Table II — Repeated measures design

		B 1	B 2
A	1	S_1 S_6	S_1 S_6
		S_2 S_7	S_2 S_7
		S_3 S_8	S_3 S_8
		S_4 S_9	S_4 S_9
		S_5 S_{10}	S_5 S_{10}
	2	S_1 S_6	S_1 S_6
		S_2 S_7	S_2 S_7
		S_3 S_8	S_3 S_8
		S_4 S_9	S_4 S_9
		S_5 S_{10}	S_5 S_{10}

Table III — Combination of independent groups and repeated measures designs

		B 1	B 2
A	1	S_1 S_6	S_1 S_6
		S_2 S_7	S_2 S_7
		S_3 S_8	S_3 S_8
		S_4 S_9	S_4 S_9
		S_5 S_{10}	S_5 S_{10}
	2	S_{11} S_{16}	S_{11} S_{16}
		S_{12} S_{17}	S_{12} S_{17}
		S_{13} S_{18}	S_{13} S_{18}
		S_{14} S_{19}	S_{14} S_{19}
		S_{15} S_{20}	S_{15} S_{20}

I
Independent groups design

II
Repeated measures design

III
Combination of independent groups and repeated measures designs

Further considerations in factorial designs

The 2 × 2 factorial design is the simplest factorial design. Using this basic factorial design, we can easily design experiments that are more and more complex. One way to increase complexity is to increase the number of levels of one or more of the independent variables. A 2 × 3 design, for example, contains two independent variables. Independent variable A has two levels, and independent variable B has three levels. The 2 × 3 design has six conditions. Table 10-2 shows a 2 × 3 factorial design with the independent variables of task difficulty (easy, hard) and anxiety (low, moderate, high).

Table 10–2   2 × 3 factorial design

Task difficulty	Anxiety			
	Low	Moderate	High	Overall means (main effect)
Easy	4	7	10	7.0
Hard	7	4	1	4.0
Overall means (main effect)	5.5	5.5	5.5	

The dependent variable is performance on the task. The numbers in each of the six cells of the design indicate the mean performance score of the group. The overall means in the margins show the main effects of each of the independent variables. The results in Table 10-2 indicate a main effect of task difficulty, because the *overall* performance score in the easy task group is higher than the hard task mean. However, there is no main effect of anxiety, because the mean performance score is the same in each of the three anxiety groups. Is there an interaction between task difficulty and anxiety? Note that increasing the amount of anxiety has the effect of increasing performance on the easy task. However, increasing anxiety *decreases* performance on the hard task. The effect of anxiety is different, depending on whether the task is easy **149** or hard. Thus, there is an interaction.

We can also increase the number of variables in the design. A 2 × 2 × 2 factorial design contains three variables, each with two levels. There are eight conditions in this design. A 2 × 2 × 3 design produces twelve conditions, while a 2 × 2 × 2 × 2 design has sixteen conditions. The rule for constructing factorial designs remains the same throughout.

A 2 × 2 × 2 factorial design is constructed in Table 10-3. The variables are:

> A: Instruction method (lecture, discussion)
> B: Class size (10, 40)
> C: Sex of student (male, female)

This is a mixed factorial design since sex of subject is a correlational variable and the other two are experimental variables. The dependent variable is performance on a standard test.

Notice that the 2 × 2 × 2 design can be seen as two 2 × 2 designs, one for the male subjects and another for the female subjects. The design yields main effects for each of the three independent variables. For example, the overall

Table 10-3   2 × 2 × 2 factorial design

Sex of subject	Male	
Instruction method	Class size	
	10	40
Lecture		
Discussion		
Sex of subject	Female	
Lecture		
Discussion		

mean for the lecture method is obtained by considering all subjects who experience the lecture method, irrespective of class size or subject sex. Similarly, the discussion method mean is derived from *all* subjects in this condition. The two means are then compared to see whether there is a significant main effect. Is one method *overall* superior to the other?

The design also allows us to look at interactions. In the $2 \times 2 \times 2$ design, we can look at the interaction between (1) method and class size, (2) method and subject sex, and (3) class size and subject sex. We can also look at a three-way interaction that involves all three independent variables. In looking at the three-way interaction, we want to determine whether the nature of the interaction between two of the variables is different, depending on the particular level of the other variable. Three-way interactions are rather complicated; fortunately, you won't encounter too many of these in your explorations of behavioral science research.

You are now prepared to understand most of the research you will see reported in the literature. After you've mastered the material presented thus far, your knowledge of research methods will be quite sophisticated.

In the final three chapters, we will turn to some issues in behavioral research—generalization of research findings, the ethics of research, and the uses of behavioral research.

STUDY QUESTIONS

1 Why would a researcher include more than one dependent variable in an experiment?

2 Why would a researcher have more than two levels of the independent variable in an experiment?

3 What is a factorial design? Why would a researcher use a factorial design?

4 What are main effects and interactions? Be able to identify the main effects and interactions in a factorial design with two independent variables. Be able to graph the results of a factorial design with two independent variables.

5 *What is a mixed factorial design? What is the value of mixed factorial designs* *in behavioral research?*

6 *Be able to identify the number of subjects required in a factorial design under: (a) completely independent groups assignment; (b) completely repeated measures assignment; and (c) both independent groups assignment and repeated measures assignment.*

7 *Be able to identify the number of conditions in a factorial design on the basis of knowing the number of independent variables and the number of levels of each independent variable.*

11
GENERALIZING RESULTS

In this chapter we will consider the problem of generalization of research findings. Can the results of a completed research project be generalized to other subject populations, to other age groups, to other ways of manipulating or measuring the variables? An experiment may have perfect *internal validity* — alternative explanations have been eliminated so that only the independent variable could have caused the results. Yet the results may have only limited generalizability—the experiment lacks *external validity*. It is absolutely necessary that an experiment have internal validity. Ideally, it should have external validity as well.

GENERALIZING TO OTHER SUBJECT POPULATIONS
Even though a researcher randomly assigns subjects to conditions, rarely are subjects randomly *selected* from the general population. Usually subjects are selected because they are available. In fact, it sometimes seems as though psychologists are interested only in the behavior of college students. In a sur- **153**

vey of two psychological journals,[1] Smart (1966) found that college students were used in 73 percent of the studies reported in one journal and in 86 percent of the studies in the other. Less than 1 percent of the studies used "samples of the general population."

Obviously, such studies use a highly restricted subject population. As Smart points out, most college students are in the age group from eighteen to twenty-four. We do not know if the results would be different for younger or older age groups. In addition, most college students are intelligent, verbal, and traditionally they have been whites from middle and upper socioeconomic backgrounds.

The problem of unrepresentative subjects is not confined to human research. A great deal of research with animals relies solely on the infamous white rat. Why? Probably because, as Beach (1950) points out, "rats are hardy, cheap, easy to rear, and well adapted to a laboratory existence." The use of other species might well lead to different conclusions about the nature of behavior.

The generalization problem can be thought of as an interaction in a factorial design. When we suggest the possibility of generalizing to other subject populations, we are asking whether there is an interaction between a type of subject variable and the treatment variable that was manipulated. Does the effect of the treatment variable differ for different subject types? Sex of subject provides a convenient example of a subject characteristic selected by the researcher. Let's suppose that a researcher uses only male subjects in an experiment on crowding and aggression (Smart found a heavy reliance on males as research subjects in his survey of two journals). Now suppose that this researcher finds a positive relationship between crowding and aggression. But the researcher actually has completed only half of a 2 × 2 mixed factorial design. If crowding was one variable and sex of subject constituted the other variable, we could then see whether a crowding × sex interaction exists.

Figure 11-1 shows four possible hypothetical outcomes of our 2 × 2 mixed factorial design. In each graph, the positive relationship between crowding and aggression for males has been maintained. In Graph A, there is no interaction—the behavior of males and females is virtually identical. The results of the original all-male study could be generalized to females. In Graph B,

---

1   The journals were the *Journal of Abnormal and Social Psychology* and the *Journal of Experimental Psychology,* both surveyed from 1962 to 1964.

there is also no interaction. The effect of crowding is identical for both sexes. **155**
Note, however, that males are, in general, more aggressive than females.
Although such a sex difference is interesting, it is not a factor in generalization,

**Figure 11-1   Outcomes of a hypothetical experiment on
crowding, sex, and aggression**

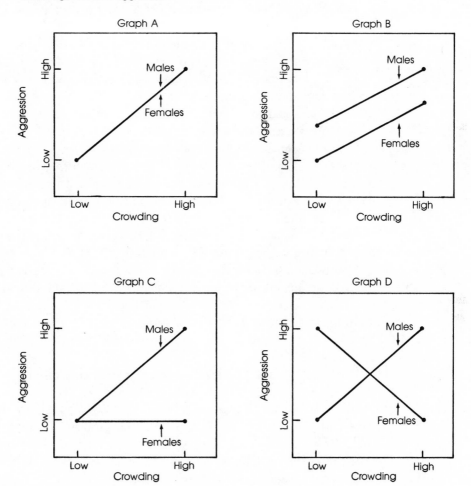

Note: The presence of an interaction indicates that the results for males cannot be generalized to females.

because the overall positive relationship between crowding and aggression is present for both males and females.

Graphs C and D do show interactions. In both of these, the original results with males cannot be generalized to females. In Graph C, there is no relationship between crowding and aggression for females. The answer to the question, "But is this true for females?" is obviously "No!" In Graph D, the interaction tells us that there is a positive relationship between crowding and aggression for males but a negative relationship between crowding and aggression for females.

Are the problems of generalizing from males to females serious enough to warrant concern? The answer must be "Yes." As it turns out, Graph D describes the data from one study (Freedman, Levy, Buchanan, & Price, 1972) on crowding and aggression. The moral of this tale of sex differences is that researchers should select both male and female subjects and include sex of subject as a factor in the experimental design.

Unfortunately, the problem of subject selection bias does not stop here. Volunteers also present a problem. It's bad enough that psychology is dependent on college sophomores; worse yet, those college sophomores often have a choice in deciding which experiments to participate in. Rosenthal (1965) has noted that different types of subjects seek out particular types of experiments. Available evidence says that, indeed, the title of the experiment does influence who signs up (Hood & Back, 1971).

Moreover, volunteers may differ in various ways from nonvolunteers. For instance, volunteers are higher self-disclosers who may be seeking opportunities to talk about themselves (Hood & Back, 1971). In addition, volunteers seem to be higher in intellectual ability and need for social approval, more unconventional, younger, and more sociable (Rosenthal, 1965; Rosenthal & Rosnow, 1969).

Finally, subjects in one locale may differ from subjects in another locale. Students at California Institute of Technology may differ from students at a nearby Los Angeles junior college. People in Iowa may differ from people in New York City. An interesting solution to this problem was recently demonstrated in a study that was done simultaneously at seven different campuses across the country (Cialdini et al., 1974). The researchers report that it was surprisingly easy to coordinate their efforts.

Subject selection bias is obviously a problem in research. The obvious solution is to consider various subject types when planning an experiment.

Subject variables can then be included in the design and data analyzed through use of the mixed designs discussed in Chapter 10. Researchers can then investigate generalizability across variables such as sex, race, IQ, and age. Although this is a difficult task, the payoff will come in greater accuracy in generalization statements.

GENERALIZING TO OTHER EXPERIMENTERS

The person who actually conducts the experiment is the source of another generalization problem. In most research, only one experimenter is used, and rarely is much attention paid to the personal characteristics of the experimenter (McGuigan, 1963). The main goal is to make sure that any influence the experimenter has on subjects is constant throughout the experiment. There is always the possibility, however, that the results are generalizable only to certain types of experimenters.

Some of the important characteristics of experimenters have been discussed by Kintz and his colleagues (1965). These include the experimenter's personality and sex and the amount of practice she or he has had being an experimenter. A friendly, warm experimenter will almost certainly produce different results from an unfriendly, cold experimenter. Subjects may behave differently with male and female experimenters. It has even been shown (Brogden, 1962) that rabbits learn faster when trained by experienced experimenters! Race of the experimenter may also have an effect on subjects' behavior. The influence of the experimenter may also depend on the characteristics of the subjects. For example, subjects seem to perform better when tested by an experimenter of the opposite sex (Stevenson and Allen, 1964).

These kinds of problems are not limited to experimenter–subject relationships. The same point could be made in discussing the relationship between a therapist and client. In fact, considerable research is being conducted on different types of therapists and their effectiveness with different types of patients (Razin, 1971).

The solution to the problem of generalizing to other experimenters is to use at least two, and preferably more, experimenters to conduct the research. Ideally, several experimenters of each sex would be used. A fine example of the use of multiple experimenters is a study by Rubin (1975), who sent several male and female experimenters to the Boston airport to study self-disclosure.

The experimenters revealed different kinds of information about themselves to passengers of both sexes and recorded the passengers' return disclosures.

EXPERIMENTER BIAS

The experimental method involves keeping all variables (other than the independent variable, of course) constant. Researchers strive to make sure that nothing but the independent variable can cause the results. For instance, it would be ludicrous to have an attractive experimenter run subjects in one condition while letting an unattractive experimenter run subjects in the other. Any difference in subjects' behavior could be attributed to the difference in the attractiveness of the experimenters, rather than to the effect of the manipulated variable.

No matter how many precautions are taken to keep extraneous variables constant, it is still possible that the experimenter may somehow treat subjects in each condition differently. This problem has been called *experimenter bias* or *experimenter expectancy effect* (Rosenthal, 1966, 1969).

Experimenter bias refers to any intentional or unintentional influence that the experimenter exerts on the subject in an attempt to confirm the hypothesis. Intentional influence might involve grossly different treatment of subjects in the various conditions, or even discarding data from subjects who do not behave in the expected way, or changing the data that a subject gives. Such behavior by an experimenter is clearly dishonest and inexcusable and rarely occurs. Nevertheless, all of us must constantly remember that honesty is the foremost characteristic of the scientist.

The *unintentional* influence of the experimenter on subjects' behavior is a more serious problem. If the experimenter knows what to expect from a subject, he or she may unwittingly communicate expectancy in surprisingly subtle ways. For instance, the experimenter may smile or show relief when a subject behaves in the right way. Or the experimenter may emphasize particular words when reading instructions. Research has shown that this kind of subtle interaction between subject and experimenter can and does occur (Rosenthal, 1967).

The problem of subtle influence on the subject is nicely shown in the case of Clever Hans, a horse whose brilliance was shown by Pfungst (1911) to be an illusion. Robert Rosenthal, a leading researcher on the problem, describes Clever Hans:

Hans, it will be remembered, was the clever horse who could solve problems of mathematics and musical harmony with equal skill and grace, simply by tapping out the answers with his hoof. A committee of eminent experts testified that Hans, whose owner made no profit from his horse's talents, was receiving no cues from his questioners. Of course, Pfungst later showed that this was not so, that tiny head and eye movements were Hans' signals to begin and to end his tapping. When Hans was asked a question, the questioner looked at Hans' hoof, quite naturally so, for that was the way for him to determine whether Hans' answer was correct. Then, it was discovered that when Hans approached the correct number of taps, the questioner would inadvertently move his head or eyes upward—just enough that Hans could discriminate the cue, but not enough that even trained animal observers or psychologists could see it.[2]

If a clever horse can respond to subtle cues, then it seems reasonable to suppose that clever humans can, too. And research has shown that experimenter expectancy can be communicated to humans by both verbal and nonverbal communication (Duncan, Rosenberg, & Finklestein, 1969; Jones & Cooper, 1971).

Solutions to the experimenter bias problem

There is still considerable controversy over whether experimenter bias is a serious problem in most psychological research (Barber & Silver, 1968; Neale & Liebert, 1973). Nevertheless, it seems wise to keep this problem in mind and to take precautions to minimize it. Clearly, experimenters should be well trained and should practice so that their behavior is constant with all subjects. However, this may not be enough, because bias can be unintentional—the experimenter may not be aware of his or her influence.

One solution would be to run subjects in all conditions *simultaneously,* so that the experimenter's behavior must be the same for all subjects. If running subjects in large groups isn't possible, it may be possible to have the experimenter be unaware of which condition the subject is in. Even better would be to use experimenters who are unaware of the researcher's hypothesis. To do this, you must hire others to conduct your resarch. Finally, automated procedures could be used, so that the experimenter does not interact at all with the subject. Everything could be done with a tape recorder or written instructions.

---

2 R. Rosenthal, Covert communication in the psychological experiment. *Psychological Bulletin,* 1967, *67,* 356–367. Copyright © 1967 by the American Psychological Association. Reprinted by permission.

Expectancy effects in the real world

One of the fascinating aspects of experimenter bias is the extent to which it can occur in real-life settings. For example, consider a teacher who expects a student to be exceptionally bright or exceptionally dumb. Could the teacher unintentionally influence the student to fulfill such expectations? Early research by Rosenthal (1966) showed that rats described to experimenters as "dull" learned more slowly than rats described as "bright." The animals were actually similar and had been randomly assigned to the bright and dull categories. Later research has shown that telling a teacher that a pupil will bloom intellectually during the next year results in an increase in the pupil's IQ score (Rosenthal & Jacobson, 1968). Another type of teacher expectancy occurs when a teacher previously taught a student's older sister or brother (Seaver, 1973). Subtle interaction patterns are probably responsible for such effects (Chaikin, Sigler, & Derlaga, 1974).

Expectancy effects are likely to occur in therapy as well. Perhaps we should consider the possibility that the astounding success of a particular therapy may be due as much to the therapist's expectation as to the technique itself!

PRETESTS AND GENERALIZATION

An important decision in planning a study is whether to give a pretest. Intuitively, pretesting seems to be a good idea. You can make sure that the groups are equivalent, and somehow it seems more satisfying to see that individuals changed their scores than it is to look only at group means on the posttest.

Pretesting, however, may limit the ability to generalize to populations that have not received a pretest. In the real world people are rarely pretested, and so this can be a serious problem[3] (Lana, 1969; Rosenblatt and Miller, 1973a).

As an example, consider an experiment on speaker credibility and attitude change toward banning fraternities from campus. A pretest measuring atti-

---

3　There is some question whether pretest generalizability is a cause for alarm. Lana reviewed the available literature and concluded that pretesting has little or no effect. However, Rosenblatt and Miller have criticized Lana. They suggest that we should be cautious in generalizing to non-pretested populations. See R. E. Lana, Pretest sensitization. In R. Rosenthal and R. Rosnow (eds.), *Artifact in behavioral research.* New York: Academic Press, 1969; P. C. Rosenblatt and N. Miller, Experimental methods. In C. G. McClintock (ed.), *Experimental social psychology.* New York: Holt, Rinehart & Winston, 1973.

tudes toward fraternities is given before the speech. Suppose there is greater attitude change in the high credibility condition. It is possible that this effect only occurs when subjects have been pretested. The pretest may indicate to subjects that attitude change is being studied. They may then figure out the researcher's hypothesis and change (or not change) their attitudes appropriately when given the posttest. If subjects are not pretested, the speaker credibility effect might be quite different.

I have just described an interaction between the variables of pretesting and credibility. This interaction prevents generalization to populations that have not been pretested. If there weren't an interaction, we could generalize to situations without a pretest. The most direct and least complicated solution to the pretest generalization problem is to eliminate the pretest. If there is a real need for a pretest, the researcher should probably include pretesting as a factor in the design. Half of the subjects would receive the pretest; the other half would receive the posttest only. The researcher can then assess generalizability by looking at the interaction between the independent variable and the pretest variable.[4]

Pretesting may have the effect of communicating the researcher's hypothesis to the subject. The subject may then behave in ways that would help confirm the hypothesis. In any experiment, there may be many cues that tell the subject what the researcher is trying to find. These cues are called *demand characteristics* of an experiment. We'll now consider the general problem of demand characteristics in some detail.

DEMAND CHARACTERISTICS

The term *demand characteristics* was coined by Martin Orne (1962) to describe those aspects of the experimental situation that affect the way subjects behave. The total setting of the experiment can be thought of as a source of cues telling the subject how to behave. Orne sees the subject as an active being who takes a problem-solving approach to the experiment. The subject tries to discover the hypothesis and usually tries to "help" by behaving in ways that confirm the hypothesis.

---

4 This has been called a "Solomon Four-Group Design." See R. L. Solomon, An extension of control group design. *Psychological Bulletin,* 1949, *46,* 137–150.

Orne (1962) feels that the subject's prime motivation is a desire to be cooperative, and his study illustrates this cooperation. The subjects were told to add a series of numbers on a sheet. When finished, the subject was to pick a card from a large stack for further instructions. Each instruction card told the subject to tear the sheet up into thirty-two pieces and to go to the next page of numbers. Thus, the subjects repeatedly destroyed their work. And apparently they continued this ridiculous task for several hours without complaint!

The problem of demand characteristics is illustrated in the typical sensory deprivation experiment. Depriving subjects of sensory input leads to such effects as hallucinations and other bizarre behavior. Orne suggests that in the typical sensory deprivation study, "the overly cautious treatment of subjects, careful screening for mental or physical disorders, awesome release forms, and, above all, the presence of a 'panic (release) button' might be more significant in producing the effects reported from sensory deprivation than the actual diminution of sensory input (1962)." Orne conducted an experiment in which subjects were placed in isolation (but not sensory deprivation) for four hours. One group had the release forms and panic button; the other group did not. Consistent with the demand characteristics hypothesis, the first group showed the typical sensory deprivation effects, but the second group did not.

There are numerous other cues in the experiment that might serve as demand characteristics. For instance, if I tell subjects that I am studying "the effects of crowding," they might interpret that as a cue to behave in ways that would confirm the hypothesis that "crowding is bad."

One way to neutralize the effects of demand characteristics is to use deception. Care can be taken to make subjects think that the experiment is studying one thing when actually it is studying something else. The experimenter may use elaborate cover stories to explain the purpose of the study and to disguise what he or she is really doing. This has become common practice in much research. Deception, however, runs counter to our concern with the ethics of experimentation. Is it ethical to lie to subjects (or to anyone), even if lying is methodologically desirable? We must also ask what happens to subjects after they have been deceived. Will they distrust psychology? Will they behave differently in future experiments? Perhaps instead of wanting to be cooperative—the motive assumed by Orne—they will try to *disconfirm* the hypothesis. We will explore the ethics issue further in the next chapter.

Another potential solution to the problem of demand characteristics is to use a postexperimental inquiry to find out whether subjects had guessed the true purpose of the experiment. The data received from subjects who had **163** accurately guessed the true purpose can then be eliminated from the experiment, or data can be analyzed with and without the data from these subjects. However, some subjects may be reluctant to tell the experimenter that they guessed the real purpose of the experiment—perhaps they are afraid of disappointing him (Freedman, Wallington, and Bless, 1967). And the experimenter's inquiry may be halfhearted. The experimenter, after all, is only human and may not really want evidence that might invalidate his study.

Clearly, it is difficult to eliminate the problem of demand characteristics. Orne has proposed using the simulator technique described in Chapter 6 as a control in hypnosis research. Presumably, the technique could be used in other studies as well. Another solution is to conduct experiments in natural situations in which subjects are not aware that their behavior is being studied. Such field experiments have become increasingly popular in recent years.

FIELD EXPERIMENTS

In a field experiment, the independent variable is manipulated in a natural setting rather than in the laboratory. Because the subjects are not aware that they are in an experiment, the problem of demand characteristics does not occur. And if the experiment is not conducted on a college campus, it may have a representative sample that can be generalized to the general population.

Field experiments have been especially popular in studying helping behavior. One such study was conducted on subway trains in New York City (Piliavin, Rodin, & Piliavin, 1969). The procedure involved a person (confederate) falling down while the train was in motion. The independent variables were race of the confederate and cause of the accident. The confederate was either black or white, and he carried either a cane or a bag containing a bottle of liquor. Presumably the fall was due to the person's bad leg or to his drunken condition. One of the interesting findings of this study is that the "drunk" was helped primarily by members of the same race, while the person with the cane was helped equally by both black and white subway riders.

The field experiment is a very attractive technique. Usually field experiments study situations that can and do occur naturally. However, the experimenter controls the situation and can run conditions in random order. He or she can achieve experimental control by keeping variables—such as the locale of the experiment—constant.

More and more, researchers have been using the field experiment to get away from the laboratory. The ingenuity of researchers in designing field experiments has been impressive. For instance, grocery bags have been dropped in front of supermarkets (Wispé & Freshley, 1971), thefts have been staged in liquor stores (Latané & Darley, 1970), and drug stores (Gelfand et al. 1973) to investigate reporting of thefts and shoplifting, and people have "luckily" found dimes in telephone coin slots (Isen & Levin, 1972). If you are interested in reading about more examples of field experimentation, you could look at one of several books of collected readings about field experiments (Bickman & Henchy, 1972; Evans & Rozelle, 1973).

REPLICATIONS: EXACT AND CONCEPTUAL

The term *exact replication* refers to an attempt to exactly reproduce the procedures of a piece of research to see if the same results are obtained. Such exact replications frequently take place within the context of generalizing results, trying to clarify some aspect of the original research, and so on. For example, there may be several explanations for a relationship that was found. More experiments are then conducted to clarify the theoretical meaning of the relationship. Suppose that an experiment shows that the recipient of a favor reciprocates that favor. There may be several explanations for this. Perhaps he reciprocates because he likes the other person; or maybe he does it out of a feeling of obligation. There may be other reasons as well. Often an exact replication of original research is done by a researcher who is trying to discover which of various explanations is correct.

Sometimes a researcher will be unable to replicate a previous finding. A single failure to replicate doesn't reveal very much, though. It is unrealistic to assume, on the basis of a single failure to replicate, that the previous research is invalid. Failures to replicate share the same problem as negative results discussed earlier. A failure to replicate *could* mean that the original results are invalid. However, it could occur because the replication attempt was flawed. Negative results can be obtained by incompetent experimenters who perhaps offended subjects, for example. It is also possible that the report of the previous research omitted some crucial aspect of the procedure (Rosenblatt & Miller, 1973b). Because this can happen, it is usually a good idea to write the researcher before attempting a replication of his or her research. In reply to such

A single failure to replicate is not adequate cause for discarding the original research finding. Repeated failures to replicate do provoke reconsideration of the validity of the earlier findings, however. Eventually we may conclude that the original results were a fluke—that a Type I error was made. This is especially likely when unsuccessful attempts to replicate results obtained earlier use not only the original procedures but different procedures as well. The use of different procedures in an attempt to replicate a research finding is called a *conceptual replication.* Conceptual replications are even more important than exact replications in furthering our understanding of behavior.

In a conceptual replication, the researcher tries to replicate the original relationship between two conceptual variables by using different procedures for manipulating or measuring the variables. Suppose you are interested in testing the hypothesis that heightened sexual arousal leads to perceiving that members of the opposite sex are more physically attractive than they ordinarily seem. In the process of testing this hypothesis, you have to *operationally define* the variables. Sexual arousal is a conceptual variable that you must manipulate. You must also devise a procedure to measure perception of physical attractiveness.

A study to test this hypothesis was conducted by Stephan, Berscheid, & Walster (1971). In their study, sexual arousal was manipulated by having one group of subjects read a seduction scene while the other group read about the sex life of herring gulls. Only male subjects were used. Subjects then rated the physical attractiveness of a female (shown in a photograph) on a response scale. The hypothesis was confirmed. Subjects who were sexually aroused did see the female as more attractive than subjects who were not aroused.

What are the problems of generalization of this finding? Obviously, we don't know whether the relationship is true for female subjects. Beyond this, however, we do not know whether we can generalize to other types of sexual arousal or other types of physical attractiveness measures. From a single study such as this, we can only say that sexual arousal, as manipulated in a *particular way,* is related to perception of physical attractiveness, as measured in a *particular way.* The results of the study support the hypothesized relationship between the two conceptual variables. However, we don't know whether other studies using different ways of arousing subjects (for example, different kinds of written passages or visual displays of erotic material) would lead to the same conclusion. We also don't know whether a different measure of perceived physical attractiveness would lead to similar results.

Simply stated, a single study only provides *support* for a relationship between the theoretical variables. A general statement relating the variables is not warranted. Such general statements are warranted only after conceptual replications have shown that the same relationship is found with a variety of procedures for manipulating or observing the variables.

Now that you are aware of conceptual replications, you can understand why the authors of textbooks usually describe relationships between variables in terms of specific studies. You should recognize that the relationships between conceptual, theoretical variables are based on specific studies.

Remember, too, that an exact replication of a study might not be obtained, although a conceptual replication might be successful. A sexual arousal manipulation that was successful twenty years ago might not be arousing now. The characteristics that are considered physically attractive change over time, and so on. And so, although the relationship between the conceptual variables may remain constant, the specific procedures used to define these variables will probably differ.

Hopefully, we can generalize from one specific study to a more general statement relating conceptual variables. This may not always be the case, however. The sexual arousal stimulated by *Playboy* nudes seems to result in perceptions of other females as *less* attractive (Carducci & Cozby, 1974). Such contradictions are frustrating, but they are also interesting and challenging. They usually lead to more studies that attempt to expand our knowledge of behavior. Science is an exciting, never-ending process. Every study answers some questions and leads to new ones. Previous research can be used now, but we must always be open to new theories, ideas, and interpretations.

This chapter on generalization has a somewhat pessimistic tone. You might be wondering whether the results of our scientific studies are of any use. If you can't generalize, what's the point of all this research? I don't think the problem is as serious as it might appear. We do have to recognize the problems of generalization, and we must try to design research to overcome these problems. However, often we *can* generalize findings from scientific research. The track record is good, and there are many reasons to believe that research will provide solutions to many practical problems that face our society. Just a few examples of the applications of psychological research demonstrate how true this is.

Research on reinforcement and behavior (behavior modification) has been applied in programs with autistic children and other institutionalized populations. Research on modeling has been used to reduce littering. Our theories and research on learning and intellectual development are being used to plan educational programs. The list could go on and on. Knowledge of the methods and findings of research conducted by behavioral scientists should enable you to *use* this research. Hopefully, you will try to find the practical implications of research and theory as you continue in your study of the behavioral sciences.

In the final chapter, we'll consider some practical aspects of research methodology. Knowledge of research methods can be a great aid in planning and evaluating programs designed to help others. First, though, we'll look at the problem of ethics in research.

STUDY QUESTIONS

1 *Why should researchers be concerned about generalizing to other subject populations? What are some of the subject population generalization problems that a researcher might confront?*

2 *What is the source of the problem of generalizing to other experimenters? How can this problem be solved?*

3 *What is an experimenter bias effect or experimenter expectancy effect? How can this problem be reduced?*

4 *Why is pretesting a problem for generalization?*

5 *What are demand characteristics? How can this problem be reduced?*

6 *What are the advantages of the field experiment technique? How does the field experiment technique differ from the field observation technique discussed in Chapter 4?*

7 *Distinguish between an exact replication and a conceptual replication. What is the value of conceptual replications?*

12

ETHICAL CONCERNS

At numerous points throughout the book, I've mentioned the concern for ethics that psychologists must have when they decide to conduct research. In this chapter, we will explore in detail the nature of ethical problems that arise in research, and we will examine some guidelines for dealing with these problems. To begin, let's consider a specific study that many of you *may* consider to be unethical.

MILGRAM'S OBEDIENCE EXPERIMENT

Stanley Milgram is a psychologist who is interested in the phenomenon of blind obedience to an authority figure. To study this subject, he conducted a series of experiments (1963, 1964, 1965). The general experimental procedure went something like this. An ad was placed in the local newspaper in New Haven, Connecticut, offering to pay $4.50 each to men who would participate in a "scientific study of memory and learning" being conducted at Yale University. A man reads the ad and reports to Milgram's laboratory at Yale. **169**

There he meets a scientist dressed in a lab coat and another subject—a middle-aged gentleman named Mr. Wallace. Mr. Wallace, as it turns out, is a confederate who is part of the experimental procedure (but the subject doesn't know this, of course). The scientist running the experiment explains that this study of "memory and learning" will involve the effects of punishment on learning. One subject will be a "teacher" who will administer the punishment, while the other subject will be the "learner." Mr. Wallace and the subject draw slips of paper to determine who will be the teacher and who will be the learner. The drawing is rigged, and the real subject is always the teacher. Mr. Wallace is always the learner.

The scientist attaches some electrodes to Mr. Wallace and then places the real subject in front of an impressive looking shock machine. The shock machine has a series of levers that—the subject is told—when pressed, will deliver shocks to Mr. Wallace. The first lever is labeled 15 volts, the second says 30 volts, then 45 volts, and so on up to 450 volts. The levers are also labeled "Slight Shock," "Moderate Shock," etcetera, up to "Danger: Severe Shock" followed by red Xs above 400 volts.

Mr. Wallace is instructed to learn a series of word pairs. Then he is given a test to see if he knows which words go together. Every time Mr. Wallace makes a mistake, the teacher is to deliver a shock as punishment. The first mistake is answered by a 15 volt shock, the second by 30 volts, and so on. Each time a mistake is made, the learner receives a greater amount of shock. Now, the learner, Mr. Wallace, never actually receives any shock, but the real subject doesn't know that. Mr. Wallace, it turns out, is not very bright, and he continues to make mistakes. When the teacher gets up to about 120 volts, Wallace begins screaming in pain and eventually yells that he wants out. What if the teacher wants to quit? This is likely to happen—the real subjects became visibly upset by the pain that Mr. Wallace was experiencing. The scientist says that the teacher *can* quit but urges him to continue, using a series of prods that stress the importance of continuing the experiment.

Although Milgram's study was presumably an experiment on memory and learning, he was really interested in learning whether subjects would continue to obey the experimenter by continuing to administer higher and higher levels of shock to the learner. What happened? In the experimental condition just described, twenty-five of forty subjects continued to deliver shock all the way to 450 volts. Milgram's study has received a great deal of publicity, and the results have challenged many of our views of our ability to defy authority.

Such results have implications for real-world situations, such as Nazi Germany and the My Lai massacre in Vietnam.

But what about the ethics of the Milgram study? What aspects of the experimental procedure might we find objectionable?

STRESS AND PSYCHOLOGICAL HARM

The first problem concerns the stress that subjects experienced while delivering intense shocks to an obviously unwilling learner. A film that Milgram made shows subjects protesting, sweating, and even laughing nervously while delivering the shocks. You might ask whether subjecting people to such a stressful experience is justified. And you might wonder whether the experience had any long-range consequences. For example, did subjects who obeyed the experimenter feel continuing remorse or begin to see themselves as cruel, inhumane people? I will present a defense of Milgram's study shortly, but first let's consider some potentially stressful research procedures.

Milgram's study required the subject to deliver electric shock to someone else. In some experiments, the subject might be on the receiving end of a shock machine. Such a procedure would involve actual physical stress, and of course great care would have to be taken to make it ethically acceptable.

More common than physical stress are procedures that involve psychological stress. For example, a subject might be told he or she will receive some extreme intensity electric shocks. The subject never actually receives the shock—it is the fear or anxiety during the waiting period that is the variable of interest. Research by Schachter employing a procedure like this showed that the anxiety produced a desire to affiliate with others during the waiting period (Schachter, 1959).

In another procedure that produces psychological stress, subjects are given unfavorable feedback about their personalities or abilities. Researchers interested in self-esteem have typically given a subject a personality test. The test is followed by an evaluation that lowers or raises the subject's self-esteem. One study went even further. After raising or lowering a male subject's self-esteem, the researcher then gave the subject evidence that he had possible homosexual tendencies (Bramel, 1962).

You can see by now that some procedures used in research involve physical or psychological stress. Whether such research should be conducted is a difficult question which we'll grapple with a little later.

DECEPTION AND THE PRINCIPLE OF INFORMED CONSENT

The Milgram experiment also illustrates the use of deception. Subjects in the Milgram experiment agreed to participate in a study of memory and learning. But they actually took part in a study on obedience. Who would imagine that a memory and learning experiment (that title does sound tame, after all) would involve delivering high intensity, painful shock to another person? Subjects in the Milgram experiment didn't know what they were letting themselves in for. The procedure lacked what is called *informed consent.* Informed consent means that the subject is given an accurate perception of the risks involved before he or she consents to participate in the experiment.

The problem of deception is not limited to laboratory research. Procedures in which an observer conceals his purposes, presence, or identity are also deceptive. For example, a sociologist named Laud Humphreys (1970) studied the behavior of male homosexuals who visit public restrooms (called tearooms). Humphreys did not participate in any homosexual activities, but rather he served as a lookout who would warn the others of possible intruders. In addition to observing the activities at the tearoom, Humphreys wrote down license plate numbers. Later, he obtained the addresses of the men, disguised himself, and visited their homes to interview them. Humphrey's procedure is certainly one way of finding out about homosexuality, but it does involve considerable deception.

Herbert Kelman (1967) has noted several problems with the use of deception. First, deception is unethical. Kelman writes:

> In our other interhuman relationships, most of us would never think
> of doing the kinds of things that we do to our subjects—exposing others
> to lies and tricks, deliberately misleading them about the purposes
> of the interaction or withholding pertinent information, making promises
> or giving assurances that we intend to disregard. We would view
> such behavior as a violation of the respect to which all fellow humans are
> entitled and of the whole basis of our relationship with them. Yet we
> seem to forget that the experimenter–subject relationship . . . is a *real*
> interhuman relationship, in which we have responsibility toward the
> subject as another human being whose dignity we must preserve.[1]

A second problem noted by Kelman is that deception may fail to achieve

---

1   H. C. Kelman, Human use of human subjects: The problem of deception in social psychological experiments. *Psychological Bulletin,* 1967, *67,* 1–11. Copyright © 1967 by the American Psychological Association. Reprinted by permission.

its intended goals. The primary justification for deceiving subjects is that knowl- **173** edge of the purpose of an experiment would contaminate the results. If the subject is unaware of the real purpose, he or she will behave more naturally. Kelman feels, however, that subjects are aware of psychologists' tricks, and that they come to experimental situations expecting to be lied to. Thus, they take nothing the researcher says at face value. Instead, subjects simply respond to the demand characteristics present in the situation. This may be an extreme statement of the problem, but it is a possibility to be concerned about.

Yet another problem with deception has been noted by Rubin (1970) and by Ring (1967). These authors point not only to the possible harmful effects of deception, but also to the motivation of some researchers who use deception. Rubin refers to "jokers wild in the lab," and Ring talks about a "fun and games" approach to research. The official justification for deception is that it provides a way of making sure that the subjects behave naturally and spontaneously, so that researchers get a better picture of real behavior. This justification is based on scientific grounds and so has some merit. Observers such as Rubin and Ring note, however, that some researchers are motivated by the desire to devise clever and elaborate experimental manipulations that are sure to capture the attention of others. Ring states that "there is a distinctly exhibitionist flavor to much current experimentation, while the experimenters often seem to equate notoriety with achievement (1967)." Rubin (1970) cites an example of research conducted at Ohio State University. The subject sits behind a large machine and is shown how to operate it by pushing the proper buttons. He is then told, "All my research money is tied up in this contraption and I'll never get my master's degree if it doesn't function properly." The machine, however, is destined to blow up—there is an explosion and the machine begins to erupt with smoke. The experimenter now says, "I'll never get my master's now . . . (choke) . . . What did you do to the machine? . . . (sob) . . . Well, I guess that ends the experiment . . . (long pause and then solemnly) . . . The machine is broken."[2] The real purpose of the experiment is to see if this experience will increase the likelihood that the subject will sign a petition being circulated by the experimenter (it does). The description of this little drama staged by the experimenter makes for amusing reading, but how amused was the subject? Deception perpetrated solely for

---

2 Excerpt from Z. Rubin, Jokers wild in the lab. *Psychology Today,* December 1970, pp. 18ff. Copyright © 1970 by Ziff-Davis Publishing Company. All rights reserved.

the amusement of others or to make yourself known must certainly be termed unethical behavior.

Earlier I said that the use of deception deprives the subject of informed consent—of the right to all information that might influence a decision to participate in a research project. Thus, if the subjects in Milgram's experiment had participated only after giving informed consent, they would first have been told that obedience was being studied and that they would be required to inflict painful shocks on another person. Informed consent is intended to eliminate the problem of deception, or at least to diminish it.

I think you can see why informed consent is not a completely satisfactory solution to the deception problem. First, knowledge that the research is studying obedience is bound to alter the subjects' behavior. Most of us don't like to think of ourselves as obedient, and so we would probably go out of our way to prove that we are not obedient. In this situation, even limited informed consent would distort the results obtained. Also, the knowledge that the experiment would involve inflicting pain might easily bias the subject sample. It is possible that only certain types of individuals would consent to participate, and we could generalize the results only to those types who agreed to participate. If this were true, anyone could say that the obedient behavior seen in the Milgram experiment occurred simply because the subjects were cruel, inhumane sadists in the first place.

DEBRIEFING

The traditional solution to the problem of deception is to thoroughly *debrief* subjects after the experiment. Debriefing has become a standard part of experimental procedure, even when there is no stress and virtually no possibility of harm to subjects. Researchers feel that participation should be an educational experience, and so they communicate their ideas about human behavior to the subjects. But is debriefing sufficient to remove any negative effects when stress and elaborate deception are involved? Let's turn again to Milgram's research.

Milgram went to great lengths to provide a thorough debriefing session. Subjects who were obedient were told that their behavior was normal and that they had acted no differently from most other subjects. They were made aware of the strong situational pressure that was exerted on them, and efforts were made to reduce any tension subjects felt. Subjects were assured that no shock was actually delivered, and there was a friendly reconciliation with the confederate, Mr. Wallace. Milgram also mailed a report of his research findings to his subjects and at the same time asked about their reactions to the experiment. The responses showed that 84 percent were glad that they had participated, and 74 percent said they had benefited from the experience. Only 1 percent said they were sorry they had participated. When subjects were interviewed by a psychiatrist a year later, no ill effects of participation could be detected. We can only conclude that debriefing did have its intended effect. Other researchers who have conducted further work on the ethics of Milgram's study reached the same conclusion (Ring, Wallston, & Corey, 1970).

Of course, you might question whether debriefing makes the research ethical. Perhaps debriefing was an adequate measure for Milgram study—a study that most social scientists see as an extremely important piece of research. But many studies that lack the significance of Milgram's research use deceptive procedures, and these present even more serious problems. Let's look at some alternatives to the use of deception in research.

ALTERNATIVES TO DECEPTION

After criticizing the use of deception in research, Kelman (1967) called for the development of alternative procedures. One procedure Kelman suggests is called *role-playing*.

Role-playing

In one role-playing procedure, the experimenter describes a situation to subjects and then asks them how they would respond to the situation. Sometimes subjects are asked to say how they themselves would behave in the situation; sometimes they are asked to predict how real participants in such a situation would behave. It isn't clear whether these two kinds of instructions produce any differences in results.

Role-playing is not generally considered to be a satisfactory alternative to deception (Freedman, 1969; Miller, 1972). One problem is that simply reading a description of a situation does not involve the subjects very deeply—they are not part of a real situation. Also, role-playing procedures seem particularly vulnerable to the problem of demand characteristics. Because the experimenter gives the subjects a complete description of the situation, the experimenter's hypothesis may be obvious to the subjects.

The most serious defect of role-playing is that—no matter what results are obtained—a critic can always say that the results would have been different if the subjects had been in a real situation. This criticism is based on the assumption that people aren't always able to accurately predict their own behavior or the behavior of others. This would be particularly true when undesirable behavior—such as conformity, obedience, or aggression—is involved. For example, if Milgram had used a role-playing procedure, how many people do you think would have predicted that they would be completely obedient? Milgram asked a group of psychiatrists to predict the results of his study, and found that even these experts could not accurately anticipate what would happen. A similar problem would arise if people were asked to predict whether they would help someone in need. Most of us would probably overestimate our altruistic tendencies.

Simulation studies

A more acceptable type of role-playing involves simulation of a real-world situation. A simulation study that impressed Kelman (1967) is the Inter-Nation Simulation, in which subjects role-play being leaders of nations. Aspects of international relations can be manipulated, and the consequences can be observed. Such simulations create high degrees of involvement, as anyone who has played an all-night game of Monopoly will appreciate.

One recent simulation study showed that even this procedure can have ethical consequences. Philip Zimbardo (1973) of Stanford University simulated a prison environment in the basement of the psychology building at Stanford. This prison came complete with cells and a room for solitary confinement. College students were recruited through an advertisement in a local newspaper, and were paid $15 per day to play the role of either a prisoner or guard for a period of two weeks. Guards were outfitted in khaki uniforms and given sunglasses and clubs. Prisoners were given numbers, loose fitting gowns, and nylon stocking caps—all of which diminished individuality. The subjects became deeply involved in their roles, so much so that Zimbardo decided that he had to stop his simulation after six days and several "mental breakdowns" among the prisoners. Zimbardo's own description is telling:

> At the end of only six days we had to close down our mock prison because what we saw was frightening. It was no longer apparent to us or most of the subjects where they ended and their roles began. The majority had indeed become "prisoners" or "guards," no longer able to

clearly differentiate between role-playing and self. There were dramatic changes in virtually every aspect of their behavior, thinking and feeling. In less than a week, the experience of imprisonment undid (temporarily) a lifetime of learning; human values were suspended, self-concepts were challenged, and the ugliest, most base, pathological side of human nature surfaced. We were horrified because we saw some boys ("guards") treat other boys as if they were despicable animals, taking pleasure in cruelty, while other boys ("prisoners") became servile, dehumanized robots who thought only of escape, of their own individual survival, and of their mounting hatred of the guards" (Zimbardo in Aronson, 1972).

This was only a simulation—subjects *knew* that they were not *really* prisoners or guards. Yet they became so involved in their roles that the guards behaved as cruelly as Milgram's subjects, and the prisoners were subjected to more psychological and physical stress than in virtually any deception experiment.

Honest experiments

Zick Rubin (1973) of Harvard University has recently described what he calls "honest" experimental strategies. None of these involve role-playing. The first strategy is one in which the subjects are made completely aware of the purposes of the research. An example is a study by Byrne, Ervin, and Lamberth (1970). These researchers told subjects that they were interested in the effectiveness of computer dating. They used a computer program to match male and female students who held either similar or dissimilar attitudes. Each couple had a Coke date, and then the researchers measured how much the members of each couple liked one another. Couples who were similar were more attracted to each other than couples who were dissimilar. The study involved no deception or misrepresentation of the purposes of the research.

A second honest strategy is used in situations in which there are explicit programs to change people's behavior. Examples cited by Rubin include educational programs, health appeals, charity drives, political campaigns, and solicitations for volunteers. In such situations, people are aware that someone is trying to change their behavior. For instance, people may voluntarily expose themselves to an appeal to quit smoking. Researchers can then investigate the effectiveness of such an appeal—for example, the amount of fear aroused (Leventhal, 1970).

Rubin also feels that many field experiments involve honest procedures.

Field experiments introduce the experimental manipulation in a natural context. An example cited by Rubin is a study in which an experimenter stared at drivers of cars while they were waiting for a red light to change (Ellsworth, Carlsmith, & Henson, 1972). These drivers crossed the intersection faster than did drivers in a control condition in which there was no staring experimenter. This particular experiment does not seem particularly unethical. We have all experienced being stared at. The researchers merely applied experimental methods in order to systematically study this situation. My own feeling is that much research in the field is honest. Researchers are observing the behavior of people in public places in everyday situations. However, just because an experiment is conducted in the field does not automatically make it ethical. An experiment in which an experimenter takes up the time of a busy salesman whose salary is dependent on commissions, or one in which subway passengers are exposed to a person who collapses would seem to have not only ethical but also legal implications (Silverman, 1975).

The last honest strategy discussed by Rubin (1973) involves situations in which a naturally occurring event presents an opportunity for research: "Nature, fate, government, and other unalterable forces often impose their will on people in random or nonsystematic ways." As an example, Rubin and Peplau (1973) were able to study the behavior of nineteen-year-old males as they received either good or bad numbers in the 1971 draft lottery. Jack Aiello (1975) studied the effects of crowding when a shortage of student housing forced Rutgers University to randomly assign entering students to crowded and uncrowded dormitory rooms. Such situations occur frequently enough so that they are worthwhile sources of data.

Assumed consent

Rubin offers a number of alternatives to deception. But what if the researcher still feels that deception is the only scientifically valid option available? A paper by Berscheid and her associates (1973) suggests a procedure that would give ethical insurance to a deceptive experiment. Berscheid suggests that a completely accurate description of the experimental procedure be given to a sample of potential subjects. These people would be asked to indicate whether, given this information, they would agree to participate in the study. If only a few of these potential subjects say they would refuse to participate (for example, less than 5 percent), then the researcher can feel confident that the actual experiment would be ethically acceptable to most people who would be involved. Although this procedure has not yet won widespread acceptance **179** among researchers, the basic idea has important possibilities (Cozby, 1974).

OTHER ETHICAL ISSUES IN RESEARCH

Stress and deception are the major sources of ethical concern in research on humans. It is important to remember that the researcher must protect the subject's anonymity, although this is an ethical principle that is rarely violated. Researchers should also try to provide subjects with a summary of the results.

Another problem concerns the voluntariness of subject participation. Most of us believe that college students are able to make free choices about whether to participate in a research subject, and about whether to walk out of research they consider unethical. But what about special subject populations such as children, mental patients, or prisoners? It seems clear that researchers must take special precautions when dealing with groups such as these.

Finally, the researcher should be punctual when arrangements have been made to meet the subject. The issue of punctuality is never discussed by psychologists, yet subjects mention it when asked about the obligations of the researcher (Epstein, Suedfeld, & Silverstein, 1973).

FORMULATION OF ETHICAL PRINCIPLES

Psychologists recognize these ethical issues and have recently adopted a set of ethical principles. These principles were formulated by a committee appointed by the American Psychological Association. The committee worked for three years and wrote two drafts before arriving at the final document. The principles are explained and discussed in detail in a booklet entitled *Ethical Principles in the Conduct of Research with Human Participants.* This valuable booklet can be obtained from the American Psychological Association. The following is a list of the ethical principles as published in a 1973 issue of the *American Psychologist:*[3]

---

3 From *American Psychologist,* 1973, *28,* 79–80. Copyright © 1973 by the American Psychological Association. Reprinted by permission. The booklet may be purchased from the American Psychological Association, 1200 Seventeenth St. N.W., Washington, D. C. 20036.

Ethical Principles in the Conduct of Research with Human Participants

1. In planning a study the investigator has the personal responsibility to make a careful evaluation of its ethical acceptability, taking into account these Principles for research with human beings. To the extent that this appraisal, weighing scientific and humane values, suggests a deviation from any Principle, the investigator incurs an increasingly serious obligation to seek ethical advice and to observe more stringent safeguards to protect the rights of the human research participant.

2. Responsibility for the establishment and maintenance of acceptable ethical practice in research always remains with the individual investigator. The investigator is also responsible for the ethical treatment of research participants by collaborators, assistants, students and employees, all of whom however, incur parallel obligations.

3. Ethical practice requires the investigator to inform the participant of all features of the research that reasonably might be expected to influence willingness to participate, and to explain all other aspects of the research about which the participant inquires. Failure to make full disclosure increases the investigator's responsibility to maintain confidentiality, and to protect the welfare and dignity of the research participant.

4. Openness and honesty are essential characteristics of the relationship between investigator and research participant. When the methodological requirements of a study necessitate concealment or deception, the investigator is required to ensure the participant's understanding of the reasons for his action and to restore the quality of the relationship with the investigator.

5. Ethical research practice requires the investigator to respect the individual's freedom to decline to participate in research or to discontinue participation at any time. The obligation to protect this freedom requires special vigilance when the investigator is in a position of power over the participant. The decision to limit this freedom increases the investigator's responsibility to protect the participant's dignity and welfare.

6. Ethically acceptable research begins with the establishment of a clear and fair agreement between the investigator and the research participant that clarifies the responsibilities of each. The investigator has the obligation to honor all promises and commitments included in that agreement.

7. The ethical investigator protects participants from physical and mental discomfort, harm, and danger. If the risk of such consequences exists, the investigator is required to inform the participant of that fact, to secure consent before proceeding, and to take all possible measures to minimize

distress. A research procedure may not be used if it is likely to cause serious and lasting harm to participants.

8. After the data are collected, ethical practice requires the investigator to provide the participant with a full clarification of the nature of the study and to remove any misconceptions that may have arisen. Where scientific or humane values justify delaying or withholding information, the investigator acquires a special responsibility to assure that there are no damaging consequences for the participant.

9. Where research procedures may result in undesirable consequences for the participant, the investigator has the responsibility to detect and remove or correct these consequences, including, where relevant, long-term aftereffects.

10. Information obtained about the research participants during the course of an investigation is confidential. When the possibility exists that others may obtain access to such information, ethical research practice requires that this possibility, together with the plans for protecting confidentiality, be explained to the participants as a part of the procedure for obtaining informed consent (American Psychological Association, 1973).

As you read these principles, you probably noticed that informed consent is considered a fundamental part of ethical practice. However, there is the recognition that fully informed consent may not be possible, and that deception may sometimes be necessary. In such cases, the researcher's responsibilities to the subject are increased. Obviously, decisions as to what should be considered ethical or unethical are not simple; there are no magic rules. Each piece of research has to be evaluated in terms of whether there are any ethical problems with the procedure, whether more ethical alternative procedures are available, and whether the importance of the study is such that the ethical problems are justified.

Many colleges and universities have instituted ethics review committees that are responsible for reviewing research proposals. These committees often use the APA ethical principles as guidelines in deciding whether to approve a particular research project. Some researchers have expressed fears that such committees will prevent much research from being conducted by routinely rejecting any proposal which lacks completely informed consent (Gergen, 1973). However, some recent data that I collected (1974) suggests that research proposals are likely to be rejected only when the research involves great amounts of physical or psychological stress *and* there is no informed consent.

It is important to note that the rejected experiments were not viewed as having a great deal of scientific importance.

So it appears that most research projects will be conducted, and at the same time use of the APA ethical principles will prevent most ethical abuses from occurring. This is as it should be, for the vast majority of research in the social sciences does not present ethical difficulties.

ETHICS AND THE USES OF PSYCHOLOGY

I would like to turn to a brief discussion of ethical implications of the possible uses of psychology. I'm sure you are aware that theoretical and technological advances in fields such as physics have yielded both positive and negative effects. Nuclear energy has many beneficial uses, but it has destructive uses as well. Laser technology has proven to be useful in medicine, yet lasers were also used to guide bombs in Vietnam.

Research in the social sciences entails similar problems. Research on learning has led to the use of behavior modification techniques in mental health fields. Psychologist B. F. Skinner[4] foresees the beneficial effects of behavioral technology on society, although others may see visions of *Clockwork Orange* or Orwell's *1984*. Currently, debate is raging over the uses of psychosurgery in the treatment of violence and aggression (Valenstein, 1974; Chorover, 1974; Mark, 1974). Neuropsychologists have been conducting the basic, theoretical research for years, and the applications of this research inevitably came. While there may be beneficial aspects of psychosurgery (for example, when used for treating individuals with histories of extreme violence), there is also the possibility of its being used as a tool for social and political repression. Society cannot escape such ethical dilemmas, and somehow we are going to have to come to grips with them.

ETHICS AND ANIMAL RESEARCH

I don't want to leave you with the impression that the question of ethics arises only in research that involves humans. In fact, strict laws and guidelines exist

---

4 A lively example of Skinner's orientation may be found in his novel, *Walden Two*. New York: Macmillan, 1948.

that govern the care of animals used in research. Such regulations deal with the need for proper housing, feeding, cleanliness, and health care, and they describe measures to be taken to make sure that the research does not involve cruelty. There are also guidelines for disposing of animals when the research is completed. Sometimes the animals can be kept as pets or maintained for other experiments. Sometimes, however, euthanasia is necessary, and here too there are guidelines concerning humane treatment. If you are considering doing research with animals, you should consult with someone who is knowledgeable about the various laws and regulations.

ETHICS AND CLINICAL PRACTICE

Ethical standards do not apply only to persons engaged in research. There is a separate set of principles for psychologists involved in practice. These principles, along with a discussion of a number of actual cases involving psychologists, can be found in a booklet entitled *Casebook on Ethical Standards of Psychologists* (American Psychological Association, 1967).[5] These principles concern regard for the moral and legal standards of the community, misrepresentations of one's qualifications, the problems of making brash public statements, and the need to protect client confidentiality and welfare. There are also principles that concern the ethics of delivering psychological services in an impersonal way, such as the radio, in newspapers, or by mail. The principles also recognize the need for proper interpretation of scores on psychological tests and the need for rules governing the security and publication of such tests.

We have seen that psychologists are greatly concerned with the ethics of research. They are also concerned with the uses of psychological knowledge. In the next chapter, we will consider some ways that research and research methods may be used to benefit society.

---

5 This booklet may be purchased from the American Psychological Association (see note 3).

STUDY QUESTIONS

1 *Discuss the major ethical issues in behavioral research: physical and psychological harm, deception, debriefing, and informed consent. How can researchers weigh the need to conduct research against the need for ethical procedures?*

2 *Why is informed consent an ethical principle? What are the problems with full informed consent? What is involved with the proposed assumed consent procedure?*

3 *What alternatives to deception are described in the text?*

4 *Describe and compare the following experimental methods: laboratory deception experiments, field experiments, and role-playing experiments. What are the advantages and disadvantages of each?*

5 *Summarize the principles embodied in the* Ethical Principles in the Conduct of Research with Human Participants.

13

THE EXPERIMENTING SOCIETY

In this chapter, we will explore some of the uses of research in the behavioral sciences. We will consider two different but compatible views of relevance. The first view argues that knowledge of theory and research in the behavioral sciences is useful to a public that is aware of this information. The second view states that all of us can become scientists and adopt an attitude that will lead us to become an experimenting society.

GIVING BEHAVIORAL SCIENCE AWAY

In 1969, George Miller of Rockefeller University delivered the presidential address to the American Psychological Association. The title of his talk was "Psychology As a Means of Promoting Human Welfare." Obviously concerned about the relevance of psychology, Miller sees the usefulness of psychology in terms of "giving psychology away" to as many people as possible. Although Miller speaks directly to the issue of the uses of psychological knowledge, his ideas are readily applicable to all areas of behavioral science. What does Miller mean by "giving psychology away?"

187

First of all, Miller rejects the idea of using psychological means to *control* the behavior of other people. He believes that the conception of psychology and psychologists as part of a powerful elite exerting control over our lives is an unfortunate one. Such a conception says that psychology is relevant but that it is not really directed at promoting human welfare.

Miller prefers to give psychological research principles away to the general public. The possession of such knowledge will make us more effective human beings and will give us greater control over our own lives. Miller states:

> Our responsibility is less to assume the role of experts and try to apply psychology ourselves than to give it away to the people who really need it—and that includes everyone. The practice of valid psychology by nonpsychologists will inevitably change people's conception of themselves and what they can do. When we have accomplished that, we will really have caused a psychological revolution.[1]

How do we give psychology away? First, there is education. This should occur not only in classrooms but should take place in all manner of formal and informal situations. Again, I quote Miller:

> In order to get started, we must begin with people where they are, not assume we know where they should be. If a supervisor is having trouble with his men, perhaps we should teach him how to write a job description and how to evaluate the abilities and personalities of those who fill the job; perhaps we should teach him the art of persuasion, or the time and place for positive reinforcement. If a ghetto mother is not giving her children sufficient intellectual challenge, perhaps we should teach her how to encourage their motor, perceptual, and linguistic skills.

Psychologists can also provide training to enable people to become paraprofessional psychologists. One recent trend is to train individuals who frequently deal with the public—bartenders, hairstylers, or taxicab drivers, for example—to recognize signs of emotional disturbances, to provide some counseling, and to know where professional help is available. In general, psychologists can impart the principles of their profession to those who are able to apply these principles to their own lives and needs.

---

1   This quotation and the quotation that follows are from G. A. Miller, Psychology as a means of promoting human welfare. *American Psychologist*, 1969, *24*, 1063–1075. Copyright © 1969 by the American Psychological Association. Reprinted by permission.

Donald Campbell of Northwestern University is, like George Miller, a past president of the American Psychological Association. He has suggested (1969) another way of giving behavioral science away. He proposes that our society take a scientific, experimental attitude when considering social reforms and innovations.

We are in a period of social innovation and reform. Government creates programs, such as Head Start, that are aimed at solving social problems. These programs are really experiments designed to achieve certain outcomes. Campbell notes, however, that the programs are rarely treated as experiments. Instead, political realities enter the picture. The political party, or the person who thought up the program, or the person hired to administer it, is placed in a precarious position. If the program fails to achieve its objectives, these people are immediately labeled as failures. We *blame* these people for the failure of the program. Obviously, then, such people have vested interests in the successes of these programs. The consequence is that the originators and administrators of such programs do not want to subject their programs to honest evaluation. Instead, they want to protect their images.

Campbell suggests that we change our conceptions of these reforms and of the people who propose and administer them. We should consider such reforms as experiments that can succeed or fail without reflecting on the competence of the people involved in the reforms. A scientist teaching at a university is not disgraced if an experiment fails; a person advocating or administering a reform program should be in the same position as the scientist. To quote Campbell:

> The political stance would become: "This is a serious problem. We propose to initiate Policy A on an experimental basis. If after five years there has been no significant improvement, we will shift to Policy B."
> By making explicit that a given problem solution was only one of several that the administrator or party could in good conscience advocate, and by having ready a plausible alternative, the administrator could afford honest evaluation of outcomes.[2]

What is the role of the social scientist in the experimenting society? Essentially, Campbell sees the social scientist as the research methodology expert

---

2 From D. T. Campbell, Reforms as experiments. *American Psychologist*, 1969, *24*, 409–429. Copyright © 1969 by the American Psychological Association. Reprinted by permission.

who tries to make sure that the reform is honestly evaluated. Every effort should be made to apply the experimental method to such reforms, so that we can learn whether the reforms are having the intended outcomes.

METHODS FOR THE EXPERIMENTING SOCIETY

Campbell recognizes that applied research, such as evaluating a specific reform program does not generally allow for the niceties of true experimental designs. However, "quasi-experimental" designs can be used that will provide ways of evaluating social reforms. Some of these quasi-experimental designs are discussed below.

Control group pretest-posttest design

This design would include an experimental and a control group, each of which would receive a pretest and a posttest. It could be diagrammed this way:

Subjects → Pretest → Reform treatment received → Posttest

Subjects → Pretest → No treatment received → Posttest

Recall that we discussed a similar design without a pretest in Chapter 5. This is not a true experimental design, because we don't have random assignment to groups—it is possible that the two groups are not equivalent. However, we have the advantage of knowing the pretest scores. Thus, we can see whether the groups were the same on the pretest. Even if the groups are not equivalent on the pretest, we can look at *changes* in scores from the pretest to the posttest. Presumably, the experimental group should show a greater change than the control group.[3]

This design could be useful in a variety of settings. For example, attitudes of staff and patients in a mental hospital could be assessed before and after a new training program is administered. A control hospital of similar size could be chosen; staff and patients there would receive the attitude measures without the new program. Even though the attitude pretest may reveal initial differences between the two hospitals, change scores would provide an indication of whether the program was effective.

3 Methods for analysis of such a design have been discussed by D. A. Kenney, A quasi-experimental approach to assessing treatment effects in the nonequivalent control group design. *Psychological Bulletin*, 1975, *82*, 345–362.

Campbell discusses at length the evaluation of one specific reform—the 1955 Connecticut crackdown on speeding. This reform was instituted after a record high number of traffic fatalities occurred in 1955. The easiest way to evaluate this reform is to compare the number of traffic fatalities in 1955 (before the crackdown) with the number of fatalities in 1956 (after the crackdown). Indeed, there was a reduction in the number of traffic deaths, from 324 in 1955 to 284 in 1956. The problem is that there are many other reasons why traffic deaths might decline, and so it is impossible to attribute all the drop to the crackdown.

One alternative is to use an interrupted time series design that would examine the traffic fatality rates over an extended period of time, both before and after the reform was instituted. Figure 13-1 shows this information for

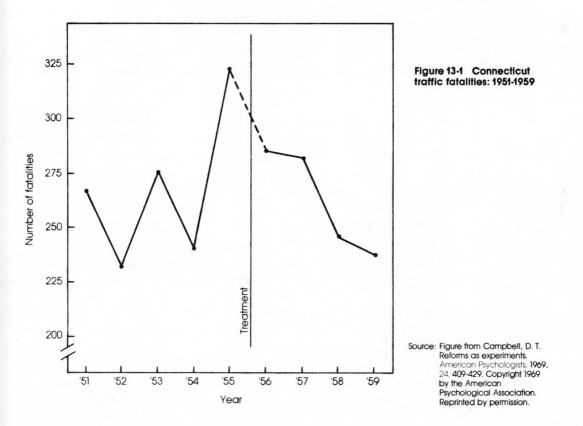

Figure 13-1 Connecticut traffic fatalities: 1951-1959

Source: Figure from Campbell, D. T. Reforms as experiments. American Psychologists, 1969, 24, 409-429. Copyright 1969 by the American Psychological Association. Reprinted by permission.

the years 1951 to 1959. Campbell argues that the drop from 1955 to 1956 does not look particularly impressive, given the great fluctuations in previous years. But notice that there is a steady downward trend in fatalities after the crackdown. Even here, Campbell sees a problem in interpretation. The drop could be due to statistical regression (see Chapter 5). Because 1955 was a record high year, the likelihood is that there would be a drop anyway.

You may recognize the similarity between Campbell's interrupted time series design and the random time series design discussed in Chapter 7. The difference between the two designs lies in the decision about when to introduce the manipulation. In the random time series design, the manipulation is introduced at a *randomly* determined point in the time sequence. In the interrupted time series design, the decision to introduce the manipulation is *not* random. In fact, the speed crackdown was instituted because 1955 was such a bad year.

Control series design

One way to improve the interrupted time series design is to find some kind of control group. In the case of the Connecticut speed crackdown, this was possible because other states had not instituted the reform. Figure 13-2 shows the same data on traffic fatalities from Connecticut plus the fatality figures of four comparable states during the same years. The fact that the fatality rates in the control states remained relatively constant, while there was a consistent decline in Connecticut, led Campbell to conclude that the crackdown did in fact have some effect.

A control group was possible in the speed crackdown evaluation because the reform had been instituted only in Connecticut. If it had been instituted across the United States, no comparison would be possible. Campbell advocates the selective institution of reforms so that comparisons with untreated groups can be made. With a little planning, the groups can be chosen systematically beforehand to allow for the most meaningful comparisons.

Random assignment in reforms

Campbell notes one situation in which the evaluation of a reform can involve true experimental techniques. This situation arises when the reform involves the allocation of scarce resources. An example would be the introduction of an innovation in medicine (for example, a new vaccine) that is in scarce supply and so not yet available to everyone. The best way to test the effects of the

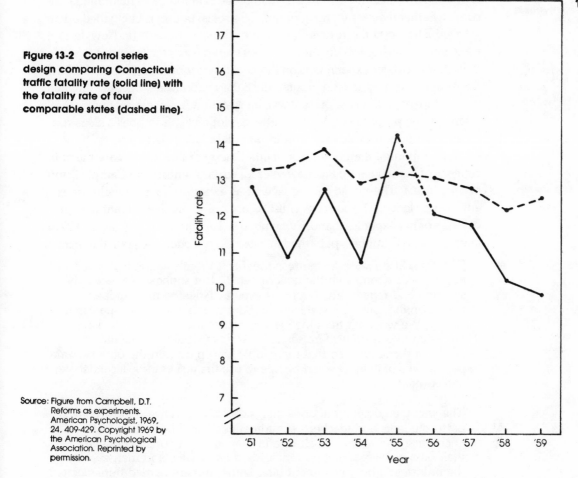

Figure 13-2   Control series design comparing Connecticut traffic fatality rate (solid line) with the fatality rate of four comparable states (dashed line).

Source: Figure from Campbell, D.T. Reforms as experiments. American Psychologist, 1969, 24, 409-429. Copyright 1969 by the American Psychological Association. Reprinted by permission.

innovation, and also the most democratic, is to randomly assign people to experimental and control groups.

CONCLUDING REMARKS

I have presented only some of Campbell's ideas and only a few examples of the kinds of reforms and social experiments that have been and can be evaluated. One social experiment with far-reaching consequences, for instance, is the negative income tax, which guarantees everyone a certain annual income whether they are working or not. This social reform is being tried out in selected cities, and the results from one of the experiments (in New Jersey) show that the guaranteed income level does *not* destroy the incentive to work. If the results of later experiments on the negative income tax continue to show this finding, we may see the program instituted nationwide, because it would be less expensive than the present welfare system. We can expect many social reforms to be proposed in the years ahead. Hopefully, Campbell's ideas concerning the honest evaluation of reforms will be taken seriously.

More important than any single methodology or new reform are the conceptions of human nature and new roles for social scientists that Campbell and Miller suggest. The public can be viewed as experts who can wisely use scientific knowledge. The social scientist is cast in the role of a servant who provides his or her expertise to those who need it. Two quotes from Tavris' (1975) interview with Campbell, published in *Psychology Today,* illustrate the point:

> [T]he typical survey asks the respondents, "What's wrong with you?" not "What's wrong with the government?" But suppose we recast the situation and regard our citizens as experts. Now the microscope is turned on the society, and it is to the citizens' interest to participate in the survey. We wouldn't treat the welfare recipient as victim or deviant, but as an expert on welfare services. And we would publish the results of the survey, so that the people who produced the data become part owners of it; they would be free to use the results in political debate, and so on.
>
> The way the government does things destroys initiative on everyone's part—students and teachers, superintendents and principals. It should encourage and reward teachers and managers for coming up with their own new ideas, support their ideas financially, and then evaluate them. Instead, the government hires some hurried, harried bureaucrats or university consultants to design a program and impose it on the participants.[4]

These new conceptions of behavioral research and methods and of scientists' roles in society offer a dramatic departure from the view of psychology as

---

4 Excerpts from C. Tavris, The experimenting society: To find programs that work, government must measure its failures. Conversation with Donald T. Campbell. *Psychology Today,* September 1975, pp. 47ff. Copyright © 1975 by Ziff-Davis Publishing Company. All rights reserved.

a way of controlling behavior. If and when these new conceptions become reality, psychology and the other social sciences really will serve to promote human welfare.

STUDY QUESTIONS

1 *What is meant by "giving psychology away?"*

2 *According to Campbell, what are the problems with society's present way of dealing with reforms? How would Campbell change the present situation?*

3 *Describe the control group pretest-posttest design. Why is this a quasi-experimental design rather than a true experimental design?*

4 *Describe the interrupted time series design and the control series design. Why is the control series design superior to the interrupted time series design?*

APPENDIX A
WRITING RESEARCH REPORTS

This appendix presents the information you will need to prepare a written report of your research. You should find this information useful in much of your classroom work. And perhaps you will even submit your written report for possible publication in a professional journal.

This section contains a number of specific rules that are followed in organizing and presenting research results. These rules are a great convenience for both the writer and the reader. They provide structure for the report, and a uniform method of presentation, which make it easier for the reader to understand and evaluate the information contained in the report.

Specific rules may vary from one discipline to another. A rule for presenting research results in psychology may not apply to the same situation in, for example, sociology research. Fortunately, the variation is usually minor. The general rules of presentation are much the same in most disciplines, and so the main problem is to make sure that such things as references and footnotes have been presented correctly.

The format presented here for writing research reports is drawn from the *Publication Manual of the American Psychological Association (2nd ed.).* The **197**

APA style is used in many journals in psychology, mental health, family relations, and education, and the general format for presentation is used in disciplines other than psychology. If you are concerned about specific rules for a particular scientific journal, consult a recent issue of the journal. If you are going to be doing a great deal of writing in APA style, you may want to purchase a copy of the *Publication Manual* through your bookstore or directly from the American Psychological Association (1200 Seventeenth Street, N.W., Washington, D. C. 20036).

The remainder of this appendix contains some general suggestions about writing style, a description of the organization of a research report, and an example of such a report. The example is an actual research article typed as it would be for submission to a journal.

WRITING STYLE

No matter what format you use to communicate information to others, writing style is important. A poorly written report that cannot be understood by others is of no value.

Clarity

Clarity in writing is essential. Be precise and clear in presenting your ideas. Eliminate jargon that most readers will not comprehend. Sometimes a researcher will develop an abbreviated notation for referring to a specific variable or procedure; such abbreviations may be convenient when communicating with others who are directly involved in your research project, but they are confusing for the general reader.

The entire report should be coherent. Ideas should be presented in an orderly, logical progression to facilitate understanding. Always remember that you are writing for someone who is being introduced to your ideas and research findings for the first time. Your choice of words, sentence structure, and general organization should be directed toward facilitating communication with this reader.

The first draft of your report is bound to be rough and will need to be improved. It is usually a good idea to reread your report a few days after writing the first draft and to make corrections that you think are necessary. At this point, you may want to get feedback from others. Find one or more people who will critically read your report and make suggestions for improvement. Do not become angry or defensive when you receive the criticism you asked for. Be prepared, then, to write several more drafts before you have a satisfactory finished product.

Acknowledging the work of others

It is extremely important to clearly separate your own words and ideas from those obtained from other sources. If you use a passage drawn from an article or book, make sure that the passage is presented as a direct quotation. There is nothing wrong with quoting another author as long as you acknowledge your source. Never present another person's idea as your own. This is plagiarism and is inexcusable. It is also unethical and sometimes illegal.

Typed copy

The typed copy of your report should be double-spaced and neat. Margins should be 1-1½ inches (2½-4 centimeters) on all sides of the page. A messy, unattractive paper detracts from the content of your report.

ORGANIZATION OF THE REPORT

A research report is organized into five major parts: abstract, introduction, method, results, and discussion. References must be listed. The report may also include tables and figures used in presenting the results. We will consider the parts of the paper in the order prescribed by APA style.

Title page

The first page of the paper lists the title, name of the author(s), and the name of the institution with which the author is affiliated. Your title should be fairly short (twelve to fifteen words at most) and should inform the reader about the nature of your research.

Abstract

The abstract is a brief summary of the research, usually about 100 to 175 words in length. It should give information on the research problem that was studied, the method used to study the problem (including information on the type of subjects), the results, and major conclusions.

The abstract should provide enough information so that the reader can decide whether to read the entire report, and it should make the report easier to comprehend when it is read. Although the abstract appears at the beginning of your report, you will probably want to wait until the body of the report is completed before you write the abstract.

APA style requires that the abstract be placed at the beginning of the report. In some disciplines the abstract is presented as a summary at the end.

Introduction

The introduction section begins on a new page with the title of your report at the top of the page. This section introduces the reader to the problem being investigated, reviews past research and theory relevant to the problem, presents the predicted outcomes of the research, and gives the method used for testing the predictions. After reading the introduction, the reader should know why you decided to do the research and how you decided to go about doing it.

The introduction starts with a description of past research and theory. An exhaustive review of past research is not necessary. Rather, you want to describe only the research and theoretical issues that are clearly related to your study. You should state explicitly how this previous work is logically connected to your research problem. This tells the reader why your research was conducted.

The final part of the introduction tells the reader exactly what hypothesis is being tested. Here you state what variables you are studying, what results you expect, and why you expect these results.

Method

The method section begins immediately after you have completed the introduction (on the same page if space permits). The method section provides the reader with detailed information about how your study was conducted. Ideally, there should be enough information in the method section to allow a reader to replicate your study.

The method section is typically divided up into a number of subsections. The nature of the subsections is determined by the nature of the research you are describing. The subsections should be organized to present the method as clearly as possible. Some of the most commonly used subsections are discussed below.

Overview   If the experimental design and procedures used in the research are complex, a brief overview of the method should be presented to help the reader understand the information that follows.

Subjects   A subsection on subjects is always necessary. The number and nature of the subjects should be described. If the subjects were humans, sex and age should be given, along with any other relevant characteristics. State explicitly how the subjects were recruited for the study. The number of subjects per group also can be included here.

In animal research, it is common practice to report the species, strain number, and other information that specifically identify the type of animal. The number of animals and the age and sex of each animal used, should be indicated. If information about care, feeding, or handling conditions in the laboratory is relevant, it should be included here.

Procedure   The procedure subsection tells the reader exactly how the study was conducted. One way to report this information is to describe, step by step, what occurred in the experiment.

The procedure subsection should tell the reader what instructions were read to (human) subjects, how the independent variables were manipulated, and how the dependent variables were measured. The methods used to control extraneous variables should also be described. These would include randomization procedures, counterbalancing, and special means that were used to keep a variable constant across all conditions. Finally, the method of debriefing subjects should be described.

It is up to you to decide how much detail to include in the procedure portion of the report. Use your own judgment to determine the importance of a specific aspect of the procedure and the amount of detail that is necessary if the reader is to clearly understand what was done in the study.

Apparatus   An apparatus subsection may be necessary if special equipment was used in the experiment. The brand name and model number of the equipment may be specified; some apparatus may be described in detail.

Other subsections   Other subsections should be included if warranted by the nature of the experiment and needed for clear presentation of the method.

Results
In the results section, you present the results as clearly as possible. When writing the results section, it is best to refer back to your predictions as stated in the introduction. The order in which your results are presented should correspond to the order of your predictions. If a manipulation check measure was made, it should be presented before your major results are described.

The results should be stated in simple sentences. For example, the results of the modeling experiment discussed in Chapter 8 might be expressed as follows:

> As predicted, the model group was significantly more aggressive than the no-model group, $F(1, 18) = 16.21$, $p < .01$. The mean aggression score in the model group was 5.20, while the no-model aggression mean was 3.10.

These two sentences inform the reader of the general pattern of the results, the obtained means, and the statistical significance of the results.

If the results are relatively straightforward, they can be presented completely in sentence form. If the study involved a complex design, tables and figures may be needed to clarify presentation of the results.

Tables and figures Tables are generally used to present large arrays of data. For example, a table might be useful in a design with several dependent measures; the means of the different groups for all dependent measures would be presented in the table. Tables are also convenient when a factorial design has been used. For example, in a $2 \times 2 \times 3$ factorial design, a table could be used to present all twelve means.

Figures are used when a visual display of the results would help the reader understand the outcome of the study. Figures may be used to illustrate a significant interaction or to show trends over time.

In APA style, tables and figures are not presented in the main body of the manuscript. Rather, they are placed at the end of the paper. Each table and figure is typed on a separate page. The presence of a table or figure in the text is indicated by describing the content of the table or figure in the text of the paper and using the following notation to show the placement of the table in the printed article.

Insert Table 1 about here

When you are writing a research report for a purpose other than for publication—for example, to fulfill a course or degree requirement—it may be more convenient to place each figure and table on a separate page within the main body of the paper. Because rules about the placement of tables and figures may vary, you should check on the proper format before writing your report.

Tables and figures are supplements to your written report of the results. They do not diminish your responsibility to clearly state the nature of the results

in the text of your report. In fact, when tables or figures are used, you must
also describe the important features of these.

Discussion of the results   It is usually *not* appropriate to discuss the implications of the results within the results section. However, the results and discussion section may be combined if the discussion is brief and greater clarity is achieved by the combination.

Discussion

The discussion section is the proper place to discuss the implications of the results. This section should begin with a statement telling whether the results support the hypothesis. If the results do support your original ideas, you should discuss how your findings contribute to knowledge of the problem that you investigated. You will want to consider the relationship between your results and past research and theory. If you did not obtain the expected results, you will want to discuss possible explanations.

The results will probably have implications for future research. If so, you should discuss the direction that future research might take. It is also possible that the results have practical implications—for example, for child-rearing, counseling, or prejudice-reduction programs. Any such practical implications should be pointed out in the discussion.

References

The references begin on a new page in your report. The references must contain complete citations for all sources mentioned in your report. Do not omit any sources from the list of references; also, do not include any sources that are not mentioned in your report.

In the body of your report, references are cited by giving the last name of the author, followed by the date of publication. The following citation methods are acceptable:

Adams (1970) found that . . .
In a recent study on aggression (Adams, 1970), . . .

Each complete citation in your reference list should contain the name of author, the title of the publication, and facts of publication. Examine the sample paper at the end of this appendix to determine the correct forms for presenting various kinds of references. The reference list in the sample follows APA style. Other disciplines may require different forms. Carefully check the rules for references before you write your report.

Final pages

The final pages of your report, if APA style is used, will contain your footnotes, tables, and figures. The footnotes come first and start on a new page. Avoid using footnotes unless they are necessary. Any tables used follow the footnotes. Each table is on a separate page. If you included figures, these are presented after the tables.

In APA style, a figure caption page is provided before each figure; the figure caption is not typed on the actual figure. This separate page is for the convenience of the printer and may not be required for student reports.

Concluding remarks

When you have completed your research report, you should feel proud of your effort. You have considered past research on a problem, conducted a research project, analyzed the results, and reported the findings. Such a research effort may result in a publication or a presentation at a convention. This is not the most important part of your research, however. What is most important is that you have acquired new knowledge. And hopefully your curiosity has been aroused so that you will want to learn even more.

RESEARCH EXAMPLE

The following paper was taken from an article published in a professional journal.[1] I hope you find the content of the article interesting, and that it will be a useful guide when you organize your research report. Pay attention to the way ideas are presented, how references are cited, and the general format for typing the final report.

The best way to learn how to write research reports is to read the research of others and to write your own reports. I hope I have provided you with enough background and information so that you can do this on your own. Good luck!

---

[1] This article was originally published in the *Journal of Personality and Social Psychology,* 1974, *29,* 80–85. Copyright © 1974 by the American Psychological Association. Reprinted (with slight modification) by permission of the American Psychological Association and Dr. Kay Deaux.

Explanations of Successful Performance on
Sex-Linked Tasks: What Is Skill for the Male
Is Luck for the Female

Kay Deaux and Tim Emswiller
Purdue University

Abstract

Male and female subjects evaluated the performance of either
a male or female stimulus person who was heard to perform in
an above-average manner on either a male- or female-related
task. Analysis of the attributions made to luck vs. skill in
explaining the performance of the stimulus person showed that,
as predicted, performance by a male on a masculine task was
more attributed to skill whereas an equivalent performance by
a female on the same task was seen to be more influenced by
luck. Contrary to prediction, the reverse did not hold true
for performance on a feminine task. Overall, males were seen
to be more skillful than females. The utility of an attributional
analysis in the study of perceived sex differences is discussed.

Explanations of Successful Performance on Sex-Linked Tasks:

What's Skill for the Male Is Luck for the Female[1]

Investigations of the evaluation of male and female
performance in equivalent situations have tended to focus on
the ratings made of the performance itself, frequently finding
that the male tends to be rated more favorably than the female
when the presented evidence is identical. Thus, presenting
rather broadly and generally described evidence about the
performance of a male or female author (Goldberg, 1968), a male
or female painter (Pheterson, Kiesler, & Goldberg, 1971), and a
male or female applicant for a study-abroad program (Deaux &
Taynor, 1971), the cited authors have found that the male's
performance tends to be rated more favorably than the female's.
One apparent exception to this depressing regularity was reported
by Pheterson et al. (1971) in a condition in which the label
winner was attached to the evidence, in this case a painting.
Under these conditions, no differences between ratings of male
and female artists emerged on measures of competence and artistic
future. We might tentatively assume, therefore, that specific
information regarding the quality of a performance will eliminate
sex-linked biases in the evaluation of that performance.

From an attributional viewpoint, however, one might question
whether the observer attaches identical causes to such equivalent
performances by a male and female actor. Analyzing differences

in the attribution of internal and external causes by performers
themselves, Feather (1969) has found a greater tendency for
females to use external attributions in explaining their performance.
Furthermore, subjects of both sexes will show greater use of
external explanations as opposed to internal when their success
or failure is unexpected rather than expected. In terms of an
observer's evaluation of a given performance, we might anticipate
that similar processes would operate. An expected performance
should be more readily attributed to ability on the part of the
performer, while an unexpected performance would more likely be
seen to be the result of chance circumstances. In fact, Weiner
et al. (Weiner, Frieze, Kukla, Reed, Rest, & Rosenbaum, 1971)
reported such data in a recent report. Information regarding
percentage of past success was provided to subjects along with
a statement of the actor's subsequent success or failure, and
subjects were asked to make attribution to luck, effort, ability,
and task difficulty in explaining the subsequent performance.
As would be expected, if the subject's expectation for the
actor's performance (based on percentage of past successes) was
high, the actor's subsequent success tended to be attributed to
ability; if expectation was low, a success was more likely to
be attributed to luck or to effort.

We would suggest that an analogous argument can be made
for the evaluation of performance by males and females in tasks
for which expectations are sex-linked, and hence are high or

low for males or females depending on the particular task.
Performance on a sex-consistent task should be more readily
attributed to internal factors such as ability, whereas
performance on a sex-inconsistent task should be more often
attributed to external factors such as chance. To test this
basic hypothesis, it is necessary to specify two tasks which
are clearly sex-linked but which in all other respects are
identical. Previous research dealing with the effect of sex
on performance evaluation has tended to use socially relevant
situations which, while realistic, are nevertheless of uncertain
sex-linkage. The present research attempted to construct two
situations which are specifically masculine- and feminine-
related, and which further are identical in terms of task
difficulty, thus eliminating this possible external attribution
for performance.

Specifically, then, we hypothesized that when individuals
are asked to evaluate the performance of a male or a female on
either a male-related or female-related task, (1) when a male
and a female perform equally well on a male-related task, the
male's performance will be more strongly attributed to skill,
while the female's performance will be more strongly attributed
to luck; (2) when a male and a female perform equally well on
a female-related task, the female's performance will be more
strongly attributed to skill, while the male's performance
will be more strongly attributed to luck.

Method

Summary of Design

The study was based on a 2 X 2 X 2 factorial independent groups design, with sex of subject, sex of stimulus person, and type of task as the independent variables. Subjects listened to a previously taped recording of either a male's or female's performance on a male- or female-linked task and then evaluated that person on several dimensions, including the attribution of luck versus ability.

Subjects

The subjects were 130 undergraduate students at Purdue University (55 males and 75 females) who participated in the experiment as one means of fulfilling a requirement for the introductory psychology class.

Procedure

Subjects reported to the experiment in groups of 6 to 12 and were seated in individual cubicles equipped with headphones, over which both instructions and experimental material were presented. The experimenter explained to the subjects that they were participating in a study designed to assess the ability of people to evaluate someone else's performance on a perceptual discrimination task. (One male and one female experimenter conducted the experiment and shared in the instructions, questionnaire collection, and debriefing.) Subjects were told that they had been randomly divided into two groups and had been assigned partners for the experiment. One half of the subjects were to be the "test-takers" of the perceptual discrimination task, while the other half of the subjects were to be the graders and evaluators of the performance of the "test-takers." In actuality, all of the subjects were evaluators, and their alleged partners were previously taped recordings by either a male or female who responded to the discrimination questions. Subjects were told that the cubicles had been wired up so that each subject in the evaluation group would hear the responses of only one of the persons from the test-taking group. To further increase credibility, a four-minute pause was inserted in the instructions at which time subjects were led to believe that the test-takers were receiving their instructions.

The test-takers' task was explained as being a series of pictures of familiar objects embedded in a camouflaged background and shown on a video screen for a time period of approximately one second. The subjects were told that they would hear the experimenter saying the question number while their partner was simultaneously receiving the visual stimulus for that question. Subjects would then hear their partner make a response by saying either "true" or "false" as to whether the object they saw on the video screen was the same as the one listed on the numbered test form in front of them. The subjects never actually saw any visual material, nor was any visual material prepared.

Subjects were provided with mimeographed answer forms presumably corresponding to those in front of the test-takers, with the difference that the answer sheets given to evaluators had the answer for each question correctly marked so that subjects could keep a record of their partner's score as he or she responded to the questions. Subjects were asked to examine the experimental material and to note that there were two tasks of 25 questions each. One task consisted of household objects and was obviously female-oriented, e.g., "This is a mop," " This is a double-boiler," etc. The other task consisted of mechanical objects and was obviously male-oriented, e.g., "This is a tire jack," "This is a wrench," etc. (Pretesting had verified that the two tasks were rated to be of equal difficulty.) Subjects were told that in order to achieve a non-biased score, the test-takers would take one task, an evaluation would be performed, and then the second task would be completed and followed by another evaluation. The experimenter randomly assigned one of the two tasks to be first. Actually, there was only one task completed during each experimental session.

The instructions given to subjects before their partner began exphasized the fact that a person's performance is influenced by factors other than intelligence, such as ability, luck, and effort. Subjects were asked to keep these factors

in mind during the performance of the task so that they could
evaluate their partner on these dimensions at the completion
of the task. The subjects were also told that they should
listen carefully for voice patterns and hesitations in their
partner's answers, for these cues would have a bearing upon
the evaluations that they would have to make later.

The taped responses which subjects heard actually followed
a predetermined random sequence of three, six, and ten second
pauses. In each case, the person whom the subject evaluated
answered 16 out of the 25 questions correctly. As subjects
had been told that the norm for this task was 12.3, the stimulus
person's performance should be seen as better than average
when compared to the norms.

Experimental Conditions

Each subject heard one of the two possible tapes (either
a male or female voice) and evaluated the confederate on one
of the two possible tasks (either male- or female-oriented).
An approximately equal number of male and female subjects
participated in each of the four sex of partner-sex of task
conditions.

Dependent variables. After subjects had heard the stimulus
person respond to each of the 25 questions on the designated
test, he or she was asked to evaluate that person's performance
on a series of 13-point scales. The major dependent variable
was a skill-luck dimension of the type used by Feather (Feather,

1969; Feather & Simon, 1971), labeled "purely luck" at one end and "purely ability" at the other with a mid-point label of "equally luck and ability."[2] The other dimensions on which subjects were asked to evaluate the stimulus person were: general performance, confidence in luck-ability rating, effort, probable performance on a similar task, general intelligence, and evaluation of the task as being better performed by males or females. In addition, subjects were asked to estimate what their own score would be if they performed the same task.

After subjects had completed these evaluation forms, they were informed that the experiment was completed. A full debriefing followed, in which the nature and purpose of the deception was explained and all questions answered.

Results

Distinctiveness of the Tasks

As a check on the manipulation of sex-linkage in the tasks, subjects were asked to rate the task on a scale labeled "females would do better" at one end and "males would do better" at the other. Analysis of variance conducted on this item showed a highly significant effect for task, F $(1,122) = 258.41$, $p < .0001$, indicating that the two tasks were clearly differentiated on a male-female dimension. In addition, the means of 3.03 and 10.19 on a scale ranging from 1 to 13 indicate approximately equal polarization of the two tasks.

As a less direct check on the manipulation, subjects were asked to estimate what their own score on the task would be, and the expected Sex of Subject by Sex of Task interaction was also significant, F (1,122) = 23.53, $p <$ .0001, with males expecting that they would do better on the masculine task while females predicted better performance for themselves on the feminine task.

Evaluations of Performance

Analysis of variance was conducted on all other response measures, and the results of the major question concerning luck versus skill can be seen in Figure 1. The accompanying analysis is presented in Table 1. As can be seen in Figure 1,

Insert Table 1 and Figure 1 about here

there were sharp differences in the attributions made to female and male stimulus persons. The overall main effect of Sex of Stimulus Person indicated that, independent of task, males were rated as more skillful than females ($p <$ .05). In addition to this main effect, the Sex of Stimulus X Sex of Task interaction was significant ($p <$ .01). As seen in Figure 1, the major cause of this interaction was the sharp difference in the ratings of male and female stimulus persons on the masculine task, while virtually no difference was found on the feminine task. Simple effects analysis (Winer, 1971) revealed that the difference between male and female stimulus persons on the masculine task was significant, F (1,122) = 12.424, $p <$ .001.

A good performance by the male was attributed to skill,
while the same performance by a female was seen to be the
result of chance. Related to this, the question dealing
with the confidence of the subject in his evaluation of luck
or skill showed only one significant main effect, that of
Sex of Stimulus Person. Subjects were more confident in their
attribution to the male than to the female stimulus person,
F (1,122) = 5.28, p = .02.

Analysis of the other dependent measures revealed some
interesting patterns. On the question dealing with simply
the level of the performance, no difference was found for
Sex of Stimulus Person. Both males and females were rated
as having performed equally well, as might be expected since
the subjects were given identical information about the norms
and observed identical performances. A significant main
effect was found for Sex of Task, however, F (1,122) = 4.81,
p = .03, such that performance on the masculine task was seen
as better than equivalent performance on the feminine task.
No other main effects or interactions were significant.

When asked to state whether the task performance was
indicative of the stimulus person's general intelligence,
subjects again favored the male. A main effect of borderline
significance for Sex of Stimulus Person, F (1,122) = 3.55,
p = .058, indicated that the good performance was seen as
more indicative of the male's general intelligence than of
the female's.

As mentioned earlier, when subjects were asked to estimate their own performance on the task, they showed expected sex-linkage predictions. In addition, however, there was a significant main effect for Sex of Subject, F (1,122) = 9.38, p = .003, males expected to do better on either task than did females. Inspection of means in the significant Sex of Subject X Sex of Task interaction showed that male subjects expected to do better than the performer (who made a score of 16) on both the feminine task (expected score = 16.38) and on the masculine task (expected score = 18.48), while female subjects expected to do better than the performer only on the feminine task (expected score on feminine task = 17.47, expected score on masculine task = 13.65).

Measures of effort and predicted performance of the stimulus person on a similar task showed no differences among conditions.

Discussion

The present study gives clear indication that equivalent performance by males and females are not explained by the same attributions. As predicted, a male's successful performance on a masculine task is explained by invoking skill on the part of the performer, while the same performance by a female tends to be more attributed to luck. In contrast to prediction, however, the reverse conditions did not hold true on the feminine task. Instead, ratings of male and female stimulus

persons were almost identical for the female task, with the
result that there was an overall main effect for men to be
seen as more skillful, independent of the task, than women.
To amplify this biasing effect, performance on a masculine
task was seen as better by subjects, despite the fact that
pretesting had shown the tasks to be rated equivalent in task
difficulty and that the score presumably obtained by stimulus
persons was identical vis-a-vis an identical norm for masculine
and feminine tasks. Such results support the popular conception
that masculine accomplishments are viewed as better
accomplishments, whether in relation to task or performer.
Further, such accomplishments, in this case an above average
performance, are seen as more indicative of the man's
intelligence than of the woman's.

It should be noted that although women were rated as more
lucky, particularly on the masculine task, these ratings were
at the mid-point of the scale, i.e., approximately equal
amounts of luck and skill were assigned. Thus, no stimulus
persons were seen as performing well primarily because of
luck, despite the fact that a true-false task should allow
such a supposition on the part of at least some subjects.
Such a tendency is consistent with our pilot study, which
also revealed a reluctance on the part of subjects to assign
luck as an explanation for a good performance. It is also
worth noting in this context that subjects were more confident

in assigning ratings to the male stimulus person, ratings
which were more polarized away from the luck factor.

The present study presents additional evidence for the
tendency of women to make lower estimates of their anticipated
performance than do males, thus confirming previous reports
of Feather (1968, 1969). While men anticipate doing better
than the person they evaluated on either a masculine or a
feminine task, women will predict a higher score for themselves
only on the feminine task, while predicting a substantially
lower score on the masculine task. (These expectations are
independent of the sex of the actor observed.) Although sex
of subject had an effect in terms of the subject's expectations
for his own performance, there was no evidence that the subject's
own sex related to his or her evaluation of either male or
female stimulus persons. In every case, the patterns of
judgment of male and female subjects were quite similar, thus
arguing against any sex-linked biases towards or against one's
own sex. Such results are consistent with previous research
in our own labs, as well as with the Bem and Bem (1970)
replication of Goldberg (1968). Males and females share the
biases equally.

The present data show that when, by clearly objective
criteria, the performance of a male and female are identical,
those performances will be rated accordingly in that we found
no difference on evaluation of performance. In a similar

vein, Pheterson et al. (1971) found no difference in judgments of competence when an authoritative judgment of the performance was supplied to subjects, i.e., the label winner. Nevertheless, people will assign different causes in explanation of that performance. If similar processes occur outside of the confines of the present experimental paradigm, then the potential discrimination against women (or any other group for whom expectations tend to be lower) may be of a more subtle nature and hence less easily eliminated by objective evidence of a good performance. Although the present study did not show these differing attributions to affect predictions regarding future performance, this failure to obtain differences may reflect some confusion on the part of the subjects as to what the similar task would be rather than evidence of no connection between explained performance and anticipated future performance. Research by Weiner and others (e.g., Weiner et al., 1971) would clearly suggest that future expectations would be affected.

It is evident that additional research is needed to explore the conditions under which differing attributions will be made to male and female performances, and the extent to which these attributions will affect future expectancies. It would also be of interest to know what the effect would be when the presented evidence indicated below average rather than above average performance. We might expect that

in such a case the male's bad performance on a feminine task
would be seen as lack of skill, while bad luck would be used
to explain failure on a sex-consistent task. A number of
similar hypotheses can be formulated, suggesting that
attribution theory is of both heuristic and conceptual value
in investigating the processes of differential evaluations
of males and females.

References

Bem, S.L., & Bem, D.J.   Case study of a non-conscious ideology:
Training the woman to know her place.   In D.J. Bem (Ed.),
Beliefs, attitudes, and human affairs.   Belmont, California:
Brooks/Cole, 1970.

Deaux, K., & Taynor, J.   Evaluation of male and female ability:
Bias works two ways.   Psychological Reports, 1973, 32,
261-262.

Feather, N.T.   Change in confidence following success or failure
as a predictor of subsequent performance.   Journal of
Personality and Social Psychology, 1968, 9, 38-46.

Feather, N.T.   Attribution of responsibility and valence of
success and failure in relation to initial confidence and
task performance.   Journal of Personality and Social
Psychology, 1969, 13, 129-144.

Feather, N.T., & Simon, J.G.   Attribution of responsibility
and valence of outcome in relation to initial confidence
and success and failure of self and other.   Journal of
Personality and Social Psychology, 1971, 18, 173-188.

Goldberg, P.   Are women prejudiced against women?   Trans-action,
1968, 5, 28-30.

Pheterson, G. I., Kiesler, S. B., & Goldberg, P. A. Evaluation
of the performance of women as a function of their sex,
achievement, and personal history. Journal of Personality
and Social Psychology, 1971, 19, 114-118.

Weiner, B., Frieze, I., Kukla, A., Reed, L., Rest, S., &
Rosenbaum, R. Perceiving the causes of success and failure.
New York: General Learning Press, 1971.

Winer, B. J. Statistical principles in experimental design.
New York: McGraw-Hill, 1971.

Footnotes

1. This article was originally published in the Journal
of Personality and Social Psychology, 1974, 29, 80-85.
Copyright 1974 by the American Psychological Association.
Reprinted (with slight modification) by permission of the
American Psychological Association and Dr. Kay Deaux.

2. In a pilot study which preceded the research reported
here, four separate dimensions were used for attributional
responses of ability, effort, task difficulty, and luck in
the manner commonly used by Weiner (Weiner et al., 1971).
On none of these four dimensions did subjects show a significant
difference by condition, however, and a rank ordering of the
importance of the four factors was identical across conditions.
These preliminary results suggested that in some instances
the differences in evaluation of male and female stimulus
persons may be fairly subtle in nature, and that a socially
desirable ranking with ability always predominating over
luck will prevail unless the subject is forced to make a
choice on a single dimension.

Table 1

Summary of Analysis of Variance on Ratings of Luck-Ability

Source	df	MS	F
A (Sex of Stimulus)	1	12.802	4.648*
B (Sex of Task)	1	2.753	1.000
C (Sex of Subject)	1	5.845	2.122
A X B	1	20.722	7.523**
A X C	1	6.844	2.485
B X C	1	3.021	1.097
A X B X C	1	4.294	1.559
Error	122	2.755	

* $p < .05$

** $p < .01$

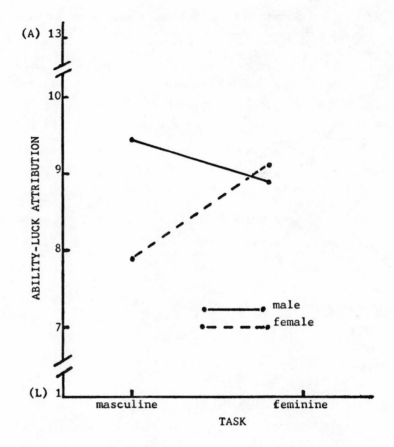

Figure 1. Ability-Luck attributions as a function of
sex of task and performer.

APPENDIX B
STATISTICAL TESTS

The purpose of this appendix is to give you the formulas and calculational procedures that will allow you to analyze data. I have not tried to include all possible statistical tests. Rather, I have attempted to include a variety of tests that should be appropriate for many of the research designs you might use.

We will examine both descriptive and inferential statistics. Before you study the statistics, however, you need to know something about the properties of measurement scales.

TYPES OF MEASUREMENT SCALES

Whenever we measure a subject on a variable, we use one of four types of measurement scales: nominal scales, ordinal scales, interval scales, and ratio scales. The type of scale used determines which statistical treatment is most appropriate for the data.

Nominal scales

Nominal scales have no numerical or quantitative properties. An obvious example would be the variable of sex. A person is classified as either male or female when sex is measured. Being male does not imply a greater amount of sexness than being female; the two levels of the sex variable are merely different. This is called a nominal scale because we simply assign *names* to different categories. Another example would be a classification of undergraduates according to major. A psychology major would not be entitled to a higher number than a history major, for instance. Even if you were to assign numbers to the different categories, the numbers would be meaningless, except for identification.

Ordinal scales

Ordinal scales are a bit more sophisticated than nominal scales because they involve quantitative distinctions. Ordinal scales allow us to rank order people or objects on the variable being measured.

One example of an ordinal scale is provided by the movie rating system used in the television section of the *Los Angeles Times*. Movies on television are given one, two, three, or four checks. The ratings are described like this:

✔ ✔ ✔ ✔ New or Old, a Classic
✔ ✔ ✔ First-Rate
✔ ✔ Flawed; May have moments
✔ Desperation Time

The rating system is not a nominal scale because the number of checks is meaningful in terms of a continuum of goodness. However, the checks allow us only to rank order the movies. A four-check movie is better than a three-check movie; a three-check movie is better than a movie with two checks, and so on. Although we have this quantitative information about the movies, we *cannot* say that the difference between a one-check and a two-check movie is always the same or that it is equal to the difference between a two- and a three-check movie. No particular value is attached to the *intervals* between the numbers used in the rating scale.

Interval scales

In an interval scale, the differences between the numbers on the scale are meaningful. Specifically, the intervals between the numbers are *equal* in size. The difference between 1 and 2 on the scale, for example, is the same as the difference between 2 and 3.

A household thermometer (Fahrenheit or centigrade) measures temperature on an interval scale. The difference between 5° C and 10° C is equal to the difference in temperature between 15° C and 20° C. However, there is no absolute zero on the scale that would indicate the absence of temperature. The zero on any interval scale is only an arbitrary reference point. The implication of this property of interval scales is that we cannot form ratios of the numbers. That is, we cannot say that one number on the scale represents twice as much (or three times as much, and so forth) temperature as another number. You cannot say, for example, that 10° C is ten times as warm as 1° C.

An example of an interval scale in the behavioral sciences might be a personality measure of a trait such as extroversion. If the measurement is an interval scale, we cannot make a statement such as "the person who scored 20 is twice as extroverted as the person who scored 10." We cannot make such a statement because there is no absolute zero point that indicates an absence of the trait that is being measured.

In the behavioral sciences, it is often difficult to know precisely whether an ordinal or an interval scale is being used. However, it is often useful to assume that the variable is being measured on an interval scale, because interval scales allow more sophisticated statistical treatments than are allowed with ordinal scales. Of course, if the measure is a rank ordering (for example, a rank ordering of students in a class on the basis of popularity), it is obvious that an ordinal scale is being used.

Ratio scales

Ratio scales do have an absolute zero point that indicates the absence of the variable being measured. Examples would include many physical measures, such as length, weight, or time. With a ratio scale, it is possible to make statements such as "a person who weighs 100 kilograms (220 pounds) weighs twice as much as a person who weighs 50 kilograms (110 pounds)."

Ratio scales are used in the behavioral sciences when variables that involve physical measures are being studied. However, most variables in the behavioral sciences are less precise and so use nominal, ordinal, or interval scale measures.

DESCRIPTIVE STATISTICS

With a knowledge of the types of measurement scales, we can now turn to a consideration of statistical techniques. We can start with ways of describing a set of scores—central tendency and variability.

Measures of central tendency

A measure of *central tendency* gives a single number that describes how an entire group scored as a whole, or on the average. Three different central tendency measures are available—the mode, the median, and the mean.

The mode The mode is the most frequently occurring score. Table B-1 shows a set of scores and the descriptive statistics that are discussed in this section. The most frequently occurring score in this data is 5: No calculations are necessary to find the mode. The mode can be used with any of the four types of measurement scales. However, it is the only measure of central tendency that can be used with nominal scale data. If you are measuring sex and find that there are one hundred females and fifty males, the mode is "female" because this is the most frequently occurring category on the nominal scale.

The median The median is the score that divides the group in half—fifty percent of the scores are below the median and 50 percent are above the median. Once the scores have been ordered from lowest to highest (as in Table B-1), the median is easily found. If there is an odd number of scores, you simply find the middle score. (For example, if there are eleven scores, the sixth score is the median, since there are five lower and five higher scores.) If there is an even number of scores, the median is the midpoint between the two middle

Table B-1   Descriptive statistics for a set of scores

Score	Descriptive statistic
1	Mode = 5
2	
4	Median = 5
4	
5	$\bar{X} = \dfrac{\Sigma X}{N} = 4.5$
5	
5	Range = 6
6	
6	$s^2 = \dfrac{\Sigma(X - \bar{X})^2}{N} = \dfrac{\Sigma X^2}{N} - \bar{X}^2 = 3.05$
7	
$\Sigma X = 45$	$s = \sqrt{s^2} = 1.75$
$\Sigma X^2 = 233$	
$N = 10$	

scores. In the data in Table B-1, there are ten scores, so the fifth and sixth scores are the two middle scores. To find the median, we add the two middle scores and divide by 2. Thus, the median in Table B-1 is

$$\frac{5+5}{2} = 5$$

The median can be used with ordinal, interval, or ratio scale data. It is most likely to be used with ordinal data, however. This is because calculation of the median considers only the rank ordering of scores and not the actual size of the scores.

The mean   The mean does take into account the actual size of the scores. Thus, the mean is based on more information about the scores than either the mode or the median. However, it is appropriate only for interval or ratio scale data.

The mean is the sum of the scores in a group divided by the number of scores. The calculational formula for the mean can be expressed as

$$\bar{X} = \frac{\Sigma X}{N}$$

where $\bar{X}$ is the symbol for the mean. In this formula, X represents a score obtained by an individual, and the Σ symbol indicates that scores are to be summed or added. The symbol ΣX can be read as "sum of the Xs" and simply is an indication that the scores are to be added. Thus, ΣX in the data from Table B-1 is

$$1 + 2 + 4 + 5 + 5 + 5 + 6 + 6 + 7 = 45$$

The N in the formula symbolizes the number of scores in the group. In our example, $N = 10$. Thus, we can now calculate the mean:

$$\bar{X} = \frac{\Sigma X}{N} = \frac{45}{10} = 4.5$$

Measures of variability

In addition to describing the central tendency of the set of scores, we also want to describe how much the scores vary among themselves. How much spread is there in the set of scores?

The range   The range is the highest score minus the lowest score. In our example, the range is 6. The range is not a very useful statistic, however, because it is based on only two scores in the distribution. It doesn't take into account all of the information that is available in the entire set of scores.

The variance and standard deviation   The variance, and a related statistic called the standard deviation, use all of the scores to yield a measure of variability. The variance indicates the degree to which scores vary about the group mean. The formula for the variance (symbolized as s^2) is

$$s^2 = \frac{\Sigma(X - \bar{X})^2}{N}$$

where $(X - \bar{X})^2$ is an individual score, X, minus the mean, $\bar{X}$, and then squared. Thus, $(X - \bar{X})^2$ is the squared deviation of each score from the mean. The Σ sign indicates that these squared deviation scores are to be summed. Finally, dividing by N gives the mean of the squared deviations. The variance, then, is the mean of the squared deviations from the group mean. (Squared deviations are used because simple deviations would add up to zero.)

The data in Table B-1 can be used to illustrate calculation of the variance. $\Sigma(X - \bar{X})^2$ is equal to

$$(1-4.5)^2 + (2-4.5)^2 + (4-4.5)^2 + (4-4.5)^2 + (5-4.5)^2 +$$
$$(5-4.5)^2 + (5-4.5)^2 + (6-4.5)^2 + (6-4.5)^2 + (7-4.5)^2 = 30.50$$

The next step is to divide $\Sigma(X - \bar{X})^2$ by N. The calculation for the variance, then, is

$$s^2 = \frac{\Sigma(X - \bar{X})^2}{N} = \frac{30.50}{10} = 3.05$$

A simpler calculational formula for the variance is

$$s^2 = \frac{\Sigma X^2}{N} - \bar{X}^2$$

where ΣX^2 is the sum of the squared individual scores, and $\bar{X}^2$ is the mean squared. You can confirm that the two formulas are identical by computing the variance using this simpler formula (remember that ΣX^2 tells you to square each score and then sum the squared scores). This simpler formula is much easier to work with when there are many scores, because each deviation doesn't have to be calculated.

The standard deviation is the square root of the variance. Because the variance uses squared scores, the variance doesn't describe the amount of variability in the same units of measurement as the original scale. The standard deviation (s) corrects this problem.

STATISTICAL SIGNIFICANCE TESTS

This section describes several statistical significance tests. All of these tests are used to determine the probability that the outcome of the research was due to the operation of random error. All use the logic of the null hypothesis discussed in Chapter 8. We will consider three significance tests in this section: The chi-square test, the Mann-Whitney U test, and the analysis of variance or F test.

Chi-square (x^2)

The chi-square (Greek letter chi, squared) test is used when dealing with nominal scale data. It is used when the data consists of frequencies—the number of subjects who fall into each of several categories.

Chi-square can be used with either the experimental or correlational method. It is used in conjunction with the experimental method when the dependent variable is measured on a nominal scale. It is used with the correlational method when both variables are measured on nominal scales.

Example   Suppose you want to know whether there is a relationship between sex and hand dominance. To do this, you sample fifty males and fifty females and ask whether they are right-handed, left-handed, or ambidextrous (used both hands with equal skill). Your data collection involves classifying each person as male or female and as right-handed, left-handed, or ambidextrous.

Fictitious data for such a study is presented in Table B-2. The frequencies labeled as "O" in each of the six cells in the table refer to the number of male and female subjects who fall into each of the three hand-dominance categories. The frequencies labeled "E" refer to frequencies that are expected if the null hypothesis is correct. It is important that each subject falls into only one of the cells when using chi-square (that is, no subject can be counted as both male and female or both right- and left-handed).

The chi-square test examines the extent to which the frequencies that are actually observed in the study differ from the frequencies that are expected if the null hypothesis is correct. The null hypothesis is that there is no relationship between sex and hand dominance: males and females do not differ on this characteristic.

Table B–2   Data for hypothetical study on sex and hand dominance: Chi-square test

Subject sex	Hand dominance			Row totals
	Right	Left	Ambidextrous	
Male	$O_1 = 15$	$O_2 = 30$	$O_3 = 5$	50
	$E_1 = 25$	$E_2 = 20$	$E_3 = 5$	
Female	$O_4 = 35$	$O_5 = 10$	$O_6 = 5$	50
	$E_4 = 25$	$E_5 = 20$	$E_6 = 5$	
Column totals	50	40	10	$N = 100$

Computations:

Cell number	$\dfrac{(O - E)^2}{E}$
1	4.00
2	5.00
3	0.00
4	4.00
5	5.00
6	0.00
$\Sigma =$	18.00

$$\chi^2 = \Sigma \frac{(O - E)^2}{E}$$
$$= 18.00$$

The formula for computing chi-square is

$$\chi^2 = \Sigma \frac{(O - E)^2}{E}$$

where O is the observed frequency in each cell, E is the expected frequency in each cell, and the symbol Σ refers to summing over all cells. The steps in calculating the value of χ^2 are described below.

Step 1. Arrange the observed frequencies in a table such as Table B-2. Note that in addition to the observed frequencies in each cell, the table presents row totals, column totals, and the total number of observations (N).

Step 2. Calculate the expected frequencies for each of the cells in the table. The expected frequency formula is

$$E = \frac{\text{Row total} \times \text{Column total}}{N}$$

where the Row Total refers to the row total for the cell, and the Column Total refers to the column total for the cell. Thus, the expected frequency for cell 1 (male right-handedness) is

$$E_1 = \frac{50 \times 50}{100} = 25$$

The expected frequencies for each of the cells are shown in Table B-2 below the observed frequencies.

Step 3. Calculate the quantity $(O - E)^2 / E$ for each cell. For cell 1, this quantity is

$$\frac{(15 - 25)^2}{25} = \frac{100}{25} = 4.00$$

Step 4. Find the value of χ^2 by summing the $(O - E)^2 / E$ values found in step 3. The calculations for obtaining χ^2 for the example data are shown in Table B-2.

Significance of chi-square The significance of the obtained χ^2 value can be evaluated by consulting a table of critical values of χ^2. A table of critical χ^2 values is presented as Table C-2 in Appendix C. The critical χ^2 values indicate the value that the *obtained* χ^2 must equal or exceed to be significant at the .10 level, the .05 level, and the .01 level.

To be able to use the table of critical values of χ^2 as well as most other statistical tables, you must understand the concept of *degrees of freedom (df)*. The critical value of χ^2 for any given study depends on the degrees of freedom. Degrees of freedom refers to the number of scores that are free to vary. In the table of categories for a chi-square test, the number of degrees of freedom is the number of cells in which the frequencies are free to vary once we know the row totals and column totals. The degrees of freedom for chi-square is easily calculated:

$$df = (R - 1)(C - 1)$$

where R is the number of rows in the table and C is the number of columns. In our example in Table B-1, there are 2 rows and 3 columns, so there are 2 degrees of freedom. In a study with 3 rows and 3 columns, there are 4 degrees of freedom, and so on.

In order to use Table C-2, find the correct degrees of freedom and then determine the critical value of χ^2 necessary to reject the null hypothesis at the chosen significance level. With 2 degrees of freedom, the obtained χ^2 value must be *equal to or greater than* the critical value of 5.991 in order to be significant at the .05 level. There is only a .05 probability that a χ^2 of 5.991 would occur if only random error is operating. Because the obtained χ^2 from our example is 18.00, we can reject the null hypothesis that there is no relationship between sex and hand dominance. (The chi-square was based on fictitious data, but it would be relatively easy for you to determine for yourself whether there is in fact a relationship.)

Concluding remarks　The chi-square test is extremely useful and is used frequently in all of the behavioral sciences. The calculational formula described is generalizable to expanded studies in which there are more categories on either of the variables. One note of caution, however: When both variables have only two categories, so that there are only two rows and two columns, the formula for calculating chi-square changes slightly. In such cases, the formula is

$$\chi^2 = \Sigma \frac{(|O - E| - .5)^2}{E}$$

where $|O - E|$ is the absolute value of $O - E$ and .5 is a constant that is subtracted for each cell.

Mann-Whitney *U* test

The Mann Whitney U test is used to test whether there is a significant difference between two groups when the subjects were measured on an ordinal scale. The two groups may have been formed using either the experimental or the correlational method. However, the Mann-Whitney U test can only be used with an independent groups design, in which the two groups are made up of different subjects.

Example　Let's say you want to test the hypothesis that only children are less aggressive than children who have at least one brother or sister. To collect your data, you go to an elementary school class and determine which pupils are only children and which have siblings. You also ask the teacher to rate each child's aggressiveness on a scale of 1 to 25 (least aggressive to most aggressive).

Before collecting your data, you determine that your aggression measure is **237** really an ordinal scale, so you decide to use the Mann-Whitney U test to evaluate your results.

Table B-3 shows fictitious results for such a study. The table shows the score the teacher gave to each child, the rank ordering of these scores, and the basic calculations for the Mann-Whitney U. It is important to keep in mind that it is the *rank order* of scores that is crucial in the U test, not the size of the actual scores on the measurement scale.

Finding the value of U involves making two calculations:

$$(1)\ N_1 N_2 + \frac{N_1 (N_1 + 1)}{2} - R_1$$

$$(2)\ N_1 N_2 + \frac{N_2 (N_2 + 1)}{2} - R_2$$

where R_1 is the sum of the ranks in the first group, R_2 is the sum of the ranks in the second group, and N_1 and N_2 refer to the number of subjects in group one and two, respectively. The value of U is the *smaller* of these two quantities. To calculate U, follow the steps below.

Step 1. Arrange the scores in each group from lowest to highest, as was done with the scores in Table B-3. Assign a rank to each of the scores. The smallest score receives a rank of 1, the next highest score receives a rank of 2, and so on. Ranks are assigned on the basis of lowest to highest, irrespective of which group the subject is in. In cases where there are tied scores, each subject receives the mean of the rank he or she occupies. For example, in Table B-2, two subjects received a score of 2. Since these subjects occupy the 2nd and 3rd ranks, each receives the same mean rank of 2.5.

Step 2. Calculate the sum of the ranks for each of the groups.

Step 3. Calculate the two quantities described above. The value of U is the *smaller* of these two quantities.

Significance of U   Critical values for determining the significance of U are shown in Table C-3. To use this table, first determine your significance level. Table C-3 is made up of three smaller tables (A, B, and C) for significance levels of .10, .05, and .01.

If you choose a .05 level of significance, use the table marked (B). Find the critical value of U for N_1 and N_2 in your study. In our example, $N_1 = 10$ and N_2

Table B–3   Data for hypothetical experiment on only children and aggression: Mann-Whitney U test

Only children		Children with siblings	
Score	Rank	Score	Rank
1	1	5	6.5
2	2.5	5	6.5
2	2.5	9	11
3	4	10	12
4	5	11	13
6	8	13	15
7	9	14	16
8	10	16	18
12	14	19	19
15	17	23	20
	$R_1 = 73$		$R_2 = 137$

$$(1)\ N_1N_2 + \frac{N_1(N_1 + 1)}{2} - R_1 \qquad (2)\ N_1N_2 + \frac{N_2(N_2 + 1)}{2} - R_2$$

$$= (10)(10) + \frac{(10)(11)}{2} - 73 \qquad = (10)(10) + \frac{(10)(11)}{2} - 137$$

$$= 82 \qquad\qquad\qquad = 18$$

Since (2) is the smaller calculation, $U = 18$

= 10. The critical value of U at the .05 level, then, is 23. To be significant, the obtained value of U must be *equal to or smaller* than the critical value. Since the obtained value of U (18) is smaller than the critical value (23), we conclude that the results are significant at the .05 level.

A note of caution: The significance of U is determined by whether the obtained U is *smaller* than the critical value. This procedure is directly opposite to the procedures used with most other significance tests (such as the chi-square test). With most tests, the obtained value must *exceed* the critical value to be significant.

Concluding remarks   The Mann-Whitney U test is very useful when the data is of an ordinal scale type and an independent groups design has been used. Other tests must be used, however, when the study used a repeated measures design. Such tests may be found in statistics texts.

Analysis of variance (F test)

The analysis of variance, or F test, is used to determine whether there is a significant difference between groups that have been measured on either interval or ratio scales. The groups may have been formed using either the experimental or the correlational method; the important thing is that at least an interval scale measure was used. The analysis of variance may be used with either independent groups or repeated measures designs. Procedures for calculating F for both types of designs are presented.

F and t   Some of you may have wondered why the t-test isn't discussed in connection with evaluating the difference between two groups, since the t-test is discussed in many statistics texts. The t-test is a straightforward, easily computed test of significance of the difference between two groups. I have chosen the F test for two reasons. First, the analysis of variance is a more general statistical procedure, since it is used when there are two *or more* levels of the independent variable. It is also used in factorial designs in which there are several independent variables. Second, when the study has only two groups, F and t are virtually identical—the value of F equals t^2 when there are only two groups. Thus, we can bypass consideration of the t-test, proceeding directly to the more general technique of analysis of variance.

The analysis of variance tests the null hypothesis that the group means are in fact equal in the population. F is a ratio of two types of variance in the data. The two variances are called systematic variance and error variance. *Systematic variance* is the deviation of the group means from the *grand mean,* which is the mean score of all subjects in all groups. Systematic variance is small when the difference between group means is small and increases as the group mean differences increase. *Error variance* is the deviation of the individual scores in each group from their respective group means (this is the type of variance discussed earlier).

If the null hypothesis is correct, these two sources of variance in the data are expected to be about equal. Thus, if the null hypothesis is correct, the ratio of systematic variance to error variance *(F)* will be about 1.0. If the population means are not equal, we expect a large systematic variance relative to the amount of error variance. In the next three sections, we'll consider the calculations involved in the analysis of variance.

Analysis of variance: One independent variable

In order to illustrate the use of the analysis of variance, let's consider a hypothetical experiment on physical distance and self-disclosure. You think that people will reveal more about themselves to an interviewer when they are sitting close to the interviewer than they will when sitting farther away. To test this idea, you conduct an experiment on interviewing. Subjects are told that interviewing techniques are being studied. Each subject is seated in a room; the interviewer comes into the room and sits at one of three distances from the subject: Close (2 feet or .61 meters), Medium (4 feet or 1.22 meters), or Far (6 feet or 1.83 meters). The distance chosen by the interviewer is the independent variable manipulation. Subjects are randomly assigned to the three distance conditions, and the interviewer's behavior is constant in all conditions. The interview consists of a number of questions, and the dependent variable is the number of personal, revealing statements made by the subject during the interview.

Fictitious data for such an experiment is shown in Table B-4. Note that this is an independent groups design with five subjects in each group. The calculations of the systematic variance and error variance involve computing the *sum of squares* for the different types of variance.

Sum of squares   Sum of squares stands for the *sum of squared deviations from the mean.* Computing an analysis of variance for the data in Table B-4 involves three sums of squares: (1) SS_{TOTAL}, the sum of squared deviations of each individual score from the grand mean; (2) SS_A, the sum of squared deviations of each of the group means from the grand mean; and (3) SS_{ERROR}, the sum of squared deviations of the individual scores from their respective group means. The "A" in SS_A is used to designate that we are dealing with the systematic variance associated with independent variable A.

The three sums of squares are deviations from a mean (recall that we calculated such deviations earlier when discussing the variance in a set of scores). We could calculate the deviations directly with the data in Table B-4, but such calculations are hard to work with so we will use simplified formulas for computational purposes. The computational formulas are:

$$SS_{TOTAL} = \Sigma X^2 - \frac{G^2}{N}$$

$$SS_A = \Sigma \frac{T_a^2}{n_a} - \frac{G^2}{N}$$

$$SS_{ERROR} = \Sigma X^2 - \Sigma \frac{T_a^2}{n_a}$$

You might note here that $SS_{TOTAL} = SS_A + SS_{ERROR}$. The nature of these formulas is considered below, and the actual computations are shown in Table B-4.

Table B-4   Data for hypothetical experiment on distance and self-disclosure: Analysis of variance

Distance (A)		
Close (A1)	Medium (A2)	Far (A3)
33	21	20
24	25	13
31	19	15
29	27	10
34	26	14
$T_{A1} = 151$	$T_{A2} = 118$	$T_{A3} = 72$
$\Sigma X_{A1}^2 = 4623$	$\Sigma X_{A2}^2 = 2832$	$\Sigma X_{A3}^2 = 1090$
$n_{A1} = 5$	$n_{A2} = 5$	$n_{A3} = 5$
$\bar{X}_{A1} = 30.20$	$\bar{X}_{A2} = 23.60$	$\bar{X}_{A3} = 14.40$

$$SS_{TOTAL} = \Sigma X^2 - \frac{G^2}{N} = (4623 + 2832 + 1090) - \frac{(151 + 118 + 72)^2}{15}$$

$$= 8545 - 7752.07$$

$$= 792.93$$

$$SS_A = \Sigma \frac{T_a^2}{n_a} - \frac{G^2}{N} = \left[\frac{(151)^2}{5} + \frac{(118)^2}{5} + \frac{(72)^2}{5} \right] - 7752.07$$

$$= 8381.80 - 7752.07$$

$$= 629.73$$

$$SS_{ERROR} = \Sigma X^2 - \Sigma \frac{T_a^2}{n_a} = 8545 - 8381.80$$

$$= 163.20$$

SS TOTAL   The formula for SS_{TOTAL} is

$$\Sigma X^2 - \frac{G^2}{N}$$

ΣX^2 is the sum of the squared scores of all subjects in the experiment. Each of the scores is squared first and then added. Thus, for the data in Table B-4, ΣX^2 is $33^2 + 24^2 + 31^2$ and so on until all of the scores have been squared and added. If you are doing the calculations by hand or with a pocket calculator, it may be convenient to find the ΣX^2 for the scores in each group and then add these up for your final computation. This is what I did for the data in the table. The G in the formula stands for the grand total of all of the scores. This involves adding up the scores for all subjects. The grand total is then squared and divided by N, the total number of subjects in the experiment. When computing the sum of squares, you should always keep the calculations clearly labeled, because you can simplify later calculations by referring to these earlier ones. Once you have computed SS_{TOTAL}, SS_A can be calculated.

SS A   The formula for SS_A is

$$\Sigma \frac{T_a^2}{n_a} - \frac{G^2}{N}$$

The T_a in this formula refers to the total of the scores in group a of independent variable A. [T_a is a shorthand notation for ΣX in each group (recall the computation of ΣX from our discussion of the mean). The T_a symbol is used to avoid having to deal with too many Σ signs in our calculational procedures.] The a is used to symbolize the particular group number; thus, T_a is a general symbol for T_1, T_2, and T_3. Looking at our data in Table B-4, $T_1 = 151$, $T_2 = 118$, and $T_3 = 72$. These are the sums of the scores in each of the groups. After T_a has been calculated, T_a^2 is found by squaring T_a. Now, T_a^2 is divided by n_a, the number of subjects in group a. Once the quantity T_a^2/n_a has been computed for each group, the quantities are summed as indicated by the Σ symbol.

Notice that the second part of the formula, G^2/N, was calculated when SS_{TOTAL} was obtained. Since we already have this quantity, it needn't be calculated again when computing SS_A. After obtaining SS_A, we can now compute SS_{ERROR}.

SS ERROR   The formula for SS_{ERROR} is

$$\Sigma X^2 - \Sigma \frac{T_a^2}{n_a}$$

Both of these quantities were calculated above in obtaining SS_{TOTAL} and SS_A. **243** To obtain SS_{ERROR}, we merely have to find these quantities and perform the proper subtraction.

As a check on the calculations, we can make sure that $SS_{TOTAL} = SS_A + SS_{ERROR}$.

The next step in the computation of the analysis of variance is to find the *mean square* for each of the sums of squares. We can then find the value of *F*. The necessary computations are shown in an analysis of variance summary table in Table B-5. Constructing a summary table is the easiest way to complete the computations.

Mean squares   After obtaining the sum of squares, it is necessary to compute the mean squares. Mean square stands for the *mean of the sum of the squared deviations from the mean* or, more simply, the mean of the sum of squares. The mean square *(MS)* is the sum of squares divided by the degrees of freedom. The degrees of freedom is determined by the number of scores in the sum of squares that are free to vary. The mean squares are the variances that are used in computing the value of *F*.

From Table B-5, you can see that the mean squares that concern us are the mean square for A (systematic variance) and the mean square for error (error variance). The formulas are

$$MS_A = SS_A/df_A$$

$$MS_{ERROR} = SS_{ERROR}/df_{ERROR}$$

where $df_A = a - 1$ (the number of groups minus one) and $df_{ERROR} = N - a$ (the total number of subjects minus the number of groups).

Table B-5   Analysis of variance summary table

Source of variance	Sum of squares	df	Mean square	F
A	SS_A	$a - 1$	SS_A/df_A	MS_A/MS_{ERROR}
Error	SS_{ERROR}	$N - a$	SS_{ERROR}/df_{ERROR}	
Total	SS_{TOTAL}	$N - 1$		
A	629.73	2	314.87	23.15
Error	163.20	12	13.60	
Total	729.93	14		

Obtaining the F value   The obtained F for the data in Table B-4 is found by dividing MS_A by MS_{ERROR}. If only random error is operating, the expected value of F is 1.0. The greater the F value, the lower the probability that the results of the experiment were due to chance error.

Significance of F   In order to determine the significance of the obtained F value, it is necessary to compare the obtained F to a critical value of F. Table C-4 in Appendix C shows critical values of F for significance levels of .10, .05, and .01. To find the critical value of F, you need to locate on the table the degrees of freedom for the numerator of the ratio (the systematic variance) and the degrees of freedom for the denominator of the F ratio (the error variance). The intersection of these two degrees of freedom on the table is the critical F value.

The appropriate degrees of freedom for our sample data are 2 and 12 (see Table B-5). The critical F value from Table C-4 is 3.89 for a .05 level of significance. For the results to be significant, the obtained F value must be equal to or greater than the critical value. Since the obtained value of F in Table B-5 is greater than the critical value, we conclude that the results are significant and reject the null hypothesis that the means of the groups are equal in the population.

Concluding remarks   The analysis of variance for one independent variable with an independent groups design can be used when there are two or more groups in the experiment. The general formulas described are appropriate for all such designs. Also, the calculations are the same whether the experimental or the correlational method is used to form the groups. The formulas are also applicable to cases in which the number of subjects in each group is not equal.

When the design of the experiment includes more than two levels of the independent variable (as in our example experiment, which had three groups), the obtained F value doesn't tell us whether any two specific groups are significantly different from one another. One way to examine the difference between two groups in such a study is to use the formula for SS_A to compute the sum of squares and the mean square for the two groups (the df in this case is $2 - 1$). When doing this, the previously calculated MS_{ERROR} should be used as the error variance term for computing F. More complicated procedures for evaluating the difference between two groups in such designs are available, but these are beyond the scope of this book.

To make sure you understand the computations involved in the analysis of variance, you may want to compute the F value for data that has been pre- viously presented (such as the modeling and aggression example given in Chapter 8). Once the basic analysis of variance technique is understood, it is not difficult to extend the analysis to designs with more than one independent variable.

Analysis of variance: Two independent variables

In this section, we will describe the computations for analysis of variance with a factorial design containing two independent variables. The formulas apply to an A $\times$ B factorial design with any number of levels of the independent variables. The formulas apply only to a completely independent groups design with different subjects in each group, and the number of subjects in each group must be equal. Once you understand this analysis, however, you should have little trouble understanding the analysis for more complicated designs with repeated measures or unequal numbers of subjects. With these limitations in mind, let's consider example data from a hypothetical experiment.

The experiment uses a 2 $\times$ 2 mixed factorial design. Variable A is the type of instruction used in a course, and variable B is the intelligence level of the students. The students are classified as either "low" or "high" intelligence on the basis of intelligence test scores, and are randomly assigned to one of two types of classes. One class uses the traditional lecture method; the other class uses an individualized learning approach involving frequent testing over small amounts of material, the use of proctors to help individual students, and a stipulation that students master each section of material before going on to the next section. The information presented to students in the two classes is identical. At the end of the course, all students take the same test, which covers all of the material presented in the course. The score on this examination is the dependent variable.

Table B-6 shows fictitious data for such an experiment with five subjects in each condition. This design allows us to evaluate three effects—the main effect of A, the main effect of B, and the A $\times$ B interaction. The main effect of A is whether one type of instruction is superior to the other; the main effect of B is whether high intelligence students score differently on the test than do low intelligence students; the A $\times$ B interaction examines whether the effect of one independent variable is different depending on the particular level of the other variable.

The computation of the analysis of variance starts with calculation of the

Table B–6   Data for hypothetical experiment on the effect of type of instruction and intelligence level on exam score: Analysis of variance

	Intelligence (B)		
	Low (B1)	High (B2)	
Traditional lecture (A1)	75 70 69 72 68	90 95 89 85 91	
	$T_{A1B1} = 354$	$T_{A1B2} = 450$	$T_{A1} = 804$
	$\Sigma X^2_{A1B1} = 25094$ $n_{A1B1} = 5$ $\overline{X}_{A1B1} = 70.80$	$\Sigma X^2_{A1B2} = 40552$ $n_{A1B2} = 5$ $\overline{X}_{A1B2} = 90.00$	$n_{A1} = 10$ $\overline{X}_{A1} = 80.40$
Individualized method (A2)	85 87 83 90 89	87 94 93 89 92	
	$T_{A2B1} = 434$	$T_{A2B2} = 455$	$T_{A2} = 889$
	$\Sigma X^2_{A2B1} = 37704$ $n_{A2B1} = 5$ $\overline{X}_{A2B1} = 86.80$	$\Sigma X^2_{A2B2} = 41439$ $n_{A2B2} = 5$ $\overline{X}_{A2B2} = 91.00$	$n_{A2} = 10$ $\overline{X}_{A2} = 88.90$
	$T_{B1} = 788$ $n_{B1} = 10$ $\overline{X}_{B1} = 78.80$	$T_{B2} = 905$ $n_{B2} = 10$ $\overline{X}_{B2} = 90.50$	

sum of squares for the following sources of variance in the data: SS_{TOTAL}, SS_A, SS_B, $SS_{A \times B}$, and SS_{ERROR}. The procedures for calculation are similar to the calculations performed for the analysis of variance with one independent variable. The numerical calculations for the example data are shown in Table B-7. We can now consider each of these calculations.

Table B–7 Computations for analysis of variance with two independent variables

$$SS_{TOTAL} = \Sigma X^2 - \frac{G^2}{N} = (25094 + 40552 + 37704 + 41439)$$
$$- \frac{(354 + 450 + 434 + 455)^2}{20}$$
$$= 144789 - 143312.45$$
$$= 1476.55$$

$$SS_A = \frac{\Sigma T_a^2}{n_a} - \frac{G^2}{N} = \frac{(804)^2 + (889)^2}{10} - 143312.45$$
$$= 143673.70 - 143312.45$$
$$= 361.25$$

$$SS_B = \frac{\Sigma T_b^2}{n_b} - \frac{G^2}{N} = \frac{(788)^2 + (905)^2}{10} - 143312.45$$
$$= 143996.90 - 143312.45$$
$$= 684.45$$

$$SS_{A \times B} = \frac{\Sigma T_{ab}^2}{n_{ab}} - \frac{G^2}{N} - SS_A - SS_B = \frac{(354)^2 + (450)^2 + (434)^2 + (455)^2}{5}$$
$$- 143312.45 - 361.25 - 684.45$$
$$= 144639.40 - 143312.45 - 361.25 - 684.45$$
$$= 281.25$$

$$SS_{ERROR} = \Sigma X^2 - \frac{\Sigma T_{ab}^2}{n_{ab}} = 144789 - 144639.40$$
$$= 149.60$$

SS TOTAL   The SS_{TOTAL} is computed in the same way as the previous analysis. The formula is

$$SS_{TOTAL} = \Sigma X^2 - \frac{G^2}{N}$$

where ΣX^2 is the sum of the squared scores of all subjects in the experiment, G is the grand total of all of the scores, and N is the total number of subjects.

It is usually easiest to calculate ΣX^2 and G in smaller steps by calculating subtotals separately for each group in the design. The subtotals are then added. This is the procedure followed in Tables B-6 and B-7.

SS A The formula for SS_A is

$$SS_A = \frac{\Sigma T_a^2}{n_a} - \frac{G^2}{N}$$

where ΣT_a^2 is the sum of the squared totals of the scores in each of the groups of independent variable A, and n_a is the number of subjects in each level of independent variable A. When calculating SS_A, we only consider the groups of independent variable A without considering the particular level of B. In other words, the totals for each group of the A variable are obtained by considering all subjects in that level of A, irrespective of which condition of B the subject may be in. The quantity G^2/N was previously calculated for SS_{TOTAL}.

SS B The formula for SS_B is

$$SS_B = \frac{T_b^2}{n_b} - \frac{G^2}{N}$$

SS_B is calculated in the same way as SS_A. The only difference is that we are calculating totals of the groups of independent variable B.

SS A $\times$ B The formula for $SS_{A \times B}$ is

$$SS_{A \times B} = \frac{\Sigma T_{ab}^2}{n_{ab}} - \frac{G^2}{N} - SS_A - SS_B$$

The sum of squares for the A $\times$ B interaction is computed by first calculating the quantity ΣT_{ab}^2. This involves squaring the total of the scores in each of the *ab* conditions in the experiment. In our example experiment in Table B-6, there are four conditions; the interaction calculation considers *all* of the groups. Each of the group totals is squared, and then the sum of the squared totals is obtained. This sum is divided by n_{ab}, the number of subjects in each group. The other quantities in the formula for $SS_{A \times B}$ have already been calculated, so the computation of $SS_{A \times B}$ is relatively straightforward.

SS ERROR The quantities involved in the SS_{ERROR} formula have already been calculated. The formula is

$$SS_{ERROR} = \Sigma X^2 - \frac{\Sigma T_{ab}^2}{n_{ab}}$$

Since these quantities were calculated previously, we merely have to perform the proper subtraction to complete the computation of SS_{ERROR}.

At this point, you may want to practice calculating the sums of squares using the data in Table B-6. As a check on the calculations, make sure that $SS_{TOTAL} = SS_A + SS_B + SS_{A \times B} + SS_{ERROR}$.

After obtaining the sums of squares, the next step is to find the mean square for each of the sources of variance. The easiest way to do this is to use an analysis of variance summary table like Table B-8.

Mean square   The mean square for each of the sources of variance is the sum of squares divided by the degrees of freedom. The formulas for the degrees of freedom and the mean square are shown in the top portion of Table B-8; the computed values are shown in the bottom portion of the table.

Obtaining the F value   The F value for each of the three sources of systematic variance (main effects for A and B, and the interaction) is obtained by dividing the appropriate mean square by the MS_{ERROR}. We now have three obtained F values and can evaluate the significance of the main effects and the interaction.

Significance of F   To determine whether an obtained F is significant, we need to find the critical value of F in Table C-4 in Appendix C. For all of the

Table B–8   **Analysis of variance summary table: Two independent variables**

Source of variance	Sum of squares	df	Mean square	F
A	SS_A	$a - 1$	SS_A/df_A	MS_A/MS_{ERROR}
B	SS_B	$b - 1$	SS_B/df_B	MS_B/MS_{ERROR}
A × B	$SS_{A\times B}$	$(a - 1)(b - 1)$	$SS_{A\times B}/df_{A\times B}$	$MS_{A\times B}/MS_{ERROR}$
Error	SS_{ERROR}	$N - ab$	SS_{ERROR}/df_{ERROR}	
Total	SS_{TOTAL}			
A	361.25	1	361.25	38.64
B	684.45	1	684.45	73.20
A × B	281.25	1	281.25	30.08
Error	149.60	16	9.35	
Total	1476.55	19		

Fs in the analysis of variance summary table, the degrees of freedom are 1 and 16. Let's assume that a .01 significance level for rejecting the null hypothesis was chosen. The critical F at .01 for 1 and 16 degrees of freedom is 8.53. If the obtained F is larger than 8.53, we can say that the results are significant at the .01 level. By referring to the obtained Fs in Table B-8, you can see that the main effects and the interaction are all significant. I'll leave it to you to interpret the main effect means and to graph the interaction. If you don't recall how to do this, you should review the material in Chapter 10.

Analysis of variance: Repeated measures

The analysis of variance computations considered thus far have been limited to independent groups designs. This section considers the computations for analysis of variance of a repeated measures design with one independent variable.

Fictitious data for a hypothetical experiment using a repeated measures design is presented in Table B-9. The experiment involves the effect of a job candidate's physical attractiveness on judgments of the candidate's competence. The independent variable is the candidate's physical attractiveness; the dependent variable is judged competence on a 10-point scale. Subjects in the experiment view two videotapes of different females performing a mechanical aptitude task that involved piecing together a number of parts. Both females do equally well, but one is physically attractive while the other is unattractive. The order of presentation of the two tapes is counterbalanced to control for order effects.

The main difference between the repeated measures analysis of variance and the independent groups analysis described earlier is that the effect of subject differences becomes a source of variance. There are four sources of variance in the repeated measures analysis of variance, and so four sums of squares are calculated:

$$SS_{TOTAL} = \Sigma X^2 - \frac{G^2}{N}$$

$$SS_A = \frac{\Sigma T_a^2}{n_a} - \frac{G^2}{N}$$

$$SS_{SUBJECTS} = \frac{\Sigma T_s^2}{n_s} - \frac{G^2}{N}$$

$$SS_{ERROR} = SS_{TOTAL} - SS_A - SS_{SUBJECTS}$$

Table B–9 Data for hypothetical experiment on attractiveness and judged competence: Repeated measures analysis of variance

Subjects	Condition (A) Unattractive candidate (A1)	Attractive candidate (A2)	T_s	T_s^2
S#1	6	8	14	196
S#2	5	6	11	121
S#3	5	9	14	196
S#4	7	6	13	169
S#5	4	6	10	100
S#6	3	5	8	64
S#7	5	5	10	100
S#8	4	7	11	121
	$T_{A1} = 39$	$T_{A2} = 52$	$\Sigma T_s^2 = 1067$	
	$\Sigma X_{A1}^2 = 201$	$\Sigma X_{A2}^2 = 352$		
	$n_{A1} = 8$	$n_{A2} = 8$		
	$\overline{X}_{A1} = 4.88$	$\overline{X}_{A2} = 6.50$		

$$SS_{TOTAL} = \Sigma X^2 - \frac{G^2}{N} = (201 + 352) - \frac{(39 + 52)^2}{16}$$

$$= 553 - 517.56$$

$$= 35.44$$

$$SS_A = \frac{\Sigma T_a^2}{n_a} - \frac{G^2}{N} = \frac{(39)^2 + (52)^2}{8} - 517.56$$

$$= 528.13 - 517.56$$

$$= 10.57$$

$$SS_{SUBJECTS} = \frac{\Sigma T_s^2}{n_s} - \frac{G^2}{N} = \frac{1067}{2} - 517.56$$

$$= 533.50 - 517.56$$

$$= 15.94$$

$$SS_{ERROR} = SS_{TOTAL} - SS_A - SS_{SUBJECTS} = 35.44 - 10.57 - 15.94$$

$$= 8.93$$

The calculations for these sums of squares are shown in the lower portion of Table B-9. The quantities in the formulas should be familiar to you by now. The only new quantity involves the calculations of $SS_{SUBJECTS}$. The term T_s^2 refers to the squared total score of each subject—that is, the squared total of the scores which each subject gives when measured in the different groups in the experiment. The quantity ΣT_s^2 refers to the sum of these squared totals for all subjects. The calculations of $SS_{SUBJECTS}$ is completed by dividing ΣT_s^2 by n_s. The term n_s refers to the number of scores that each subject gives. Since our hypothetical experiment has two groups, $n_s = 2$. The total for each subject is based on two scores.

An analysis of variance summary table is shown in Table B-10. The procedures for computing the mean squares and obtaining F are similar to our previous calculations. Note that the mean square and F for the subjects' source of variance are not computed. There is usually no reason to know or care whether subjects differ significantly from each other. The ability to calculate this source of variance does have the advantage of reducing the amount of error variance—in an independent groups design, subject differences are part of the error variance. Because there is only one score per subject in the independent groups design, it is impossible to estimate the influence of subject differences.

Table B-10 Analysis of variance summary table: Repeated measures design

Source of variance	Sum of squares	df	Mean square	F
A	SS_A	$a - 1$	SS_A/df_A	MS_A/MS_{ERROR}
Subjects	$SS_{SUBJECTS}$	$s - 1$	—	
Error	SS_{ERROR}	$(a - 1)(s - 1)$	SS_{ERROR}/df_{ERROR}	
Total	SS_{TOTAL}	$N - 1$		
A	10.57	1	10.57	8.26
Subjects	15.94	7	—	
Error	8.93	7	1.28	
Total	35.44	15		

I'll leave it to you to use the summary table and the table of critical F values to determine whether the difference between the two groups is significant. The procedures are identical to those discussed previously.

Analysis of variance: Conclusion

The analysis of variance is a very useful test that can be extended to any type of factorial design, including those that use both independent groups and repeated measures in the same design. The method of computing analysis of variance is much the same regardless of the complexity of the design. A section on analysis of variance as brief as this cannot hope to cover all of the many aspects of such a general statistical technique. I hope, though, that you now have the background to compute an analysis of variance and to understand the more detailed discussions of analysis of variance in advanced statistics texts.

MEASURES OF STRENGTH OF ASSOCIATION

The final part of this appendix considers several measures of the strength of association between two variables. These measures are called *correlation coefficients*. Three correlation coefficients are considered: the contingency coefficient, the Spearman rank-order correlation coefficient, and the Pearson product-moment correlation coefficient.

Contingency coefficient

The contingency coefficient *(C)* is a measure of strength of association for nominal data. It is computed after obtaining the value of chi-square. The formula for C is

$$C = \sqrt{\frac{\chi^2}{N + \chi^2}}$$

Thus, the value of C for the sex and hand dominance study analyzed above (Table B-2) is

$$C = \sqrt{\frac{18}{100 + 18}} = \sqrt{.153} = .39$$

Since the significance of the obtained chi-square value has already been determined by using Table C-2 in Appendix C, no further significance testing of C is necessary.

Spearman rank-order correlation coefficient

The Spearman rank-order correlation coefficient *(rho)* is used to measure the strength of association between pairs of variables measured on an ordinal scale. In order to use *rho,* pairs of observations must be made on each subject. These observations must be in terms of ranks; if scores rather than ranks are obtained from each subject, the scores must be converted to ranks.

Example   Suppose you are interested in the dominance rankings of a group of boys in an institutional care setting. You wish to know whether the dominance ranks during the day shift are related to the dominance ranks during the night shift, when different staff members are present. To obtain pairs of observations, you determine the dominance rank of each boy during the day shift and again during the night shift.

Fictitious data for such a study, along with calculations for Spearman's *rho,* are presented in Table B-11. The seven subjects in the study were assigned

Table B-11   Data for hypothetical study on the relationship between dominance rank during the day and night shifts: Spearman *rho*

Subject (initials)	Rank during day shift	Rank during night shift	d	d^2
B.W.	2	1	1	1
G.N.	4	3	1	1
S.P.	1	2	−1	1
R.A.	6	5	1	1
D.G.	7	7	0	0
C.M.	5	6	−1	1
J.J.	3	4	−1	1
				$\Sigma d^2 = 6$

Computation: $rho = 1 - \dfrac{6\Sigma d^2}{N^3 - N} = 1 - \dfrac{(6)(6)}{343 - 7}$

$$= 1 - \frac{36}{336}$$

$$= 1 - .107$$

$$= .893$$

ranks ranging from 1 (highest in dominance) to 7 (lowest in dominance). The
calculational formula for *rho* is

$$rho = 1 - \frac{6\ \Sigma d^2}{N^3 - N}$$

where *d* is the difference between each subject's rank on the first observation and the rank on the second observation. The quantity d^2 is obtained by squaring each subject's rank difference The quantity Σd^2 is simply the total of all subjects' squared rank differences. *N* refers to the number of paired ranks, and N^3 is *N* cubed, or $N \times N \times N$. Once the value of *rho* has been obtained, the significance of *rho* can be determined.

Significance of rho   In order to test the null hypothesis that the correlation in the population is 0.00, we can consult a table of critical values of *rho*. Table C-5 in Appendix C shows critical values for .10, .05, and .01 significance levels. To use the table, find the critical value of *rho* for *N* the number of paired observations. The obtained value of *rho* must be greater than the critical value to be significant. The critical value at the .05 level for our example data (*N* = 7) is .786 (plus or minus). Since the obtained value of *rho* is larger than the critical value, we conclude that the dominance rankings are significantly correlated.

Pearson product-moment correlation coefficient

The Pearson product-moment correlation coefficient *(r)* is used to find the strength of the relationship between two variables that have been measured on interval scales.

Example   Suppose you want to know what variables are related to attendance of the meetings of sensitivity training (or growth) groups. You've noticed that some people regularly come to every meeting while others show up only occasionally. You decide to conduct a study on this problem. In your study, you measure participants in a sensitivity group on the variables of need for affiliation (a personality trait) and the number of meetings attended. The affiliation variable is measured by giving a personality test at the first meeting of a group that will meet weekly for fifteen weeks. During the fifteen-week period, you keep a record of the number of meetings attended by each participant. After obtaining the pairs of observations for each member of the group, a Pearson *r* can be computed to measure the strength of relationship between affiliation need and attendance at group meetings.

Table B-12 presents fictitious data from such a study along with the calculations for r. The calculational formula for r is

$$r = \frac{N\Sigma XY - \Sigma X\Sigma Y}{\sqrt{N\Sigma X^2 - (\Sigma X)^2} \sqrt{N\Sigma Y^2 - (\Sigma Y)^2}}$$

where X refers to a subject's score on variable X, and Y is a subject's score on variable Y. In Table B-12, the affiliation personality test score is variable X, and the attendance score is variable Y. In the formula, N is the number of paired observations (that is, the number of subjects measured on both variables).

The calculation of r involves a number of arithmetic operations on the X and Y scores. ΣX is simply the sum of the scores on variable X. ΣX^2 is the sum of the squared scores on X (each score is first squared and then the sum of the squared scores is obtained). The quantity $(\Sigma X)^2$ is the square of the sum of the scores: The total of the X scores (ΣX) is first calculated and then this total is squared. It is important to not confuse the two quantities, ΣX^2 and $(\Sigma X)^2$. The same calculations are made, using the Y scores, to obtain ΣY, ΣY^2, and $(\Sigma Y)^2$. To find ΣXY, each subject's X score is multiplied by the score on Y; these values are then summed for all subjects. Once these calculations have been made, r is computed by using the formula for r given above.

At this point, you may wish to carefully examine the calculations shown in Table B-12, to familiarize yourself with the procedures for computing r. You might then try calculating r from another set of data, such as the seating pattern and exam score study shown in Table 9-1 in Chapter 9.

Significance of r   To test the null hypothesis that the population correlation coefficient is in fact 0.00, we consult a table of critical values of r. Table C-5 in Appendix C shows critical values of r for .10, .05, and .01 levels of significance. To find the critical value, you first need to determine the degrees of freedom. The df for the significance test for r is $N - 2$. In our example study on affiliation and group attendance, the number of paired observations is 10, so the df = 8. For 8 degrees of freedom, the critical value of r at the .05 level of significance is .632 (plus or minus). The obtained r must be greater than the critical r to be significant. Since our obtained r (from Table B-12) of .567 is less than the critical value, we do not reject the null hypothesis.

Notice that we do not reject the null hypothesis in this case, even though the magnitude of r is fairly large. It is possible, however, that a significant correlation would be obtained with a larger sample size.

Table B-12   Data for hypothetical study on need for affiliation and attendance at group meetings: Pearson _r_

Subject identification number	Affiliation score (X)	Meetings attended (Y)	XY
01	4	10	40
02	6	15	90
03	7	8	56
04	8	9	72
05	8	7	56
06	12	10	120
07	14	15	210
08	15	13	195
09	15	15	225
10	17	14	238
	$\Sigma X = 106$	$\Sigma Y = 116$	$\Sigma XY = 1302$
	$\Sigma X^2 = 1308$	$\Sigma Y^2 = 1434$	
	$(\Sigma X)^2 = 11236$	$(\Sigma Y)^2 = 13456$	

Computation:

$$r = \frac{N\Sigma XY - \Sigma X \Sigma Y}{\sqrt{N\Sigma X^2 - (\Sigma X)^2}\ \sqrt{N\Sigma Y^2 - (\Sigma Y)^2}}$$

$$= \frac{10(1302) - (106)(116)}{\sqrt{10(1308) - 11236}\ \sqrt{10(1434) - 13456}}$$

$$= \frac{13020 - 12296}{\sqrt{13080 - 11236}\ \sqrt{14340 - 13456}}$$

$$= \frac{724}{\sqrt{1844}\ \sqrt{884}}$$

$$= \frac{724}{1276.61}$$

$$= .567$$

You now have a basis for computing a number of statistical tests. The basic calculations for these tests are not difficult, but the calculations become tedious with large amounts of data. The development of computer analysis of research data has reduced much of the labor involved in making the calculations. If you are planning to pursue advanced studies in the behavioral sciences, you will probably want to become familiar with the use of computers.

APPENDIX C
STATISTICAL TABLES

To obtain a series of random numbers, enter the table at any arbitrary point and read in sequence either across or down.

RANDOM ASSIGNMENT PROCEDURE

Order your subjects in some way. This could be by name or in order from first to last. Let's say that you have three groups and want five subjects per group, for a total of fifteen subjects. Below are fifteen subjects ordered from first to fifteenth. Enter the random number table and assign a number to each subject (if there is a duplicate number, ignore it and use the next number in the sequence). In the example below, the table was entered in the upper left-hand corner and was read in a down direction. Now assign subjects to groups: The five subjects who receive the lowest random numbers are assigned to group 1, the next five subjects are assigned to group 2, and the five subjects with the **259** highest numbers are assigned to group 3. These general procedures can be followed with any number of groups in an experiment.

Subject order	Random number	Group assignment
1	10	1
2	37	2
3	08	1
4	99	3
5	12	1
6	66	2
7	31	1
8	85	3
9	63	2
10	73	2
11	98	3
12	11	1
13	83	2
14	88	3
15	99	3

RANDOM SAMPLING

Obtain a list of all members of your population. Enter the random number table and assign a random number to each member of the population. Determine your desired sample size (N). Your sample, then, is comprised of the first N individuals. For example, if you want to take a random sample of 15 faculty at your school, use the random number table to give each faculty member a number. The fifteen faculty with the lowest numbers would be selected for the sample.

Table C-1   Random numbers

```
10 09 73 25 33   76 52 01 35 86   34 67 35 48 76   80 95 90 91 17   39 29 27 49 45
37 54 20 48 05   64 89 47 42 96   24 80 52 40 37   20 63 61 04 02   00 82 29 16 65
08 42 26 89 53   19 64 50 93 03   23 20 90 25 60   15 95 33 47 64   35 08 03 36 06
99 01 90 25 29   09 37 67 07 15   38 31 13 11 65   88 67 67 43 97   04 43 62 76 59
12 80 79 99 70   80 15 73 61 47   64 03 23 66 53   98 95 11 68 77   12 17 17 68 33

66 06 57 47 17   34 07 27 68 50   36 69 73 61 70   65 81 33 98 85   11 19 92 91 70
31 06 01 08 05   45 57 18 24 06   35 30 34 26 14   86 79 90 74 39   23 40 30 97 32
85 26 97 76 02   02 05 16 56 92   68 66 57 48 18   73 05 38 52 47   18 62 38 85 79
63 57 33 21 35   05 32 54 70 48   90 55 35 75 48   28 46 82 87 09   83 49 12 56 24
73 79 64 57 53   03 52 96 47 78   35 80 83 42 82   60 93 52 03 44   35 27 38 84 35

98 52 01 77 67   14 90 56 86 07   22 10 94 05 58   60 97 09 34 33   50 50 07 39 98
11 80 50 54 31   39 80 82 77 32   50 72 56 82 48   29 40 52 42 01   52 77 56 78 51
83 45 29 96 34   06 28 89 80 83   13 74 67 00 78   18 47 54 06 10   68 71 17 78 17
88 68 54 02 00   86 50 75 84 01   36 76 66 79 51   90 36 47 64 93   29 60 91 10 62
99 59 46 73 48   87 51 76 49 69   91 82 60 89 28   93 78 56 13 68   23 47 83 41 13

65 48 11 76 74   17 46 85 09 50   58 04 77 69 74   73 03 95 71 86   40 21 81 65 44
80 12 43 56 35   17 72 70 80 15   45 31 82 23 74   21 11 57 82 53   14 38 55 37 63
74 35 09 98 17   77 40 27 72 14   43 23 60 02 10   45 52 16 42 37   96 28 60 26 55
69 91 62 68 03   66 25 22 91 48   36 93 68 72 03   76 62 11 39 90   94 40 05 64 18
09 89 32 05 05   14 22 56 85 14   46 42 75 67 88   96 29 77 88 22   54 38 21 45 98

91 49 91 45 23   68 47 92 76 86   46 16 28 35 54   94 75 08 99 23   37 08 92 00 48
80 33 69 45 98   26 94 03 68 58   70 29 73 41 35   53 14 03 33 40   42 05 08 23 41
44 10 48 19 49   85 15 74 79 54   32 97 92 65 75   57 60 04 08 81   22 22 20 64 13
12 55 07 37 42   11 10 00 20 40   12 86 07 46 97   96 64 48 94 39   28 70 72 58 15
63 60 64 93 29   16 50 53 44 84   40 21 95 25 63   43 65 17 70 82   07 20 73 17 90

61 19 69 04 46   26 45 74 77 74   51 92 43 37 29   65 39 45 95 93   42 58 26 05 27
15 47 44 52 66   95 27 07 99 53   59 36 78 38 48   82 39 61 01 18   33 21 15 94 66
94 55 72 85 73   67 89 75 43 87   54 62 24 44 31   91 19 04 25 92   92 92 74 59 73
42 48 11 62 13   97 34 40 87 21   16 86 84 87 67   03 07 11 20 59   25 70 14 66 70
23 52 37 83 17   73 20 88 98 37   68 93 59 14 16   26 25 22 96 63   05 52 28 25 62

04 49 35 24 94   75 24 63 38 24   45 86 25 10 25   61 96 27 93 35   65 33 71 24 72
00 54 99 76 54   64 05 18 81 59   96 11 96 38 96   54 69 28 23 91   23 28 72 95 29
35 96 31 53 07   26 89 80 93 54   33 35 13 54 62   77 97 45 00 24   90 10 33 93 33
59 80 80 83 91   45 42 72 68 42   83 60 94 97 00   13 02 12 48 92   78 56 52 01 06
46 05 88 52 36   01 39 09 22 86   77 28 14 40 77   93 91 08 36 47   70 61 74 29 41

32 17 90 05 97   87 37 92 52 41   05 56 70 70 07   86 74 31 71 57   85 39 41 18 38
69 23 46 14 06   20 11 74 52 04   15 95 66 00 00   18 74 39 24 23   97 11 89 63 38
19 56 54 14 30   01 75 87 53 79   40 41 92 15 85   66 67 43 68 06   84 96 28 52 07
45 15 51 49 38   19 47 60 72 46   43 66 79 45 43   59 04 79 00 33   20 82 66 95 41
94 86 43 19 94   36 16 81 08 51   34 88 88 15 53   01 54 03 54 56   05 01 45 11 76
```

Source: From tables of the Rand Corporation from *A Million Random Digits with 100,000 Normal Deviates* (New York: The Free Press, 1955) by permission of the Rand Corporation.

Table C-1   Random numbers (continued)

09	18	82	00	97	32	82	53	95	27	04	22	08	63	04	83	38	98	73	74	64	27	85	80	44
90	04	58	54	97	51	98	15	06	54	94	93	88	19	97	91	87	07	61	50	68	47	66	46	59
73	18	95	02	07	47	67	72	62	69	62	29	06	44	64	27	12	46	70	18	41	36	18	27	60
75	76	87	64	90	20	97	18	17	49	90	42	91	22	72	95	37	50	58	71	93	82	34	31	78
54	01	64	40	56	66	28	13	10	03	00	68	22	73	98	20	71	45	32	95	07	70	61	78	13
08	35	86	99	10	78	54	24	27	85	13	66	15	88	73	04	61	89	75	53	31	22	30	84	20
28	30	60	32	64	81	33	31	05	91	40	51	00	78	93	32	60	46	04	75	94	11	90	18	40
53	84	08	62	33	81	59	41	36	28	51	21	59	02	90	28	46	66	87	95	77	76	22	07	91
91	75	75	37	41	61	61	36	22	69	50	26	39	02	12	55	78	17	65	14	83	48	34	70	55
89	41	59	26	94	00	39	75	83	91	12	60	71	76	46	48	94	97	23	06	94	54	13	74	08
77	51	30	38	20	86	83	42	99	01	68	41	48	27	74	51	90	81	39	80	72	89	35	55	07
19	50	23	71	74	69	97	92	02	88	55	21	02	97	73	74	28	77	52	51	65	34	46	74	15
21	81	85	93	13	93	27	88	17	57	05	68	67	31	56	07	08	28	50	46	31	85	33	84	52
51	47	46	64	99	68	10	72	36	21	94	04	99	13	45	42	83	60	91	91	08	00	74	54	49
99	55	96	83	31	62	53	52	41	70	69	77	71	28	30	74	81	97	81	42	43	86	07	28	34
33	71	34	80	07	93	58	47	28	69	51	92	66	47	21	58	30	32	98	22	93	17	49	39	72
85	27	48	68	93	11	30	32	92	70	28	83	43	41	37	73	51	59	04	00	71	14	84	36	43
84	13	38	96	40	44	03	55	21	66	73	85	27	00	91	61	22	26	05	61	62	32	71	84	23
56	73	21	62	34	17	39	59	61	31	10	12	39	16	22	85	49	65	75	60	81	60	41	88	80
65	13	85	68	06	87	64	88	52	61	34	31	36	58	61	45	87	52	10	69	85	64	44	72	77
38	00	10	21	76	81	71	91	17	11	71	60	29	29	37	74	21	96	40	49	65	58	44	96	98
37	40	29	63	97	01	30	47	75	86	56	27	11	00	86	47	32	46	26	05	40	03	03	74	38
97	12	54	03	48	87	08	33	14	17	21	81	53	92	50	75	23	76	20	47	15	50	12	95	78
21	82	64	11	34	47	14	33	40	72	64	63	88	59	02	49	13	90	64	41	03	85	65	45	52
73	13	54	27	42	95	71	90	90	35	85	79	47	42	96	08	78	98	81	56	64	69	11	92	02
07	63	87	79	29	03	06	11	80	72	96	20	74	41	56	23	82	19	95	38	04	71	36	69	94
60	52	88	34	41	07	95	41	98	14	59	17	52	06	95	05	53	35	21	39	61	21	20	64	55
83	59	63	56	55	06	95	89	29	83	05	12	80	97	19	77	43	35	37	83	92	30	15	04	98
10	85	06	27	46	99	59	91	05	07	13	49	90	63	19	53	07	57	18	39	06	41	01	93	62
39	82	09	89	52	43	62	26	31	47	64	42	18	08	14	43	80	00	93	51	31	02	47	31	67
59	58	00	64	78	75	56	97	88	00	88	83	55	44	86	23	76	80	61	56	04	11	10	84	08
38	50	80	73	41	23	79	34	87	63	90	82	29	70	22	17	71	90	42	07	95	95	44	99	53
30	69	27	06	68	94	68	81	61	27	56	19	68	00	91	82	06	76	34	00	05	46	26	92	00
65	44	39	56	59	18	28	82	74	37	49	63	22	40	41	08	33	76	56	76	96	29	99	08	36
27	26	75	02	64	13	19	27	22	94	07	47	74	46	06	17	98	54	89	11	97	34	13	03	58
91	30	70	69	91	19	07	22	42	10	36	69	95	37	28	28	82	53	57	93	28	97	66	62	52
68	43	49	46	88	84	47	31	36	22	62	12	69	84	08	12	84	38	25	90	09	81	59	31	46
48	90	81	58	77	54	74	52	45	91	35	70	00	47	54	83	82	45	26	92	54	13	05	51	60
06	91	34	51	97	42	67	27	86	01	11	88	30	95	28	63	01	19	89	01	14	97	44	03	44
10	45	51	60	19	14	21	03	37	12	91	34	23	78	21	88	32	58	08	51	43	66	77	08	83
12	88	39	73	43	65	02	76	11	84	04	28	50	13	92	17	97	41	50	77	90	71	22	67	69
21	77	83	09	76	38	80	73	69	61	31	64	94	20	96	63	28	10	20	23	08	81	64	74	49
19	52	35	95	15	65	12	25	96	59	86	28	36	82	58	69	57	21	37	98	16	43	59	15	29
67	24	55	26	70	35	58	31	65	63	79	24	68	66	86	76	46	33	42	22	26	65	59	08	02
60	58	44	73	77	07	50	03	79	92	45	13	42	65	29	26	76	08	36	37	41	32	64	43	44

Table C-2   Critical values of chi-square

Degrees of freedom	Probability level		
	.10	.05	.01
1	2.706	3.841	6.635
2	4.605	5.991	9.210
3	6.251	7.815	11.345
4	7.779	9.488	13.277
5	9.236	11.070	15.086
6	10.645	12.592	16.812
7	12.017	14.067	18.475
8	13.362	15.507	20.090
9	14.684	16.919	21.666
10	15.987	18.307	23.209
11	17.275	19.675	24.725
12	18.549	21.026	26.217
13	19.812	22.362	27.688
14	21.064	23.685	29.141
15	22.307	24.996	30.578
16	23.542	26.296	32.000
17	24.769	27.587	33.409
18	25.989	28.869	34.805
19	27.204	30.144	36.191
20	28.412	31.410	37.566

Source: Table adapted from Fisher and Yates, *Statistical Tables for Biological, Agricultural, and Medical Research.* 6th ed. London: Longman, 1974. Reprinted by permission.

Table C-3   Critical values of the Mann-Whitney *U*

(A)
.10 probability level

N_2 \ N_1	7	8	9	10	11	12	13	14	15	16	17	18	19	20
3	2	3	3	4	5	5	6	7	7	8	9	9	10	11
4	4	5	6	7	8	9	10	11	12	14	15	16	17	18
5	6	8	9	11	12	13	15	16	18	19	20	22	23	25
6	8	10	12	14	16	17	19	21	23	25	26	28	30	32
7	11	13	15	17	19	21	24	26	28	30	33	35	37	39
8	13	15	18	20	23	26	28	31	33	36	39	41	44	47
9	15	18	21	24	27	30	33	36	39	42	45	48	51	54
10	17	20	24	27	31	34	37	41	44	48	51	55	58	62
11	19	23	27	31	34	38	42	46	50	54	57	61	65	69
12	21	26	30	34	38	42	47	51	55	60	64	68	72	77
13	24	28	33	37	42	47	51	56	61	65	70	75	80	84
14	26	31	36	41	46	51	56	61	66	71	77	82	87	92
15	28	33	39	44	50	55	61	66	72	77	83	88	94	100
16	30	36	42	48	54	60	65	71	77	83	89	95	101	107
17	33	39	45	51	57	64	70	77	83	89	96	102	109	115
18	35	41	48	55	61	68	75	82	88	95	102	109	116	123
19	37	44	51	58	65	72	80	87	94	101	109	116	123	130
20	39	47	54	62	69	77	84	92	100	107	115	123	130	138

Table C-3 Critical values of the Mann-Whitney *U* (continued)

(B)
.05 probability level

N_2 \ N_1	7	8	9	10	11	12	13	14	15	16	17	18	19	20
3	1	2	2	3	3	4	4	5	5	6	6	7	7	8
4	3	4	4	5	6	7	8	9	10	11	11	12	13	13
5	5	6	7	8	9	11	12	13	14	15	17	18	19	20
6	6	8	10	11	13	14	16	17	19	21	22	24	25	27
7	8	10	12	14	16	18	20	22	24	26	28	30	32	34
8	10	13	15	17	19	22	24	26	29	31	34	36	38	41
9	12	15	17	20	23	26	28	31	34	37	39	42	45	48
10	14	17	20	23	26	29	33	36	39	42	45	48	52	55
11	16	19	23	26	30	33	37	40	44	47	51	55	58	62
12	18	22	26	29	33	37	41	45	49	53	57	61	65	69
13	20	24	28	33	37	41	45	50	54	59	63	67	72	76
14	22	26	31	36	40	45	50	55	59	64	67	74	78	83
15	24	29	34	39	44	49	54	59	64	70	75	80	85	90
16	26	31	37	42	47	53	59	64	70	75	81	86	92	98
17	28	34	39	45	51	57	63	67	75	81	87	93	99	105
18	30	36	42	48	55	61	67	74	80	86	93	99	106	112
19	32	38	45	52	58	65	72	78	85	92	99	106	113	119
20	34	41	48	55	62	69	76	83	90	98	105	112	119	127

Table C-3   Critical values of the Mann-Whitney U (continued)

(C)
.01 probability level

N_2 \ N_1	7	8	9	10	11	12	13	14	15	16	17	18	19	20
3	-	-	0	0	0	1	1	1	2	2	2	2	3	3
4	0	1	1	2	2	3	3	4	5	5	6	6	7	8
5	1	2	3	4	5	6	7	7	8	9	10	11	12	13
6	3	4	5	6	7	9	10	11	12	13	15	16	17	18
7	4	6	7	9	10	12	13	15	16	18	19	21	22	24
8	6	7	9	11	13	15	17	18	20	22	24	26	28	30
9	7	9	11	13	16	18	20	22	24	27	29	31	33	36
10	9	11	13	16	18	21	24	26	29	31	34	37	39	42
11	10	13	16	18	21	24	27	30	33	36	39	42	45	48
12	12	15	18	21	24	27	31	34	37	41	44	47	51	54
13	13	17	20	24	27	31	34	38	42	45	49	53	56	60
14	15	18	22	26	30	34	38	42	46	50	54	58	63	67
15	16	20	24	29	33	37	42	46	51	55	60	64	69	73
16	18	22	27	31	36	41	45	50	55	60	65	70	74	79
17	19	24	29	34	39	44	49	54	60	65	70	75	81	86
18	21	26	31	37	42	47	53	58	64	70	75	81	87	92
19	22	28	33	39	45	51	56	63	69	74	81	87	93	99
20	24	30	36	42	48	54	60	67	73	79	86	92	99	105

Table C-4   Critical values of F

df for denominator	α	\multicolumn{12}{c}{df for numerator}
		1	2	3	4	5	6	7	8	9	10	11	12
1	.25	5.83	7.50	8.20	8.58	8.82	8.98	9.10	9.19	9.26	9.32	9.36	9.41
	.10	39.9	49.5	53.6	55.8	57.2	58.2	58.9	59.4	59.9	60.2	60.5	60.7
	.05	161	200	216	225	230	234	237	239	241	242	243	244
2	.25	2.57	3.00	3.15	3.23	3.28	3.31	3.34	3.35	3.37	3.38	3.39	3.39
	.10	8.53	9.00	9.16	9.24	9.29	9.33	9.35	9.37	9.38	9.39	9.40	9.41
	.05	18.5	19.0	19.2	19.2	19.3	19.3	19.4	19.4	19.4	19.4	19.4	19.4
	.01	98.5	99.0	99.2	99.2	99.3	99.3	99.4	99.4	99.4	99.4	99.4	99.4
3	.25	2.02	2.28	2.36	2.39	2.41	2.42	2.43	2.44	2.44	2.44	2.45	2.45
	.10	5.54	5.46	5.39	5.34	5.31	5.28	5.27	5.25	5.24	5.23	5.22	5.22
	.05	10.1	9.55	9.28	9.12	9.01	8.94	8.89	8.85	8.81	8.79	8.76	8.74
	.01	34.1	30.8	29.5	28.7	28.2	27.9	27 7	27.5	27.3	27.2	27.1	27.1
4	.25	1.81	2.00	2.05	2.06	2.07	2.08	2.08	2.08	2.08	2.08	2.08	2.08
	.10	4.54	4.32	4.19	4.11	4.05	4.01	3.98	3.95	3.94	3.92	3.91	3.90
	.05	7.71	6.94	6.59	6.39	6.26	6.16	6.09	6.04	6.00	5.96	5.94	5.91
	.01	21.2	18.0	16.7	16.0	15.5	15.2	15.0	14.8	14.7	14.5	14.4	14.4
5	.25	1.69	1.85	1.88	1.89	1.89	1.89	1.89	1.89	1.89	1.89	1.89	1.89
	.10	4.06	3.78	3.62	3.52	3.45	3.40	3.37	3.34	3.32	3.30	3.28	3.27
	.05	6.61	5.79	5.41	5.19	5.05	4.95	4.88	4.82	4.77	4.74	4.71	4.68
	.01	16.3	13.3	12.1	11.4	11.0	10.7	10.5	10.3	10.2	10.1	9.96	9.89
6	.25	1.62	1.76	1.78	1.79	1.79	1.78	1.78	1.78	1.77	1.77	1.77	1.77
	.10	3.78	3.46	3.29	3.18	3.11	3.05	3.01	2.98	2.96	2.94	2.92	2.90
	.05	5.99	5.14	4.76	4.53	4.39	4.28	4.21	4.15	4.10	4.06	4.03	4.00
	.01	13.7	10.9	9.78	9.15	8.75	8.47	8.26	8.10	7.98	7.87	7.79	7.72
7	.25	1.57	1.70	1.72	1.72	1.71	1.71	1.70	1.70	1.69	1.69	1.69	1.68
	.10	3.59	3.26	3.07	2.96	2.88	2.83	2.78	2.75	2.72	2.70	2.68	2.67
	.05	5.59	4.74	4.35	4.12	3.97	3.87	3.79	3.73	3.68	3.64	3.60	3.57
	.01	12.2	9.55	8.45	7.85	7.46	7.19	6.99	6.84	6.72	6.62	6.54	6.47
8	.25	1.54	1.66	1.67	1.66	1.66	1.65	1.64	1.64	1.63	1.63	1.63	1.62
	.10	3.46	3.11	2.92	2.81	2.73	2.67	2.62	2.59	2.56	2.54	2.52	2.50
	.05	5.32	4.46	4.07	3.84	3.69	3.58	3.50	3.44	3.39	3.35	3.31	3.28
	.01	11.3	8.65	7.59	7.01	6.63	6.37	6.18	6.03	5.91	5.81	5.73	5.67
9	.25	1.51	1.62	1.63	1.63	1.62	1.61	1.60	1.60	1.59	1.59	1.58	1.58
	.10	3.36	3.01	2.81	2.69	2.61	2.55	2.51	2.47	2.44	2.42	2.40	2.38
	.05	5.12	4.26	3.86	3.63	3.48	3.37	3.29	3.23	3.18	3.14	3.10	3.07
	.01	10.6	8.02	6.99	6.42	6.06	5.80	5.61	5.47	5.35	5.26	5.18	5.11
10	.25	1.49	1.60	1.60	1.59	1.59	1.58	1.57	1.56	1.56	1.55	1.55	1.54
	.10	3.29	2.92	2.73	2.61	2.52	2.46	2.41	2.38	2.35	2.32	2.30	2.28
	.05	4.96	4.10	3.71	3.48	3.33	3.22	3.14	3.07	3.02	2.98	2.94	2.91
	.01	10.0	7.56	6.55	5.99	5.64	5.39	5.20	5.06	4.94	4.85	4.77	4.71

Table C-4   Critical values of F   (continued)

df for denominator	α	\(df for numerator\) 1	2	3	4	5	6	7	8	9	10	11	12
11	.25	1.47	1.58	1.58	1.57	1.56	1.55	1.54	1.53	1.53	1.52	1.52	1.51
	.10	3.23	2.86	2.66	2.54	2.45	2.39	2.34	2.30	2.27	2.25	2.23	2.21
	.05	4.84	3.98	3.59	3.36	3.20	3.09	3.01	2.95	2.90	2.85	2.82	2.79
	.01	9.65	7.21	6.22	5.67	5.32	5.07	4.89	4.74	4.63	4.54	4.46	4.40
12	.25	1.46	1.56	1.56	1.55	1.54	1.53	1.52	1.51	1.51	1.50	1.50	1.49
	.10	3.18	2.81	2.61	2.48	2.39	2.33	2.28	2.24	2.21	2.19	2.17	2.15
	.05	4.75	3.89	3.49	3.26	3.11	3.00	2.91	2.85	2.80	2.75	2.72	2.69
	.01	9.33	6.93	5.95	5.41	5.06	4.82	4.64	4.50	4.39	4.30	4.22	4.16
13	.25	1.45	1.55	1.55	1.53	1.52	1.51	1.50	1.49	1.49	1.48	1.47	1.47
	.10	3.14	2.76	2.56	2.43	2.35	2.28	2.23	2.20	2.16	2.14	2.12	2.10
	.05	4.67	3.81	3.41	3.18	3.03	2.92	2.83	2.77	2.71	2.67	2.63	2.60
	.01	9.07	6.70	5.74	5.21	4.86	4.62	4.44	4.30	4.19	4.10	4.02	3.96
14	.25	1.44	1.53	1.53	1.52	1.51	1.50	1.49	1.48	1.47	1.46	1.46	1.45
	.10	3.10	2.73	2.52	2.39	2.31	2.24	2.19	2.15	2.12	2.10	2.08	2.05
	.05	4.60	3.74	3.34	3.11	2.96	2.85	2.76	2.70	2.65	2.60	2.57	2.53
	.01	8.86	6.51	5.56	5.04	4.69	4.46	4.28	4.14	4.03	3.94	3.86	3.80
15	.25	1.43	1.52	1.52	1.51	1.49	1.48	1.47	1.46	1.46	1.45	1.44	1.44
	.10	3.07	2.70	2.49	2.36	2.27	2.21	2.16	2.12	2.09	2.06	2.04	2.02
	.05	4.54	3.68	3.29	3.06	2.90	2.79	2.71	2.64	2.59	2.54	2.51	2.48
	.01	8.68	6.36	5.42	4.89	4.56	4.32	4.14	4.00	3.89	3.80	3.73	3.67
16	.25	1.42	1.51	1.51	1.50	1.48	1.47	1.46	1.45	1.44	1.44	1.44	1.43
	.10	3.05	2.67	2.46	2.33	2.24	2.18	2.13	2.09	2.06	2.03	2.01	1.99
	.05	4.49	3.63	3.24	3.01	2.85	2.74	2.66	2.59	2.54	2.49	2.46	2.42
	.01	8.53	6.23	5.29	4.77	4.44	4.20	4.03	3.89	3.78	3.69	3.62	3.55
17	.25	1.42	1.51	1.50	1.49	1.47	1.46	1.45	1.44	1.43	1.43	1.42	1.41
	.10	3.03	2.64	2.44	2.31	2.22	2.15	2.10	2.06	2.03	2.00	1.98	1.96
	.05	4.45	3.59	3.20	2.96	2.81	2.70	2.61	2.55	2.49	2.45	2.41	2.38
	.01	8.40	6.11	5.18	4.67	4.34	4.10	3.93	3.79	3.68	3.59	3.52	3.46
18	.25	1.41	1.50	1.49	1.48	1.46	1.45	1.44	1.43	1.42	1.42	1.41	1.40
	.10	3.01	2.62	2.42	2.29	2.20	2.13	2.08	2.04	2.00	1.98	1.96	1.93
	.05	4.41	3.55	3.16	2.93	2.77	2.66	2.58	2.51	2.46	2.41	2.37	2.34
	.01	8.29	6.01	5.09	4.58	4.25	4.01	3.84	3.71	3.60	3.51	3.43	3.37
19	.25	1.41	1.49	1.49	1.47	1.46	1.44	1.43	1.42	1.41	1.41	1.40	1.40
	.10	2.99	2.61	2.40	2.27	2.18	2.11	2.06	2.02	1.98	1.96	1.94	1.91
	.05	4.38	3.52	3.13	2.90	2.74	2.63	2.54	2.48	2.42	2.38	2.34	2.31
	.01	8.18	5.93	5.01	4.50	4.17	3.94	3.77	3.63	3.52	3.43	3.36	3.30
20	.25	1.40	1.49	1.48	1.46	1.45	1.44	1.43	1.42	1.41	1.40	1.39	1.39
	.10	2.97	2.59	2.38	2.25	2.16	2.09	2.04	2.00	1.96	1.94	1.92	1.89
	.05	4.35	3.49	3.10	2.87	2.71	2.60	2.51	2.45	2.39	2.35	2.31	2.28
	.01	8.10	5.85	4.94	4.43	4.10	3.87	3.70	3.56	3.46	3.37	3.29	3.23

Table C-4 Critical values of F (continued)

df for denominator	α	\multicolumn{12}{c}{df for numerator}
		1	2	3	4	5	6	7	8	9	10	11	12
22	.25	1.40	1.48	1.47	1.45	1.44	1.42	1.41	1.40	1.39	1.39	1.38	1.37
	.10	2.95	2.56	2.35	2.22	2.13	2.06	2.01	1.97	1.93	1.90	1.88	1.86
	.05	4.30	3.44	3.05	2.82	2.66	2.55	2.46	2.40	2.34	2.30	2.26	2.23
	.01	7.95	5.72	4.82	4.31	3.99	3.76	3.59	3.45	3.35	3.26	3.18	3.12
24	.25	1.39	1.47	1.46	1.44	1.43	1.41	1.40	1.39	1.38	1.38	1.37	1.36
	.10	2.93	2.54	2.33	2.19	2.10	2.04	1.98	1.94	1.91	1.88	1.85	1.83
	.05	4.26	3.40	3.01	2.78	2.62	2.51	2.42	2.36	2.30	2.25	2.21	2.18
	.01	7.82	5.61	4.72	4.22	3.90	3.67	3.50	3.36	3.26	3.17	3.09	3.03
26	.25	1.38	1.46	1.45	1.44	1.42	1.41	1.39	1.38	1.37	1.37	1.36	1.35
	.10	2.91	2.52	2.31	2.17	2.08	2.01	1.96	1.92	1.88	1.86	1.84	1.81
	.05	4.23	3.37	2.98	2.74	2.59	2.47	2.39	2.32	2.27	2.22	2.18	2.15
	.01	7.72	5.53	4.64	4.14	3.82	3.59	3.42	3.29	3.18	3.09	3.02	2.96
28	.25	1.38	1.46	1.45	1.43	1.41	1.40	1.39	1.38	1.37	1.36	1.35	1.34
	.10	2.89	2.50	2.29	2.16	2.06	2.00	1.94	1.90	1.87	1.84	1.81	1.79
	.05	4.20	3.34	2.95	2.71	2.56	2.45	2.36	2.29	2.24	2.19	2.15	2.12
	.01	7.64	5.45	4.57	4.07	3.75	3.53	3.36	3.23	3.12	3.03	2.96	2.90
30	.25	1.38	1.45	1.44	1.42	1.41	1.39	1.38	1.37	1.36	1.35	1.35	1.34
	.10	2.88	2.49	2.28	2.14	2.05	1.98	1.93	1.88	1.85	1.82	1.79	1.77
	.05	4.17	3.32	2.92	2.69	2.53	2.42	2.33	2.27	2.21	2.16	2.13	2.09
	.01	7.56	5.39	4.51	4.02	3.70	3.47	3.30	3.17	3.07	2.98	2.91	2.84
40	.25	1.36	1.44	1.42	1.40	1.39	1.37	1.36	1.35	1.34	1.33	1.32	1.31
	.10	2.84	2.44	2.23	2.09	2.00	1.93	1.87	1.83	1.79	1.76	1.73	1.71
	.05	4.08	3.23	2.84	2.61	2.45	2.34	2.25	2.18	2.12	2.08	2.04	2.00
	.01	7.31	5.18	4.31	3.83	3.51	3.29	3.12	2.99	2.89	2.80	2.73	2.66
60	.25	1.35	1.42	1.41	1.38	1.37	1.35	1.33	1.32	1.31	1.30	1.29	1.29
	.10	2.79	2.39	2.18	2.04	1.95	1.87	1.82	1.77	1.74	1.71	1.68	1.66
	.05	4.00	3.15	2.76	2.53	2.37	2.25	2.17	2.10	2.04	1.99	1.95	1.92
	.01	7.08	4.98	4.13	3.65	3.34	3.12	2.95	2.82	2.72	2.63	2.56	2.50
120	.25	1.34	1.40	1.39	1.37	1.35	1.33	1.31	1.30	1.29	1.28	1.27	1.26
	.10	2.75	2.35	2.13	1.99	1.90	1.82	1.77	1.72	1.68	1.65	1.62	1.60
	.05	3.92	3.07	2.68	2.45	2.29	2.17	2.09	2.02	1.96	1.91	1.87	1.83
	.01	6.85	4.79	3.95	3.48	3.17	2.96	2.79	2.66	2.56	2.47	2.40	2.34
200	.25	1.33	1.39	1.38	1.36	1.34	1.32	1.31	1.29	1.28	1.27	1.26	1.25
	.10	2.73	2.33	2.11	1.97	1.88	1.80	1.75	1.70	1.66	1.63	1.60	1.57
	.05	3.89	3.04	2.65	2.42	2.26	2.14	2.06	1.98	1.93	1.88	1.84	1.80
	.01	6.76	4.71	3.88	3.41	3.11	2.89	2.73	2.60	2.50	2.41	2.34	2.27
∞	.25	1.32	1.39	1.37	1.35	1.33	1.31	1.29	1.28	1.27	1.25	1.24	1.24
	.10	2.71	2.30	2.08	1.94	1.85	1.77	1.72	1.67	1.63	1.60	1.57	1.55
	.05	3.84	3.00	2.60	2.37	2.21	2.10	2.01	1.94	1.88	1.83	1.79	1.75
	.01	6.63	4.61	3.78	3.32	3.02	2.80	2.64	2.51	2.41	2.32	2.25	2.18

Table C-5   Critical values of *Rho* (Spearman rank-order correlation coefficient)

N	.10	.05	.01
	Level of Significance α†		
5	.90	1.00	
6	.83	.89	1.00
7	.71	.79	.93
8	.64	.74	·.88
9	.60	.68	.83
10	.56	.65	.79
11	.52	.61	.77
12	.50	.59	.75
13	.47	.56	.71
14	.46	.54	.69
15	.44	.52	.66
16	.42	.51	.64
17	.41	.49	.62
18	.40	.48	.61
19	.39	.46	.60
20	.38	.45	.58
21	.37	.44	.56
22	.36	.43	.55
23	.35	.42	.54
24	.34	.41	.53
25	.34	.40	.52
26	.33	.39	.51
27	.32	.38	.50
28	.32	.38	.49
29	.31	.37	.48
30	.31	.36	.47

†α is halved for a one-sided test.

Table C-6   Critical values of *r* (Pearson product-moment correlation coefficient)

df	Level of significance for two-tailed test		
	.10	.05	.01
1	.988	.997	.9999
2	.900	.950	.990
3	.805	.878	.959
4	.729	.811	.917
5	.669	.754	.874
6	.622	.707	.834
7	.582	.666	.798
8	.549	.632	.765
9	.521	.602	.735
10	.497	.576	.708
11	.476	.553	.684
12	.458	.532	.661
13	.441	.514	.641
14	.426	.497	.623
15	.412	.482	.606
16	.400	.468	.590
17	.389	.456	.575
18	.378	.444	.561
19	.369	.433	.549
20	.360	.423	.537
25	.323	.381	.487
30	.296	.349	.449
35	.275	.325	.418
40	.257	.304	.393
45	.243	.288	.372
50	.231	.273	.354
60	.211	.250	.325
70	.195	.232	.303
80	.183	.217	.283
90	.173	.205	.267
100	.164	.195	.254

Source: Table adapted from R. A. Fisher, *Statistical Methods for Research Workers.* 14th ed. New York: Hafner Press, 1973. Reprinted by permission.

GLOSSARY

Archival data
Currently existing sources of information that are available to a researcher.

Area sampling
The random selection of a sample of geographic areas from a population of such areas.

Assumed consent
An alternative to informed consent in deception research. Consent is assumed on the basis of high rates of consent among subjects given accurate information about the experiment.

Carry-over effect
A problem that may occur in repeated measures designs if the effects of one treatment are still present when the next treatment is given.

Central tendency
A single number or value that describes the typical or central score among a set of scores.

Conceptual replication
Replication of research using different procedures for manipulating or measuring the variables.

Confederate
A person posing as a subject in an experiment who is actually part of the experiment. **273**

Confounding
Failure to control for the effects of a third variable in an experimental design.

Construct validity
The degree to which a measurement device accurately measures the theoretical construct it is designed to measure.

Correlation coefficient
An index of how strongly two variables are related to each other in a group of subjects.

Correlational method
A method of determining whether two variables are related by measurement or observation of the variables.

Counterbalancing
A method of controlling for order effects in a repeated measures design by either including all orders of treatment presentation or randomly determining the order for each subject.

Criterion validity
The degree to which a measurement device accurately predicts behavior on a criterion measure.

Cross-cultural research
Research that studies the relationship between variables across different cultures.

Debriefing
Explanation of the purposes of the research that is given to subjects following their participation in the research.

Degrees of freedom (df)
The number of observations that are free to vary given that there are certain restrictions placed on the set of observations.

Demand characteristics
Cues that inform the subject how he or she is expected to behave.

Dependent variable
The variable that is the subject's response to, and dependent upon, the level of the manipulated independent variable.

Electroencephalograph (EEG)
An apparatus that measures the electrical activity of the brain.

Error variance
Random variability in a set of scores that is not the result of the independent variable. Statistically, the variability of each score from its group mean.

Experimental method
A method of determining whether variables are related in which the researcher manipulates the independent variable and controls all other variables either by randomization or by direct experimental control.

Experimenter bias (expectancy)

Any intentional or unintentional influence that the experimenter exerts upon subjects in order to confirm the hypothesis under investigation.

External validity

The degree to which the results of an experiment may be generalized.

F test (analysis of variance)

A statistical significance test for determining whether two or more means are significantly different. F is the ratio of systematic variance to error variance.

Face validity

The degree to which a measurement device appears to accurately measure a variable.

Factorial design

A design in which all levels of each independent variable are combined with all levels of the other independent variables. A factorial design allows investigation of the separate main effects and interactions of two or more independent variables.

Filler items

Items included in a questionnaire measure to help disguise the true purpose of the measure.

Frequency distribution

An arrangement of a set of scores from lowest to highest that indicates the number of times each score was obtained.

Frequency polygon

A graphic display of a frequency distribution in which the frequency of each score is plotted on the vertical axis with the plotted points connected by straight lines.

Functional design

An experiment containing many levels of the independent variable in order to determine the exact functional relationship between the independent and dependent variables.

Galvanic Skin Response (GSR)

The electrical conductance of the skin that changes when sweating occurs.

Haphazard sampling

Selecting subjects in a haphazard manner, usually on the basis of availability, and not with regard to having a representative sample of the population; a type of non-probability sampling.

History

As a threat to the internal validity of an experiment, refers to any outside event that is not part of the manipulation that could be responsible for the results.

Independent variable

The variable that is manipulated in order to observe its effect on the dependent variable.

Independent groups design

An experiment in which different subjects are assigned to each group. Also called between-subjects design.

Inferential statistics

Statistics designed to determine whether results based on sample data are generalizable to a population.

Informed consent

In research ethics, the principle that subjects in an experiment be informed in advance of all aspects of the research that might influence their decision to participate.

Instrument decay

As a threat to internal validity, the possibility that a change in the characteristics of the measurement instrument is responsible for the results.

Interaction effect

The differeing effect of one independent variable on the dependent variable, depending on the particular level of another independent variable.

Internal validity

The certainty with which results of an experiment can be attributed to the manipulation of the independent variable rather than to some other, confounding variable.

Interrupted time series design

A design in which the effectiveness of a treatment is determined by examining a series of measurements made over an extended time period both before and after the treatment is introduced. The treatment is not introduced at a random point in time.

Interviewer bias

Intentional or unintentional influence exerted by an interviewer in such a way that the actual or interpreted behavior of respondents is consistent with the interviewer's expectations.

Main effect

The direct effect of an independent variable on a dependent variable.

Manipulation check

A measure used to determine whether the manipulation of the independent variable has had its intended effect on a subject.

Matched random assignment

A method of assigning subjects to groups in which pairs of subjects are first matched on some characteristic and then individually assigned randomly to groups.

Maturation

As a threat to internal validity, the possibility that any naturally occurring change within the individual is responsible for the results.

Mean

A measure of central tendency, obtained by summing scores and then dividing the sum by the number of scores.

Measurement error
: The degree to which a measurement deviates from the true score value.

Median
: A measure of central tendency; the middle score in a distribution of scores that divides the distribution in half.

Mode
: A measure of central tendency; the most frequent score in a distribution of scores.

Monotonic relationship
: Any relationship between variables in which increases in the independent variable are accompanied by consistent increases in the dependent variable.

Mortality
: The loss of subjects who decide to leave the experiment. Mortality is a threat to internal validity when the mortality rate is related to the nature of the experimental manipulation.

Nonmonotonic relationship
: Any relationship between two variables in which increases in the independent variable are accompanied by both increases and decreases in the dependent variable.

Nonsignificant results
: Results that are probably due to error factors and indicative of a decision to not reject the null hypothesis.

Nonprobability sampling
: Type of sampling procedure in which one cannot specify the probability that any member of the population will be included in the sample.

Null hypothesis
: The hypothesis, used for statistical purposes, that the variables under investigation are not related in the population, that any observed effect based upon sample results is due to random error.

Operational definition
: Definition of a concept that specifies the operations used to measure or manipulate the concept.

Order effect
: In a repeated measures design, the effect that the order of introducing treatment has on the dependent variable.

Partial correlation
: The correlation between two variables with the influence of a third variable statistically controlled for.

Pilot study
: A small-scale study conducted prior to conducting an actual experiment; designed to test and refine procedures.

Placebo group
In drug research, a group given an inert substance to assess the psychological effect of receiving a treatment.

Population
The defined group of individuals from which a sample is drawn.

Predictor measure
A measure that is used to predict behavior on another measure.

Probability
The likelihood that a given event (among a specific set of events) will occur.

Probability sampling
Type of sampling procedure in which one is able to specify the probability that any member of the population will be included in the sample.

Quota sampling
A sampling procedure in which the sample is chosen to reflect the numerical composition of various subgroups in the population. A haphazard sampling technique is used to obtain the sample.

Random assignment
Assigning subjects to groups in a random manner such that assignment is determined entirely by chance.

Random error
An unexplained and unsystematic variability from a true score.

Random time series design
A design in which the effectiveness of a randomly introduced treatment is determined by examining a series of measurements made over an extended time period both before and after the treatment is introduced.

Randomization
Controlling for the effects of extraneous variables by insuring that the variables operate in a manner determined entirely by chance.

Rare event
An event that has a low probability of occurrence.

Reliability
The degree to which a measure is consistent.

Repeated measures design
An experiment in which the same subjects are assigned to each group. Also called within-subjects design.

Replication
Repeating a research study to determine whether the results can be duplicated.

Research hypothesis
The hypothesis that the variables under investigation are related in the population, that the observed effect based on sample data is true in the population.

Response set
A pattern of individual response to questions on a self-report measure in a way that is not related to the content of the questions.

Role-playing
A procedure for studying behavior in which individuals are asked to indicate how they would respond to a given situation rather than being observed in action in the situation.

Sampling
The process of choosing members of a population to be included in a sample.

Selection differences
Differences in the type of subjects who comprise each group in an experimental design; this situation occurs when subjects select which group they are to be assigned to.

Sensitivity
The ability of a measure to detect differences between groups.

Significance level
The probability of rejecting the null hypothesis when it is true.

Significant result
An outcome of a study that has a low probability of occurrence if the null hypothesis is true; a result that leads to a decision to reject the null hypothesis.

Simple random sampling
A sampling procedure in which each member of the population has an equal probability of being included in the sample.

Simulator group
In hypnosis research, a group that is not actually hypnotized but whose members are instructed to act as if they were hypnotized.

Single-subject experiment
An experiment in which the effect of the independent variable is assessed using data from a single subject.

Standard deviation
The square root of the variance.

Stratified random sampling
A sampling procedure in which the population is divided into strata followed by random sampling from each stratum.

Stratum (pl. strata)
Subdivision of a population based on specified characteristics of its members.

Systematic variance
Variability in a set of scores that is the result of the independent variable. Statistically, the variability of each group mean from the grand mean of all subjects.

Time-lagged correlation

The correlation between one variable measured at time 1 and another variable measured at time 2.

Theoretical internal validity

The certainty with which the results of an experiment can be attributed to an underlying theoretical construct used to explain those results.

True score

An individual's actual score on a variable being measured, as opposed to the score the individual obtained on the measure itself.

Type I error

An incorrect decision to reject the null hypothesis when it is true.

Type II error

An incorrect decision to accept the null hypothesis when it is false.

Validity

The degree to which a measurement instrument measures what it is intended to measure.

Variability

The amount of dispersion of scores about some central value.

Variable

A general class or category of objects, events, or situations within which specific instances are found to vary.

Variance

A measure of the variability of scores about a mean; the mean of the sum of squared deviations of scores from the group mean.

REFERENCES

Aiello, J. Field studies of crowding. Paper presented at the meeting of the Western Psychological Association, Sacramento, California, 1975.

American Psychological Association. *Casebook on ethical standards of psychologists.* American Psychological Association, 1967.

————. Ethical principles in the conduct of research with human participants. *American Psychologist,* 1973, *28,* 79–80.

Aristotle. Rhetoric. In *Aristotle, rhetoric, and poetics,* translated by W. Rhys Roberts. New York: Modern Library, 1954.

Aronson, E. *The social animal.* San Francisco: W. H. Freeman, 1972.

————, & Carlsmith, J. M. Experimentation in social psychology. In G. Lindzey & E. Aronson (Eds.), *Handbook of social psychology.* Vol. 2. Reading, Mass.: Addison-Wesley, 1968.

————, Willerman, B., & Floyd, J. The effect of a pratfall on increasing interpersonal attractiveness. *Psychonomic Science,* 1966, *4,* 227–228.

Barber, T. X., & Silver, M. J. Fact, fiction, and the experimenter bias effect. *Psychological Bulletin Monograph Supplement,* 1968, *70,* 1–29.

Beach, F. A. The snark was a boojum. *American Psychologist,* 1950, *5,* 115–124.

Bem, S. L. A measure of psychological androgyny. *Journal of Consulting and Clinical Psychology,* 1974, *42,* 155–162.

————. Sex-role adaptability: One consequence of psychological androgyny. *Journal of Personality and Social Psychology,* 1975, *31,* 634–643.

Berscheid, E., Baron, R. S., Dermer, M., & Libman, M. Ethical principles in the conduct of research with human participants. *American Psychologist,* 1973, *28,* 913–925.

Bickman, L., & Henchy, T. (Eds.) *Beyond the laboratory: Field research in social psychology.* New York: McGraw-Hill, 1972.

Bramel, D. A dissonance theory approach to defensive projection. *Journal of Abnormal and Social Psychology,* 1962, *64,* 121–129.

Brehm, J. *A theory of psychological reactance.* New York: Academic Press, 1966.

Brock, T. C. On interpreting the effects of guilt on compliance. *Psychological Bulletin,* 1969, *72,* 138–145.

Brogden, W. J. The experimenter as a factor in animal conditioning. *Psychological Reports,* 1962, *11,* 239–242.

Byrne, D., Ervin, C. R., & Lamberth, J. Continuity between the experimental study of attraction and real-life computer dating. *Journal of Personality and Social Psychology,* 1970, *16,* 157–165.

Campbell, D. T. Reforms as experiments. *American Psychologist,* 1969, *24,* 409–429.

———, & Stanley, J. C. *Experimental and quasi-experimental designs for research.* Chicago: Rand McNally, 1966.

Carducci, B. J., & Cozby, P. C. Judgments of female attractiveness following exposure to erotic material. Paper presented at the meeting of the Western Psychological Association, San Francisco, 1974.

Carlsmith, J. M., & Gross, A. E. Some effects of guilt on compliance. *Journal of Personality and Social Psychology,* 1969, *11,* 240–244.

Chaikin, A. L., Sigler, E., & Derlega, V. J. Nonverbal mediators of teacher expectancy effects. *Journal of Personality and Social Psychology,* 1974, *30,* 144–149.

Chaikin, A. L., Derlega, V. J., Bayma, B., & Shaw, J. Neuroticism and disclosure reciprocity. *Journal of Consulting and Clinical Psychology,* 1975, *43,* 13–19.

Chorover, S. L. The pacification of the brain. *Psychology Today,* May 1974, pp. 59–61, 63–64, 66, 69.

Cialdini, R. B., Borden, R., Walker, M. R., Freeman, S., Shuma, P., Braver, S. L., Ralls, M., Floyd, L., Reynolds, L., Crandall, R., & Jellison, J. M. Wearing the warm glow of success: A (football) field study. *Proceedings of the Division of Personality and Social Psychology,* 1974, *1,* 13–15.

Cozby, P. C. A study of ethical decision-making in psychological research. Unpublished manuscript. 1974.

Darley, J. M., & Latané, B. Bystander intervention in emergencies: Diffusion of responsibility. *Journal of Personality and Social Psychology,* 1968, *8,* 377–383.

deCharms, R., & Moeller, G. H. Values expressed in American children's readers: 1800–1950. *Journal of Abnormal and Social Psychology,* 1962, *64,* 136–142.

Dion, K. K., Berscheid, E., & Walster, E. What is beautiful is good. *Journal of Personality and Social Psychology,* 1972, *24,* 285–290.

Driscoll, R., Davis, K. E., & Lipetz, M. E. Parental interference and romantic love: The Romeo and Juliet effect. *Journal of Personality and Social Psychology,* 1972, *24,* 1–10.

Duncan, S., Rosenberg, M. J., & Finklestein, J. The paralanguage of experimenter bias. *Sociometry,* 1969, *32,* 207–219.

Ellsworth, P. C., Carlsmith, J. M., & Henson, A. The stare as a stimulus to flight in human beings: A series of field experiments. *Journal of Personality and Social Psychology,* 1972, *21,* 302–311.

Epstein, Y. M., Suedfeld, P., & Silverstein, S. J. The experimental contract: Subjects' expectations of and reactions to some behaviors of experimenters. *American Psychologist,* 1973, *28,* 212–221.

Eron, L. D., Huesmann, L. R., Lefkowitz, M. M., & Walder, L. O. Does television violence cause aggression? *American Psychologist,* 1972, *27,* 253–263.

Evans, R. I., & Rozelle, R. M. (Eds.) *Social psychology in life.* (2nd ed.) Boston: Allyn & Bacon, 1973.

Freedman, J. L. Role-playing: Psychology by consensus. *Journal of Personality and Social Psychology,* 1969, *13,* 107–114.

———, Klevansky, S., & Ehrlich, P. R. The effect of crowding on human task performance. *Journal of Applied Social Psychology,* 1971, *1,* 7–25.

———, Levy, A. S., Buchanan, R. W., & Price, J. Crowding and human aggressiveness. *Journal of Experimental Social Psychology,* 1972, *8,* 528–548.

———, Wallington, S. A., & Bless, E. Compliance without pressure: The effect of guilt. *Journal of Personality and Social Psychology,* 1967, *7,* 117–124.

Gelfand, D. M., Hartmann, D. P., Walder, P., & Page, B. Who reports shoplifters: A field-experimental study. *Journal of Personality and Social Psychology,* 1973, *25,* 276–285.

Gergen, K. J. The codification of research ethics: Views of a Doubting Thomas. *American Psychologist,* 1973, *28,* 907–912.

Guilford, J. P. *Fundamental statistics in psychology and education.* New York: McGraw-Hill, 1965.

Hayes, W. L. *Statistics for psychologists.* New York: Holt, Rinehart, & Winston, 1963.

Henle, M., & Hubbell, M. B. "Egocentricity" in adult conversation. *Journal of Social Psychology,* 1938, *9,* 227–234.

Hilgard, E. R. Pain as a puzzle for psychology and physiology. *American Psychologist,* 1969, *24,* 103–113.

Hood, T. C., & Back, K. W. Self-disclosure and the volunteer: A source of bias in laboratory experiments. *Journal of Personality and Social Psychology,* 1971, *17,* 130–136.

Horner, M. S. Femininity and successful achievement. In J. M. Bardwick, E. Douvan, M. S. Horner, & D. Gutmann (Eds.), *Feminine personality and conflict.* Belmont, Calif.: Brooks/Cole, 1970.

Hovland, C., & Weiss, W. The influence of source credibility on communication effectiveness. *Public Opinion Quarterly,* 1951, *15,* 635–650.

Humphreys, L. *Tearoom trade.* Chicago: Aldine, 1970.

Isen, A. M., & Levin, P. F. The effect of feeling good on helping: Cookies and kindness. *Journal of Personality and Social Psychology,* 1972, *21,* 384–388.

Jones, R., & Cooper, J. Mediation of experimenter effects. *Journal of Personality and Social Psychology,* 1971, *20,* 70–74.

Jourard, S. M. The effects of experimenters' self-disclosure on subjects' behavior. In C. Spielberger (Ed.), *Current topics in community and clinical psychology.* New York: Academic Press, 1969.

Kelley, H. H. Attribution theory in social psychology. In D. Levine (Ed.), *Nebraska symposium on motivation, 1967.* Lincoln: University of Nebraska Press, 1967.

Kelman, H. C. Human use of human subjects: The problem of deception in social psychological experiments. *Psychological Bulletin,* 1967, *67,* 1–11.

Kenney, D. A. Cross-lagged panel correlation: A test for spuriousness. *Psychological Bulletin,* 1975, *82,* 887–903.

————. A quasi-experimental approach to assessing treatment effects in the nonequivalent control group design. *Psychological Bulletin,* 1975, *82,* 345–362.

Kintz, N. L., Delprato, D. J., Mettee, D. R., Persons, C. E., & Schappe, R. H. The experimenter effect. *Psychological Bulletin,* 1965, *63,* 223–232.

Lana, R. E. Pretest sensitization. In R. Rosenthal & R. Rosnow (Eds.), *Artifact in behavioral research.* New York: Academic Press, 1969.

Langer, E. J., & Abelson, R. P. A patient by any other name . . . : Clinical group difference in labeling bias. *Journal of Consulting and Clinical Psychology,* 1974, *42,* 4–9.

Latané, B., & Darley, J. M. *The unresponsive bystander: Why doesn't he help?* New York: Appleton-Century-Crofts, 1970.

Leventhal, H. Findings and theory in the study of fear communications. In L. Berkowitz (Ed.), *Advances in experimental social psychology.* Vol. 5. New York: Academic Press, 1970.

Lieberman, M. A., Yalom, I. D., & Miles, M. B. *Encounter groups: First facts.* New York: basic Books, 1973.

McGuigan, F. J. The experimenter: A neglected stimulus object. *Psychological Bulletin,* 1963, *60,* 421–428.

McMillen, D. L. Transgression, self-image, and compliant behavior. *Journal of Personality and Social Psychology,* 1971, *20,* 176–179.

Mark, V. H. A psychosurgeon's case *for* psychosurgery. *Psychology Today,* July 1974, pp. 28, 30, 33, 84, 86.

Mead, M. *Coming of age in Samoa.* New York: Morrow, 1938.   **285**

Milgram, S. Behavioral study of obedience. *Journal of Abnormal and Social Psychology,* 1963, *67,* 371–378.

_____. Group pressure and action against a person. *Journal of Abnormal and Social Psychology,* 1964, *69,* 137–143.

_____. Some conditions of obedience and disobedience to authority. *Human Relations,* 1965, *18,* 57–76.

Miller, A. G. Role-playing: An alternative to deception? *American Psychologist,* 1972, *27, 623*–636.

Miller, G. A. Psychology as a means of promoting human welfare. *American Psychologist,* 1969, *24,* 1063–1075.

Monahan, L., Kuhn, D., & Shaver, P. Intrapsychic versus cultural explanations of the "fear of success" motive. *Journal of Personality and Social Psychology,* 1974, *29,* 60–64.

Mosteller, F., & Wallace, D. L. *Inference and disputed authorship: The Federalist.* Reading, Mass.: Addison-Wesley, 1964.

Neale, J. M., & Liebert, R. M. *Science and behavior.* Englewood Cliffs, N. J.: Prentice-Hall, 1973.

Orne, M. T. The nature of hypnosis: Artifact and essence. *Journal of Abnormal and Social Psychology,* 1959, *58,* 277–299.

_____. On the social psychology of the psychological experiment: With particular reference to demand characteristics and their implications. *American Psychologist,* 1962, *17,* 776–783.

Pfungst, O. *Clever Hans (the horse of Mr. von Osten): A contribution to experimental, animal, and human psychology.* Translated by C. L. Rahn. New York: Holt, 1911. Republished 1965.

Piliavin, I. M., Rodin, J., & Piliavin, J. A. Good samaritanism: An underground phenomenon? *Journal of Personality and Social Psychology,* 1969, *4,* 289–299.

Razin, A. M. A-B variable in psychotherapy. *Psychological Bulletin,* 1971, *75,* 1–21.

Ring, K. Experimental social psychology: Some sober questions about frivolous values. *Journal of Experimental Social Psychology,* 1967, *3,* 113–123.

_____, Wallston, K., & Corey, M. Mode of debriefing as a factor affecting subjective reaction to a Milgram-type obedience experiment: An ethical inquiry. *Representative Research in Social Psychology,* 1970, *1,* 67–88.

Rokeach, M., Homant, R., & Penner, L. A value analysis of the disputed Federalist Papers. *Journal of Personality and Social Psychology,* 1970, *16,* 245–250.

Rosenblatt, P. C., & Miller, N. Experimental methods. In C. G. McClintock (Ed.), *Experimental Social Psychology.* New York: Holt, Rinehart, & Winston, 1973a.

_____, _____. Problems and anxieties in research design and analysis. In C. G. McClintock (Ed.), *Experimental social psychology.* New York: Holt, Rinehart, & Winston, 1973b.

Rosenhan, D. On being sane in insane places. *Science,* 1973, *179,* 250–258.

Rosenthal, R. The volunteer subject. *Human Relations,* 1965, *18,* 389–406.

――――. *Experimenter effects in behavior research.* New York: Appleton-Century Crofts, 1966.

――――. Covert communication in the psychological experiment. *Psychological Bulletin,* 1967, *67,* 356–367.

――――. Interpersonal expectations: Effects of the experimenter's hypothesis. In R. Rosenthal & R. L. Rosnow (Eds.), *Artifacts in behavioral research.* New York: Academic Press, 1969.

――――, & Jacobson, L. *Pygmalion in the classroom: Teacher expectation and pupils' intellectual development.* New York: Holt, Rinehart, & Winston, 1968.

――――, & Rosnow, R. L. The volunteer subject. In R. Rosenthal and R. Rosnow (Eds.), *Artifact in behavioral research.* New York: Academic Press, 1969.

Rubin, Z. Jokers wild in the lab. *Psychology Today,* December 1970, pp. 18, 20, 22–24.

――――. Designing honest experiments. *American Psychologist,* 1973, *28,* 445–448.

――――. Disclosing oneself to a stranger: Reciprocity and its limits. *Journal of Experimental Social Psychology,* 1975, *11,* 233–260.

――――, & Peplau, L. A. Belief in a just world and reactions to another's lot: A study of participants in the national draft lottery. *Journal of Social Issues,* 1973, *29,* 73–93.

Schachter, S. *The psychology of affiliation.* Stanford, Calif.: Stanford University Press, 1959.

Seaver, W. B. Effects of naturally induced teacher expectancy effects. *Journal of Personality and Social Psychology,* 1973, *28,* 333–342.

Sidman, M. *Tactics of scientific research.* New York: Basic Books, 1960.

Silverman, I. Nonreactive methods and the law. *American Psychologist,* 1975, *30,* 764–769.

Skinner, B. F. *Science and human behavior.* New York: Macmillan, 1953.

――――. *Walden Two.* New York: Macmillan, 1948.

Smart, R. Subject selection bias in psychological research. *Canadian Psychologist,* 1966, *7,* 115–121.

Solomon, R. L. An extension of control group design. *Psychological Bulletin,* 1949, *46,* 137–150.

Stephan, W., Berscheid, E., & Walster, E. Sexual arousal and heterosexual perception. *Journal of Personality and Social Psychology,* 1971, *20,* 93–101.

Stevenson, H. W., & Allen, S. Adult performance as a function of sex of experimenter and sex of subject. *Journal of Abnormal and Social Psychology,* 1964, *68,* 214–216.

Tavris, C. The experimenting society: To find programs that work, government must **287** measure its failures. Conversation with Donald T. Campbell. *Psychology Today,* September 1975, pp. 47, 50–53, 55–56.

Valenstein, E. S. *Brain control: A critical examination of brain stimulation and psycho-surgery.* New York: Wiley, 1974.

Vitz, P. C. Preference for different amounts of visual complexity. *Behavioral Science,* 1966, *11,* 105–114.

Walster, E. Assignment of responsibility for an accident. *Journal of Personality and Social Psychology,* 1966, *3,* 73–80.

Watson, R. I., Jr. Investigation into deindividuation using a cross-cultural survey technique. *Journal of Personality and Social Psychology,* 1973, *25,* 342–345.

Webb, E. J., Campbell, D. T., Schwartz, R. D., & Sechrest, R. *Unobtrusive measures: A survey of nonreactive research in social science.* Chicago: Rand McNally, 1966.

Wispé, L., & Freshley, H. Race, sex, and sympathetic helping behavior: The broken bag caper. *Journal of Personality and Social Psychology,* 1971, *17,* 59–64.

Zimbardo, P. G. The human choice: Individuation, reason, and order versus de-individuation, impulse, and chaos. In W. J. Arnold & D. Levine (Eds.), *Nebraska symposium on motivation, 1969.* Lincoln: University of Nebraska Press, 1970.

――――. The psychological power and pathology of imprisonment. In E. Aronson & R. Helmreich. *Social psychology.* New York: Van Nostrand, 1973.

INDEX